The Queen *of* America

The Queen

JEFFERSONIAN AMERICA
Jan Ellen Lewis, Peter S. Onuf, and Andrew O'Shaughnessy, Editors

of America

MARY CUTTS'S
LIFE OF DOLLEY MADISON

Edited by Catherine Allgor

University of Virginia Press   *Charlottesville and London*

University of Virginia Press
© 2012 by the Rector and Visitors of the University of Virginia
All rights reserved
Printed in the United States of America on acid-free paper

First published 2012
First paperback edition published 2018
ISBN 978-0-8139-4181-3 (paper)

9 8 7 6 5 4 3 2 1

The Library of Congress has cataloged the hardcover edition as follows:

Library of Congress Cataloging-in-Publication Data

Cutts, Mary Estelle Elizabeth, 1814–1856.
   The queen of America : Mary Cutts's life of Dolley Madison / edited by Catherine
Allgor.
     p.   cm. — (Jeffersonian America)
   Includes two transcriptions of Mary Estelle Elizabeth Cutts's manuscript as well as
a study of Cutts's authorship and women's historical writing in the nineteenth century.
   Includes bibliographical references and index.
   ISBN 978-0-8139-3298-9 (cloth : alk. paper)
   1. Madison, Dolley, 1768–1849. 2. Presidents' spouses—United States—
Biography. 3. Cutts, Mary Estelle Elizabeth, 1814–1856. 4. Women historians—
United States—Biography. 5. Historiography—Social aspects—United States—
History—19th century. 6. Sex role—United States—History—19th century. I. Allgor,
Catherine, 1958–. II. Title.
   E342.2.M2C87 2012
   973.5'1092—dc23
   [B]

                                                              2011050258

To RALPH KETCHAM, collector of Dolley's papers, who made Dolley
Madison a woman who made history;
and to NANCY F. COTT, pioneer in the history of women and gender, who
made me a woman who made history

Contents

Foreword by Cokie Roberts

We have here a detective story. Or, as Catherine Allgor more elegantly puts it in her introduction to the Mary Cutts manuscripts, a work of "historical detection." Luckily for us readers we have three excellent sleuths on the case. They are seeking to uncover the true story of the first full-scale biography of Dolley Madison, written in two versions by her niece Mary Estelle Elizabeth Cutts, and what it tells us—and fails to tell us—about one of the most powerful women in our history.

Catherine Allgor, who in addition to the introduction to the manuscripts provides us with the opening essay, authored the preeminent Dolley Madison biography, *A Perfect Union: Dolley Madison and the Creation of the American Nation*. Attempting to learn more about Mary Cutts, Allgor turned to someone who is used to digging out the truth: Elizabeth Dowling Taylor's *A Slave in the White House: Paul Jennings and the Madisons* (2012) looks at a little-examined aspect of Dolley and James Madison's lives. And Holly Cowan Shulman, who in her essay examines the evidence in the Cutts manuscripts, has given us the opportunity to find out for ourselves what the famous First Lady was like by painstakingly putting Dolley Madison's correspondence online. The Dolley Madison Digital Edition, which Shulman edits, contains cartons of clues for historical detectives.

Piecing together those clues is especially difficult when it comes to women's history. Most American women did not leave behind properly preserved correspondence, much less speeches or pamphlets or memoirs. And the families, libraries, universities, and historical societies that act as careful custodians of men's documents often ignore and even misplace whatever their collections may have by way of women's writings. That's why Mary Cutts intrigues us. She did something highly unusual—she gathered up what correspondence of Dolley's she could find and then set about portraying for posterity the importance of her aunt's role in history.

But Cutts was somewhat thwarted in her efforts both by her subject and by herself—because they were both women. She, a proper mid-nineteenth-century member of the privileged class, could not draw attention to herself at a time when that was considered unseemly for females. And Cutts couldn't describe her aunt as what she really was—a political power—because that, too, would have been unladylike. We don't read here about the woman who campaigned so vigorously for her husband in 1812 that James G. Blaine later declared, "Mrs. Madison saved the administration of her husband," unequivocally concluding, "but for her DeWitt Clinton would have been chosen President in 1812."[1] The dutiful niece instead reduces Dolley's political skill, Allgor tells us, to innate charm. It wasn't that the First Lady was manipulating men who could be helpful to her husband—it was just that she couldn't help dazzling them. Dolley herself promoted the idea that she was simply an amiable southern belle. When Henry Clay gushed, "Everybody loves Mrs. Madison," she coyly replied that was because "Mrs. Madison loves everybody."[2] Those of us who have read her mail know that's not true.

But is Mary Cutts's version of history, with all of its omissions and pretensions, really any less true than many of the biographies of famous men? When I read letters the Founding Fathers wrote to each other, I am often put off by how self-conscious they are. These men knew their correspondence would be preserved and published and wrote accordingly. It's usually only in the letters to their wives or mothers or sisters, the letters that are often not included in the renderings of the great events of history, that we get a real sense of these men as flesh-and-blood humans, not marble and bronze deities. As Dolley Madison aged and became, in Taylor's telling, "a living icon of the age of the Founders" and in Allgor's, "a relict of the Republic," she, too, became self-conscious in her writings. Her letters to her nieces took on a more proper tone as she realized that, like her husband's papers that she was working to have published, hers, too, might be read by the public. When the novelist and journalist Margaret Bayard Smith chose to include a much-pleased Dolley in the *National Portrait*

1. Catherine Allgor, *A Perfect Union: Dolley Madison and the Creation of the American Nation* (New York: Henry Holt, 2006), 278.

2. Carl Sferrazza Anthony, *First Ladies: The Saga of the Presidents' Wives and Their Power, 1789–1961* (New York: William Morrow, 1990), 83.

Gallery of Distinguished Americans, Allgor reveals that Dolley told her nieces to send her old friend Smith just *their* letters from her, the ones she had written with care, not her earlier letters to their mother filled with her "unvarnished opinions and feelings on different subjects."[3]

Fortunately, we have some of those earlier letters. And thanks to Shulman, we have easy access to them. Through them and other women's letters and through the letters of men to women, we have a much more complete history than we do through most accounts. We find out, for instance, in one of those letters to her sister that Dolley wanted hidden, about the French ambassador to Washington when Madison was secretary of state: "I have heared sad things of Turreau—that he whiped his wife & abused her before all his servants."[4] Women cared about such things and found them worthy of chronicling. When we do follow the clues in locating women's letters, we learn not just what wars were fought on the battlefield but what deprivations were felt on the home front. We know not just about men meeting in Philadelphia to craft our charters but about women in Boston and Charleston and Richmond bearing and often burying those men's babies and caring for their mothers while still providing crucial political reporting from their cities and colonies. We know not just about the diplomatic missions of statesmen serving abroad but also what the women observed of the cultures of foreign countries, and what they gleaned in court circles. Women writing to each other recount affairs of state in one sentence and then describe what everyone is wearing in the next. Through them we get a much fuller picture of the world surrounding the men.

And through the men's letters to women, when they thought no one else would read them, we learn what these great statesmen feared or found funny. It's a tender, heart-wrenched John Adams we meet when he discovers the baby Abigail's been expecting is stillborn. It's a John Marshall worthy of sitcom stardom who tells his wife that he has managed to arrive for a court term in Raleigh without any breeches. And, unlike in his public statements, it's a totally frank Secretary of State James Madison who outlines the foreign affairs situation to Dolley, who was in Philadelphia and desperate for news: "If a general war takes place in Europe Spain will probably be less disposed to insult us; and England less sparing of her insults.

3. Dolley Payne Todd Madison to Margaret Bayard Smith, 31 Aug. 1834, Dolley Madison Digital Edition.

4. Dolley Madison to Anna Payne Cutts, 4 June 1805, Dolley Madison Digital Edition.

Whether a war will be forced by either is more than can be foreseen....
The power however of deciding questions of war and providing measures
that will make or meet it, lies with Congress, and that is always our answer
to newsmongers."[5] The press would get one answer, his wife the real one,
but he was warning her to stick to the talking points if she encountered
"newsmongers."

Mary Cutts was well aware of her aunt's influence and power, though
propriety prevented her from using those words. Living in Washington,
she knew that Dolley had been assigned her own honorary seat in Congress; she was well aware that her beloved relative was the first private
citizen invited to send a telegram; she saw that the great men of the era
continued to call on Mrs. Madison and to enlist her in their causes even
when she was old and impoverished. Dolley ruled the capital city until her
death, which was announced by the *Daily National Intelligencer* on July
14, 1849: "All of our own country and thousands in other lands will need
no language of eulogy to inspire a deep and sincere regret when they learn
the demise of one who touched all hearts by her goodness and won the
admiration of all by the charms of dignity and grace."[6] Congress adjourned
so members could attend America's biggest state funeral up to that time.
Members of the House and Senate joined the president of United States,
along with his cabinet, the Diplomat Corps, the Supreme Court, military
officers, District of Columbia officials, plus "citizens and strangers" in paying homage to the woman who had come to epitomize what we now call
the First Lady.

So Cutts understood whom she was heralding. She didn't just pen some
flowery paean to her aunt; she took the trouble of locating and transcribing
the correspondence of the woman she referred to as "the ornament of his
[James Madison's] house." Mary Cutts did her historical detective work,
though she shrouded her evidence in the language of her time. Even so,
the dutiful niece couldn't find a publisher, despite rewriting parts of her
draft to make it more "masculine." No matter how she changed her copy,
it was still about a woman, and no one bought it. Still, Cutts's work did not
go for naught. Her own niece, Lucia Cutts, took the manuscripts and produced an unsatisfactory version that at least gave future Dolley Madison
biographers some access to her letters, some slight insight into how her

5. James Madison to Dolley Madison, 6 Nov. 6, 1805, Dolley Madison Digital
Edition.

6. www.congressionalcemetery.org/first-lady-dolley-p-madison.

contemporaries saw this persuasive and perennially admired woman. But it has taken until now for the originals to appear in print. From them, and the essays giving them context, we can fill in a historical gap left open too long. In history, thankfully, seldom can you say, "case closed," but these pages make it possible for us to conclude "case considered and understood."

Acknowledgments

This volume was made possible by support from the Academic Senate and the Center for Ideas and Society, both at the University of California at Riverside, and by an Evelyn Davis Green Fellowship at the Radcliffe Institute for Advanced Study at Harvard University. The volume editor would also like to thank Nancy F. Cott, Carl and Lily Pforzheimer Foundation Director, and Ellen M. Shea, Head of Public Services, both of the Schlesinger Library of the Radcliffe Institute for Advanced Study at Harvard University; Barbara Bair, Manuscript Division, and Jeff Flannery, Head of the Manuscript Reading Room, both of the Library of Congress; J. C. A. Stagg, Editor in Chief, and David Mattern, Senior Associate Editor, both of the Papers of James Madison; Peter Drummey and Stephen T. Riley, Librarians, Tracy Potter, Reference Librarian, and Anna Cook, Assistant Reference Librarian, all of the Massachusetts Historical Society.

Michael Quinn, Director, and Lynne Dakin Hastings, Vice President for Museum Programs, both of James Madison's Montpelier, generously shared Montpelier's resources and hospitality. Judith S. Graham of the Adams Family Papers at the Massachusetts Historical Society and Jacobus Kats, Support Technician, University of California at Riverside, helped greatly with technical issues.

Very special thanks to Penelope J. Kaiserlian, Director, Ellen Satrom, Managing Editor, and the Rector and Visitors of the University of Virginia for their always constant support of my work. This is my second project with Richard K. Holway, History and Social Science Editor, and Mark H. Saunders, Director of Marketing. We conceived of this volume over a cocktail-laden dinner in Seattle, and the intoxication has never waned. Most academics wish they could be more "productive"; I do, too, if only to have more opportunities to work with Dick and Mark. If patience is a sign of saintliness, Mark Mones, Assistant Managing Editor, and Raennah Mitchell, Acquisitions Assistant, earned canonization as they shepherded us toward publication. Thanks to everyone in the production department who, once more, made it all a thing of beauty, and to Susan Murray, Copy Editor, who doled out expertise and good humor in equal measure.

Finally, Andrew S. Jacobs, Scott E. Casper, and Rosemarie Zagarri offered this volume early and steady guidance, as well as considerable intellectual insight. Thank you. Errors are unavoidable, even with the best counsel; any lapses are my own.

Abbreviations

CM I	Cutts Memoir I, Schlesinger Library, Radcliffe Institute for Advanced Study at Harvard University
CM II	Cutts Memoir II, Cutts Family Papers, Library of Congress
	Page numbers in note citations to CM I and CM II refer to the typeset texts on pp. 87–195 of this volume
DLC	Library of Congress
DMDE	Dolley Madison Digital Edition, Rotunda, the Electronic Imprint of the University of Virginia Press (Charlottesville: University of Virginia Press, 2004–present), http://rotunda.upress.virginia.edu/dmde
DPM, *Selected Letters*	*The Selected Letters of Dolley Payne Madison,* edited by David B. Mattern and Holly C. Shulman (Charlottesville: University of Virginia Press, 2003)
DPTM	Dolley Payne Todd Madison
MEEC	Mary Estelle Elizabeth Cutts

The Queen *of* America

Introduction

In her memoir of her famous aunt, First Lady Dolley Madison, written sometime in the early 1850s, Mary Estelle Elizabeth Cutts illustrates the "quaintness" of the "olden days," and the young Dolley's ladylike upbringing, with a story. The ladies of the time were "so particular . . . about the complexion" that little Dolley traveled to school not only with a white sun-bonnet sewn on her head, but in long white gloves and "sometimes even a white linen mask."[1] The arresting image of the little ghost girl, moving between trees and through the meadows of the Virginia countryside like a miniature phantom is too good a metaphor to resist.

The best stories have ghosts, and in the pages that follow, this will be but one moment that Dolley's life will flicker between sun and shadows, not the last time she will be the ghost at the center of her own story. How else can you describe a "memoir" by a woman who couldn't have known the events about which she writes, except as the work of a ghostwriter? But the ghosts go deeper—even after two drafts of her biography of Dolley Payne Todd Madison, Mary Cutts will express herself *"dissatisfied!"* convinced it is her own inadequacies as a writer that prevented a full rendering of the woman she loved and admired.[2] But she is only half-right. It is true that her recollections of her aunt (and her aunt's recollections) still leave for frustrated historians a Dolley as elusive as any specter. But it is not Mary's lack of writerly ability that doomed her, but the layers of social and cultural gender repression that shaped the way Mary felt about how she had to present her aunt. Indeed, like the heavy skirts that were the fashion in Mary's day, the strictures of "ladyhood" were a dragging weight, not only on the task Mary set herself, but on her sense of her own fitness for that task.

1. CM I, 90.   2. CM II, 194.

Surely it is not an accident that some of the best ghost stories of the nineteenth century were written by women. Across the Atlantic, in 1847, two years before Dolley Madison's death and probably shortly before Mary took to her pen, Charlotte Brontë released to the world one of the greatest "scream in the night" tales ever written, *Jane Eyre.* Up in Massachusetts, a young poet, perhaps during the years Mary wrote, began trailing around her Homestead, all in white. She would go to declare: "Nature is a Haunted House / Art a House that tries to be haunted."[3] With the intensification of Victorianism in England and the "cult of true womanhood" in the United States, no wonder female writers responded to the restrictions and boundedness of the lives dictated for them by dealing in the immaterial, the "evanescent" (one of Emily Dickinson's favorite words), and with worlds beyond this one. Dolley reacted to this world by using Mary as her medium; Mary responded by using the disguise of ladyhood to hide her aunt's historical significance.

At the heart of every ghost story lies a mystery—something ghost stories have in common with the discipline of history. Mysteries demand detectives, and, along with telling a fascinating story, this volume is an exercise in historical detection. Learning to find, evaluate, and use evidence in order to make meaning lies at the core of the historical enterprise. As Annette Gordon Reed demonstrated in her work on the Jefferson–Hemings controversy, studying underrepresented groups—women of all classes and races, people of color, poor and lower-class people—brings a different perspective on the question of evidence.[4] Historians of these groups have worked to uncover the voices of people rarely heard in history, and in doing so, have discovered that their "documents" (written or not) offer new kinds of information beyond that found in the more traditional documentation left by elite white men. Such studies also demand new techniques for evaluating and questioning the pieces left from the past.

This volume is divided into two parts, "Contexts" and "Texts." The first section, "Contexts," begins with my essay, which discusses the model of the "vanishing lady" and provides the cultural and historical context for Mary's attempt to make history. I make the case for why she is worth our study, especially as Mary's account isn't necessarily factually accurate. If

3. Emily Dickinson to Thomas Wentworth Higginson, Spring 1876, (L459A), quoted in Emily Dickinson, *The Letters of Emily Dickinson,* ed. Thomas H. Johnson, 3 vols. (Cambridge: Belknap Press of Harvard University Press, 1965), 554.

4. Annette Gordon Reed, *Thomas Jefferson and Sally Hemings: An American Controversy* (Charlottesville: University of Virginia Press, 1998).

we can't trust the evidence Mary offers us as fact, what do her memoirs reveal? Certainly more than she intended. Mary Cutts's manuscripts are as much about a mid-nineteenth-century woman writer as they are about an early republican First Lady.

Holly C. Shulman, the editor of the Dolley Madison Digital Edition, takes up the question of historical evidence in the two documents. Who is a reliable witness? How do we understand the evidence they have to offer? For decades, historians and biographers have taken Mary's stories at face value, as a source of information only. But, as Shulman's evidence shows, things are not always what they seem, and it is a rare writer who doesn't have a secret or two to hide.

Elizabeth Dowling Taylor begins our journey into the document by gathering the bits of extant data about Mary Estelle Elizabeth Cutts, presenting them as a life that was at once exceptional and representative. By the accident of birth, Mary Cutts traveled in exalted circles and, from a place of comparative privilege, harbored the ambition to be a writer—hardly the experience of most women in any age. Still, her exceptional existence was shaped by the universal institution of marriage, albeit in a negative way, as she chose to stay as "Miss Cutts."

The second section, "Texts," forms the heart of this volume. The team of Lee Langston-Harrison, Catherine Allgor, and James T. Connolly has transcribed the two versions of Mary's manuscript, following the highest documentary editorial standards. The order in which the two versions were written is a scholarly guess. It is not even clear if one account is a first draft and the other a final draft; the two accounts may actually be one. What is clear is that they differ from each other in significant ways. The first centers around Dolley Madison the person; perhaps prompted by professionals around her, Mary made what we conjecture to be the second draft. With its focus on James Madison and his retirement, this draft conforms more closely to what they understood to be "real history." "Texts" ends with Mary's last words on the subject of what she called her "little undertaking."

And the ghosts go on. Mary died before she could find a publisher for her account and would become, in effect, a real "ghost writer," as her own niece, Lucia Beverly Cutts, would publish her version of Mary's memoir. *The Memoirs and Letters of Dolly Madison, Wife of James Madison, President of the United States* (1886), drawn largely from both manuscripts, not only perpetuated the misspelling of her kinswoman's name, but Lucia eschewed the unladylike privileges of authorship, choosing to identify herself as any proper woman would, by her relation to others. What was good for her subject ("Wife of James Madison") was good for her. This first full-length treatment of Dolley Madison's life was authored by "a grand-niece." Understandably, those who study Dolley have often conflated the two women. In PBS's recent *American Experience* film *Dolley Madison,* a single actor, identified as Lucia and dressed in the fashion of the late nineteenth century, gives voice to Mary's words.

It is, then, not only fitting, but fair that Mary finally makes her bid for history in this collection. As women of the twentieth and twenty-first centuries, the authors of these essays have had the chance to be what Mary could not be—a professional historian. It is an honor and privilege that we can use our intellectual and professional resources to help Mary Cutts's voice be heard.

Contexts

The Lady Vanishes

Mary Estelle Elizabeth Cutts's Memoir
of Dolley Payne Todd Madison

CATHERINE ALLGOR

A Box of Treasures

In addition to the more traditional letters and paper documents, the Cutts-Madison Collection at the Massachusetts Historical Society (MHS) contains several intriguing artifacts, including a collection of calling cards and an autograph album.[1] The album is a fine example of its genre; many ladies and young gentlemen kept such albums in the nineteenth century. The Cutts Collection also houses a more singular piece, a little box that at first glance resembles a coffin.

A closer look reveals that it is a beautifully crafted rosewood box with four compartments. The lid is glassed at the compartments, each of which contains a lock of hair. A small brass plate fixed below each window-lid identifies from whose head each lock of hair was taken—George Washington, James Madison, Dolley Madison, and John Quincy Adams.

This little relict came to the MHS as a gift in December 1916, from Moorfield Storey, a generous benefactor to the society and its collections.[2] The locks of hair came from Richard Cutts, representative from Massachusetts from 1801 to 1813; Storey seems to have commissioned the box to hold them. The artifact is intriguing for several reasons—as a custom commission, the piece is truly one of a kind, and its contents reflect the nineteenth-century totemic fascination with hair that we moderns find disconcerting. But for the historian of women's lives and gender, the box's most compelling feature lies below the main exhibit. Under each compart-

---

1. Cutts-Madison Collection, Massachusetts Historical Society, Boston.
2. Storey's gift is recorded in *The Proceedings of the Massachusetts Historical Society*, 3rd ser., 50 (Oct. 1916–17): 81–82.

ment is a little drawer holding the small screw of paper that had been the original container for the hair.

Before they had been literally enshrined, these hirsute souvenirs had been collected and rolled in paper by Richard Cutts's daughter, Mary Estelle Elizabeth Cutts, in her role as an amateur historian. However, Mary Cutts's hair collection and her collection of calling cards of the Washington elite (for that and the autograph album were hers as well) were not her only historical products. She is also the author of a memoir of her famous aunt, Dolley Payne Todd Madison; actually, Mary wrote two versions of a memoir that differ from each other in significant ways. In a time when women did not boldly declare themselves the subjects (rather than objects) of history or routinely avail themselves of the historical voice, Mary's nineteenth-century "recollection" represents both her and Dolley Madison's bid for historical significance. But like the little box, her more traditional forms of history-making have their own hidden compartments, albeit intellectual ones.

Women played a large part in Dolley's life; after her death, women would mediate between Dolley and the public. Much of what history knows about Dolley Madison would be controlled by women who knew and loved her, and then by generations of women who were convinced of her importance, though (until recently) without the theoretical tools they needed to understand why. Without question, the work of Mary Estelle Elizabeth Cutts represents the most significant account of Dolley Madison's life and would become the foundation for all subsequent work.

Calling Mary's writing a "memoir" is troublesome since the word implies that these are her own memories. Since the first version of Mary's account starts before Dolley's birth, with much of the action occurring before Mary's own time, the reader could surmise that the information came from Dolley herself. While Dolley was undoubtedly a source, it is also clear that Mary exercised strong editorial control of the draft, and sometimes the lines dividing author, source, and editor blur. But no matter—whether filtered, edited, or downright invented, these memoirs are the closest to Dolley's autobiographical voice left to history. And, as Holly C. Shulman notes in her essay, the lies they tell are as important as the facts they impart.

In addition to its intrinsic value as a primary document of a leading Founding figure, the Cutts memoir is also an outstanding example of pre-twentieth-century women's history. In telling her aunt's story, making the case for a lady's historical significance without making her seem unladylike, Mary Cutts and her work embody the contradictions of writing about public women in an age before mainstream feminism. In her account, Mary tries to demonstrate Dolley's historical significance while also depicting her as an example of the best of American womanhood, even as the definition of "woman" was in contest and in flux between the years Dolley Madison flourished and the time of Mary's writing.

This essay explores how Mary worked around and through her paradoxical task, using a variety of techniques, all of which "cover" power with feminine language, themes, and tropes. Indeed, this strategy became a kind of language itself—a feminine, domestic argot in which women (and some men) would couch their discussions of issues involving reform and social change, most notably abolition.

Virginia Woolf said that all historians interested in telling the truth about the past needed to answer two questions—Who does the housework? and Who has the money? Susan Pedersen, biographer of the British politician Eleanor Rathbone, invokes a famous Hitchcock movie, cautioning all biographers of prominent women to watch for "the vanishing ladies," the ones to whom Woolf's queries tacitly refer. Such a group can include mothers who equip a daughter for a life of achievement; daughters who channel their ambitions through dynastic marriages; companions who act as "wives" to other women; spinster sisters or aunts who, though they seem to live on the edge of families, can fund their female relatives' dreams.[3] One could add another question to Woolf's queries—Who is left to tell the tale? Mary Cutts is the primary "vanishing lady" in Dolley's life. As in Pedersen's examples, she makes Dolley's life possible, but not through money or housework; rather, she puts Dolley in the historical canon, in a place next to the luminaries with whom she shares the little rosewood box. And, like all ladies, vanishing and not, Mary qualifies as a woman forgotten by history, barely registering on the documentary record.

3. Susan Pedersen, "The Ladies Vanish: Writing the Life of Eleanor Rathbone," presentation, Radcliffe Institute Fellows' Series, Sept. 24, 2002. Using this model, Dolley Madison Payne, Mary's beloved sister, is also a woman who makes another woman's life possible. Maine senator John Fairfield reported on her death in 1838: "Dolly, I understand, has left her property principally to Mary, which was between two and three thousand dollars, so that with what Mary had before, she is comfortably off" (John Fairfield to Anna Paine Fairfield, Dec. 20, 1838, *The Letters of John Fairfield*, ed. Arthur G. Stapes [Lewiston, Me.: Lewiston Journal Company, 1922], 245).

The Vanishing Lady

Mary Estelle Elizabeth Cutts was born on September 16, 1814, the second daughter and sixth child of Representative Richard Cutts and his wife, Anna Payne Todd Cutts. Anna Payne Cutts was the apple of her big sister Dolley's eye. Because Anna had lived since childhood with Dolley, beginning when Dolley was married to her first husband, John Todd, and then during her marriage to James Madison, Dolley looked upon her as a "daughter-sister."[4] Indeed, Anna named her first daughter, born in 1811, after Dolley. The second daughter was also named for family members. "Mary" had been the name of the sisters' mother and a middle sister, both deceased. The interjection of "Estelle" within the traditional coupling of "Mary Elizabeth" might reflect the fad of fashionable names for girls in the early nineteenth century.[5] Mary was raised in Washington City during the last years of the Madison administration, beginning what would be a lifelong, loving relationship with Dolley Madison, typical of the kind of supportive and intimate relations Dolley enjoyed with all her female kin.

Not much is known about Mary Cutts's early life, though due to her parents' position, she enjoyed a highly privileged childhood. The prose, spelling, and handwriting of her letters reflect a careful schooling. Southerners did not put much store in educating women, but her mother was not just a southerner, she was a Quaker, and, like other Quaker children of both sexes, the Payne girls had received above-average educations. The northern states, especially Massachusetts, were more progressive about female education, so between her Quaker-raised mother and her Massachusetts father, Mary had as good an education as any young woman could expect.

As one can also surmise from Elizabeth Dowling Taylor's biographical essay in this collection, young Mary Cutts led a rather dashing life. She spent much of her time in Washington, D.C., in Boston, and with her paternal family at Cutts Island, Maine. Mary seemed to identify more with the southern half of her family, but as she grew, she came to discover and appreciate her New England roots. No doubt her sense of "southernness" was influenced by the presence of her mother's family during her early years, especially her charismatic Aunt Dolley. Though Mary was born too late to enjoy the Madisons' White House—she was three years old when James

4. DPTM to Anna Payne Cutts, 18 May 1804, DMDE.
5. Letters written to her during her adulthood suggest that Mary may have styled herself with the more glamorous "Estelle."

and Dolley left Washington City in 1817—Mary Cutts became a regular visitor at Montpelier, the Madison family's countryseat. After the Madisons retired to Montpelier, the rural retreat rapidly became a major tourist destination, so that Mary Cutts and her older sister, Dolley Payne Madison Cutts, enjoyed many opportunities to meet and mix with the famous, the infamous, and the celebrated.[6]

The most significant demographic fact about Mary's adult life is that she did not marry. This was not usual for white women of her time, especially women of the elite classes, whose marriage into other ruling families was expected as part of a larger pattern of class formation. It is not clear why Mary did not wed; it may be that she was having too good a time. While other "spinsters" lived on sufferance in siblings' homes, Mary continued to live a cosmopolitan life with her parents in Washington. She did sometimes serve in the spinsterly profession of "companion," but, significantly, not for Dolley, who after James's death in 1836 desperately needed a young person to lean on. That duty fell to yet another niece, Annie Payne, a daughter of Dolley's brother John C. Payne. Dolley informally adopted Annie as a young woman; because the Payne family had initially settled in Louisa County, Virginia, Dolley had not known Annie from childhood as she had done Mary. Why Dolley did not enlist Mary is not clear; perhaps the choice was Mary's. Being a companion to her Aunt Dolley meant long months of isolation at Montpelier; instead, Mary companioned Louisa Catherine Johnson Adams, wife and then widow of John Quincy Adams in the capital city.

Mary was very close to her sister, Dolley Payne Madison Cutts, and Aunt Dolley seems to have regarded them as much of a pair. Her letters to them in the 1820s are full of affection, as well as advice and instruction. Though it is subtle, there is a hint that Dolley regarded Mary as the more flighty of the two, showing a slight preference for her namesake, whom she treated as a more thoughtful and serious young person.[7]

6. In 1839, when Mary Cutts was almost twenty-five, Louisa Catherine Johnson Adams characterized her as one of those "southern girls" (Louisa Catherine Johnson Adams, [1 July 1839], "Adventures of A Nobody," Adams Family Papers, Massachusetts Historical Society).

7. Louisa Catherine Johnson Adams's assessment may reflect Dolley's, describing Mary as "an amiable girl full of kind feeling but wanting in energy of character. The southern girls are almost all so who have no slaves!" Johnson Adams may have meant that because she had had no slaves to command, Mary's character lacked a certain force (Louisa Catherine Johnson Adams, [1 July 1839], "Adventures of A Nobody,"

Dolley Madison was a pivotal player in the years-long project of transcribing, editing, and publishing James Madison's papers, so perhaps it is not surprising that after his death, Dolley Madison gave thought to her own treatment in the historical record.[8] Her letters to her nieces in the 1830s took on an elevated tone; the advice Dolley imparted had, in style and substance, the sense of a handbook for young ladies. Dolley also turned to more literary pursuits, a sanctioned sphere for a lady to "speak" publicly. Once, in a letter to sister Anna, Dolley characterized herself as "always a dreamer you know," and in her later years, she turned her hand to poetry.[9] She also asserted her own place in history, answering queries about the old White House and publicly claiming her role in saving the famous Washington portrait during the British invasion of 1814.

Moreover, in the 1840s, Dolley was being treated like a historical artifact herself. A "relict of the Republic," as well as of James Madison (widows were called "relicts"), Dolley served as a figurehead on many public occasions, such as the dedication of the Washington Monument. Presidents and other political leaders claimed the imprimatur of her presence at receptions, as did Samuel F. B. Morse, who bestowed on her the honor of sending the first private telegraph message on his new invention. The members of the House of Representatives voted to give her her own seat on the House floor, and she received a special-edition medal cast in silver commemorating the War of 1812. No wonder that, in 1846, the *Boston Cultivator* dubbed her "one of [Virginia's] monuments."[10]

On one hand, that Dolley should consider writing her story is completely understandable. The leaders of the Revolutionary and Founding generations had long understood that they were making history and treated their correspondence and private writings thusly. Men and women such as John and Abigail Adams not only preserved letters received, but copied correspondence into letterbooks. In a time of uncertain mail delivery (espe-

---

Adams Family Papers, Massachusetts Historical Society). Thank you to Judith Graham, Series Editor, Louisa Catherine Adams Diary, Adams Family Papers, Massachusetts Historical Society.

8. For more on Dolley's role in the publication of James Madison's letters, see Holly C. Shulman, "'A Constant Attention': Dolley Madison and the Publication of the Papers of James Madison, 1836–1837," *Virginia Magazine of History and Biography* 118, no. 1 (Jan. 2010): 40–70.

9. DPTM to Anna Payne Cutts, 23 Apr. [1827], DMDE.

10. Anonymous, *Boston Cultivator*, 4 Apr. 1846, 4.

cially for those, like the Adamses, who corresponded transatlantically), this practice ensured that future scholars, if not the actual recipients of the lost letters, got the full historical picture.

On the other hand, many factors militated against Dolley Madison taking up the pen on her own behalf. The primary circumstance was her femaleness. Women had only a tenuous claim on history in the best of times; in the middle of the nineteenth century, new social, political, and economic gender patterns dictated a more private role for women. As a proper lady, Dolley was in an untenable position. Her culture understood politics as the main topic of history, and while even as a proper eighteenth-century lady, Dolley could not discuss politics openly, the Revolutionary backlash against political women that was fully entrenched by the 1830s made such discussion even more taboo. No wonder that even as she was correcting a newspaper account that named Charles Carroll as the savior of the Washington portrait, claiming that "the merit in this case belongs to me," she also protested: "I acted thus because of my respect for General Washington—not that I felt a desire to gain laurels."[11]

In 1834, Dolley got her chance to be a full-fledged historical subject when the journalist and writer Margaret Bayard Smith was commissioned to write an entry on her for the four-volume *National Portrait Gallery of Distinguished Americans*. Dolley was both flattered and fearful, worrying about "egoism," but also that she would not receive due credit for her rightful accomplishments. She almost drove Bayard Smith to distraction, at once pledging her cooperation—"Should any particular be desired, I will endeavor to furnish it"—and then genteelly stonewalling her for years.[12]

Dolley enlisted Mary and Dolley Cutts to help gather documents, urging them to show Bayard Smith their own correspondence with her, those letters full of elegantly expressed wisdom, but *not* her earlier letters to their mother, which had "my unvarnished opinions and feelings on different subjects." Dolley had secrets to hide; she may also have had an antipathy for the admittedly snoopy Margaret Bayard Smith. Though Dolley confided to Bayard Smith that she preferred "[her] pen" above that of "any

11. DPTM to Robert G. L. DePeyster, 11 Feb. 1848, cited in DPM, *Selected Letters*, 387. For more on the backlash, see Rosemarie Zagarri, *Revolutionary Backlash: Women and Politics in the Early American Republic* (Philadelphia: University of Pennsylvania Press, 2007).

12. DPTM to Margaret Bayard Smith, 31 Aug. 1834, quoted in DPM, *Selected Letters*, 305–6.

other" for this task, she also had previously characterized Margaret to her sister as "a *curious* body—& tho she appears affectinate & frank, I think she is *dangerious.*"[13]

All of these factors may explain Dolley's reticence, but whatever the cause, in the end, Bayard Smith had to resort to her own memories of Dolley to flesh out the piece. However, Dolley did supply Margaret with a good likeness of her and passed on at least one document that she, quite rightly, figured would make her historical legacy—the famous letter to a sister (probably her middle sister, Lucy) on the eve of the British invasion. The letter documents the last hours in the old White House, while conveying the urgency and danger in the capital city. But even this document was filtered—Dolley did not give Margaret an original copy, but rather, a fair copy that Margaret reproduced.

Whatever her feelings about Bayard Smith, Dolley could have no quarrel with the finished sketch, which put her in a most flattering light.[14] Perhaps buoyed by the positive reception garnered by the piece, Dolley began, probably at some point in the mid- to late 1840s, a project that, though short of a full-fledged memoir, was the closest she could come to full disclosure. Historians do not know exactly when Dolley turned to Mary to be her amanuensis or what her thought processes were around the decision. Like many transactions involving women, this one is covered by the private nature of female worlds. In truth, Dolley might have preferred Mary's sister to undertake this task of documenting her life, but Dolley Madison Cutts had died in 1838 at the age of twenty-seven. Mary Estelle Elizabeth Cutts would have to do.

13. DPTM to MBS, 31 Aug. 1834, quoted in DPM, *Selected Letters*, 305–6; DPTM to Anna Payne Cutts, 6 June 1829, quoted in DPM, *Selected Letters*, 278. A remark of Bayard Smith's to her own sister shows that Dolley was right to fear what information the journalist could have used, but also that Dolley should have trusted her old friend: "In the last Portrait gallery—you will see my memoir of Mrs. Madison—all I say is true—but I have not of course told the whole truth" (Margaret Bayard Smith to Maria Bayard Boyd, 6 Feb. 1836, Margaret Bayard Smith Papers, DLC).

14. For more on the 1814 letter, see David B. Mattern, "Dolley Madison Has the Last Word: The Famous Letter," *White House History* 4 (Fall 1998): 38–43; and Margaret Bayard Smith, "Mrs. Madison," *The National Portrait Gallery of Distinguished Americans*, ed. James Herring and James B. Longacre, 4 vols. (New York: Hermon Bancroft, 1836), 3:1.

The Problem with Memory

In Mary Cutts's remembrances, as with all memoirs, there are problems, with memory and accuracy, with wishes and anxieties, and with layers of meanings (intended and unintended). The problems begin with the structural. It is not even clear what the relationship is between the two memoirs, if, in fact, there are two. We divide Mary's writing into two sections because what comprises "Cutts Memoir I" is two bound sections that presently reside at the Schlesinger Library of the Radcliffe Institute for Advanced Study at Harvard University.[15] Though no doubt originals exist somewhere, the pages that make up what we call "Cutts Memoir II" are scattered throughout a microfilm in the Cutts Family Papers Collection, located in the Manuscript Division of the Library of Congress.

Scholars have long treated these accounts as two different versions, rather than one long narrative, because, though they cover different time periods in Dolley's life, there is overlap during the Madisons' most politically active years. Cutts Memoir I begins with Dolley's family and her childhood and ends at the end of the War of 1812. Cutts Memoir II begins with the election of 1800 and the 1801 arrival of the Madisons in Washington and continues a little past the death of Dolley Madison in 1849. With two seemingly separate bundles of writing in hand, scholars have made the leap that one is a first draft and the other a final draft.

A good argument for considering the writings as sequential drafts is that, in correspondence with the publisher Henry D. Gilpin, Mary indicates that she has, indeed, rewritten her work at some point in her process. Her other publisher friends, Jared and Mary Crowninshield Silsbee Sparks, "advised her" with a "great many useful hints—among others to bring in as much of people of her [Dolley Madison's] day—and historical personages— as I could—this I have endeavored to do with accuracy." Mary admitted: "I found without them that the narrative would in many places flag— especially the sixteen years—passed in Washington." For his part, Jared Sparks "advised me to put in all I could about Mr. Madison to strengthen

15. That the pages of the Schlesinger draft are bound reinforces the impression that Cutts Memoir I is a stand-alone draft, especially compared to the loose pages that make up Cutts Memoir II. But it does not follow that Mary did this binding; it could have happened any time after her death. Though the Schlesinger draft is in two bound sections, it is clearly one document, as indicated by the paper, the writing, and the internal pagination, as well as continuity in the narrative.

the whole." Mary mentions that she "quoted from orations &c delivered by Mr: Ingersoll and Gov: Barbour—printed only in newspapers—and forgotten." Mary sounds like many a professional historian as she defends her findings: "What I said about P. H. [probably Patrick Henry] I knew was common place but I thought that of Aaron Burr was new!"[16]

From these bits of information Mary related on the eve of her intended publication, it might seem that one could figure out which draft was the second and final one, but not so. Cutts Memoir I contains the most about Dolley's early life, but also all the bits of "real history" Mary dutifully wove in, especially about the War of 1812. Cutts Memoir II features "all I could about Mr. Madison," as the narrative goes into the 1830s and 1840s, when Mary had her own memories of James Madison. Indeed, Cutts Memoir I could be said to be more about Dolley, and Cutts Memoir II is more about James, at least up until his death. What argues against Cutts Memoir II being the draft Mary intended to publish is that apparently Mary skips the Madison presidency and the war altogether, discussing the Madisons' role in the Jefferson administration and then moving directly to retirement!

Even following Mary's more concrete clues is frustrating. The enriched sections about "historical personages" seem to be a feature of Cutts Memoir II, as does as the Barbour oration, but the sections on Aaron Burr and Patrick Henry appear in Cutts Memoir I. As far as content goes, it seems most likely that she intended the piece to be one; that is, overlap notwithstanding, the two memoirs are not subsequent drafts, but rather, are two sections of a single book. Until the originals of Cutts Memoir II surface, and perhaps not even then, it is impossible to conjecture what Mary intended.

For now, we treat the two accounts as separate, making Cutts Memoir I the first simply by chronology—it begins earlier than the other account. For our purposes, Cutts Memoir I, with its focus on Dolley Madison's early life, engages the questions of memory and evidence most potently. In the case of Cutts Memoir I, questions abound. Whose memories are they? For instance, in discussing Dolley's early life, Mary's source is presumably Dolley, but perhaps other people served as primary sources as well. One of those sources was Dolley's old friend Frances Dandridge Henley Lear. According to Mary, "When this tribute to the memory of her early friend

16. Mary Sparks to Mary Cutts, 6 June 1856, Cutts-Madison Papers, Massachusetts Historical Society; Mary Cutts to Henry D. Gilpin, [10 June 1856], Cutts-Madison Papers, Massachusetts Historical Society. To read these crucial letters in their entirety, see the last section in this volume, "The Last Letters."

was suggested, she heartily seconded the suggestion and gave what information she could," including letters.[17]

And even if the stories came from Dolley herself, it is not clear whether they are recollected especially for this project or if Mary relies on oft-repeated anecdotes or family lore. Mary herself writes, when relaying a childhood incident: "these and other tales of her childhood she often told her neices, seventy years afterwards."[18] Not only does the historian have to rely on Dolley's memory, and Mary's memory of Dolley, but also it is clear that some of the information about Dolley's early life is wrong, deliberately fabricated by either woman. Of course, though the accuracy of an account counts, the distortions and downright deceptions often prove more revealing than the literal truth.

Mary makes no claim that her "memories" of Dolley's life form a complete biography, though surely she must have had some aspirations toward comprehensiveness, since she begins in Dolley's childhood and covers many time periods that she herself could not have witnessed. Mary has the instincts of a good historian, following a "Life and Letters" model, with transcriptions of primary sources, chiefly letters.[19] Still, Mary will not cover all subjects. Though Dolley's son by her first marriage, John Payne Todd, and his troubles were a large part of Dolley's life, the allusions to Payne (as he was aptly, if ironically, known) that Mary makes are vague and formulaic. This is not to say that Mary avoided controversial topics; rather, she focused on other parts of Dolley's life that proved problematic, both personally and politically, including her father's character, her relations with the Quakers, her well-known love of luxury and dress, and her involvement in politics, among others. And all the while, Mary strove to make her case for Dolley's historical significance.

Names and Places

As was standard in her time, Mary Cutts begins her biography/memoir with lineage. Her job (and Dolley's) in this not-so-brief discussion of Dolley's pedigree is to establish her indisputable position as one of the First Families of Virginia. This is not difficult, though her grandparents were newcomers to the area. By the eighteenth century, there were many fami-

17. CM I, 107.   18. Ibid., 90.

19. Some of Mary's transcriptions have proved invaluable to present-day historians, as they are the only extant copies.

lies of long standing in Virginia, a fact that counted, but it was no disgrace to be a recent arrival in such a new country. In fact, being close to the Mother Country carried a cachet of its own—a status that even a revolution failed to alter.

As regards the paternal side, having an "English gentleman of wealth and education" for a grandfather, as Josias Payne is depicted, will do the trick (though Mary mistakenly tags Josias with his brother's name—John). Just to be sure, Mary tosses in a "Sir Thomas Fleming" and a Scottish earl. Over several handwritten pages, Mary traces various branches of Dolley's family tree down to a tangle of Winstons and Dabneys and Coleses.[20]

Mary follows this biographical convention for two reasons, one general, one particular. The general reason lies in the belief in blood. The "degrees" of blood determined the closeness of relatives; "blood" itself was supposed to "carry" not only physical but also psychological traits, and a particular configuration of "blood traits" defined a family and the individuals within it. The fact that southern families, like all families, seem to contain equal numbers of scoundrels and felons, as well as shining heroes and model citizens, did not dissuade Mary. By invoking her ancestors in worshipful ways, Mary Cutts asserts that "breeding" destined Dolley to be a leader in society.

Another reason for the tortured path through the Coles-Winston-Dabney-Syme-Payne tangle lies in the endpoint that Mary reaches—the famed orator and statesman Patrick Henry, who was a "near relative." As Shulman notes, Mary spends a disproportionate amount of time on Henry, in contrast to the rest of Dolley's kin. Mary demonstrates that Patrick Henry was connected to Dolley by nature—"inborn genius, such as his, constitute[s] its [the country's] true aristocracy"—and nurture—"Reared under similar auspices in Hanover County [Virginia], afterward meeting in Philadelphia."[21]

Having introduced Patrick Henry, Mary expounds on his sterling qualities, and the narrative seems to lose Dolley. But Mary focuses on traits that Patrick shares with Dolley, qualities that won them both public renown—eloquence (though Dolley's was of a more personal kind), physical courage, and an almost magical effect on people. Mary could have been speaking of her aunt when she enthused: "History furnishes but few examples of such patriotism, with the power of swaying the minds of men, of carrying them away with him by the power of eloquence, and the might of right! which he so powerfully depicted, and so modest and unselfish a nature withal!"[22]

20. CM I, 87–88.   21. Ibid., 88.   22. Ibid.

As is so often said of Dolley (and Mary says so later in the document), Patrick "was dazzled by neither power, nor dignity." Like Patrick Henry, Dolley knew what it meant to "serve[]... in perilous times," as she did during the War of 1812, "when to be highest was only to be exposed foremost to the bolt of the dreaded enemy, or at some conjuncture of civil danger." Like Dolley, Patrick rose to meet circumstances, and, quite rightly, "Virginia is proud of this son, who seemed to spring into existance as a meteor when most needed by his country and who by the power of truth led them to assert their rights and shake off the trammels with which England would bind her Colonies more tightly to herself!"[23]

Mary uses Patrick Henry as a mirror, reflecting his luster indirectly onto his kinswoman, establishing Dolley's importance while allowing her to remain modest and politically neutral. Establishing historical importance by reflection is a well-known tack in women's history in the past and the present. Still, she cannot resist asserting the overt political connection when she says that Dolley "might well be proud" of Patrick Henry, in "a Republican Country." Mary's first choice for party affiliation was "Democratic," no doubt a reflection of her own political time. In the 1850s, southern Democrats traced their party to Jefferson and Jackson. But Mary crossed out the word "Democratic" in her draft, replacing it with "Republican," the word that Thomas Jefferson and James Madison embraced as their own.[24] Though "Republican" had its own meanings in her time, no doubt Mary was striving for historical accuracy. It should be noted that, in the extant copy of the memoir, Mary's niece Lucia B. Cutts who would publish parts of the memoir in her own compilation, has drawn a line through this first section, possibly making the editorial decision that the Henry section was a digression.

Mary had a more urgent personal task in her relation of Dolley's early life, and, significantly, it is in these sections that Dolley's editorial hand appears. Perhaps motivated by vanity, Dolley shaves off four years from her birth year. More intriguingly, the memoir states that Dolley was born "while on a visit to North Carolina." In the first draft of this version of the memoir, Mary, obviously speaking for Dolley, claims that the visit was to Dolley's paternal relations in North Carolina. Apparently, this was too big a whopper for Lucia Cutts to countenance (there is no record that John Payne even had relations in that state), so, with a cross-out, Lucia amends the sentence to "a visit."[25]

23. Ibid., 88.   24. Ibid.   25. Ibid., 89.

Whatever the embellishment or correction, the tale is not true. The Paynes were not visiting North Carolina; they had emigrated there as part of a group of Quakers moving to the North Carolina frontier. That John Payne sold his Virginia land demonstrates that this was intended to be a long-term, if not permanent, relocation. It is not clear what happened in North Carolina, but evidence exists that John Payne may have failed in business; whatever the truth, land sales, again, tell their tale. The Paynes moved back with almost indecent haste, selling their North Carolina lands at a loss. They returned to Virginia, where at least they could count on help from the Payne and Coles families.

Still, Mary's misstatement is precisely the information that Dolley sent Margaret Bayard Smith in the early 1830s. On one of the few occasions that Dolley sent along any personal data to Bayard Smith, she wrote: "My family are all Virginians except myself, who was born in N. Carolina whilst my Parents were there on a visit of one year, to an Uncle."[26] Some have suggested that perhaps Dolley was not lying because she did not know the true circumstances of her birth; this seems unlikely, given subsequent events, but even on the face of it, the story does not hold water. Not only did kin-conscious Dolley know she had no uncle in North Carolina, but a yearlong visit seems extreme, even by southern visiting standards.

So why did Dolley lie? To protect her father? Perhaps so, though tensions between father and daughter later in the document cast some doubt on that motive. Perhaps Dolley obfuscated in order to remove the whiff of failure and poverty around the whole episode? This seems more likely, given what seems to be the primary motivation of this part of the narrative—the need to make Dolley the Most American of Americans, a Virginia aristocrat. Again, hers was a culture that set a great deal of store by birth and blood, and, though she modestly marks herself as a North Carolinian, by insisting that she had been born in North Carolina during a "visit," Dolley could keep her Virginia origin virtually unsullied.

Such a motive might also explain another puzzling untruth, centering around Dolley's name. Mary relates that the little girl born on May 20, 1772 (not 1768, Dolley's real birth date), "was named Dorothy in compliment to her mother's Aunt Mrs. John Henry. As she grew up the name was getting out of fashion, and she ever afterwards wrote it Dolley and so she was called." But she was not born "Dorothy"; she was "Dolley" from the start. "Dolley" appears on her birth records and in the few full signatures extant,

26. DPTM to MBS, 31 Aug. 1834, quoted in DPM, *Selected Letters*, 306.

most notably on her marriage certificates and various wills. And "Dolley" has the last word—it is the name on her grave marker at Montpelier.[27]

Coming from the horse's mouth, so to speak, no wonder that well into the twentieth century, biographers have insisted that her name was "Dorothy." For two major biographers of Dolley, Maud Wilder Goodwin and Allen C. Clark (who also edited her letters), even "Dorothy" was neither distinguished nor glamorous enough an appellation. They asserted that her parents named her "Dorothea," for an illustrious relation, Dorothea Spotswood Dandridge.[28] However, Dorothea Spotswood, being only ten years old at the time of Dolley's birth, would have had little opportunity to acquire much luster. This curious, long-held conviction may have stemmed from an inability to accept such a "frivolous" name for a lady so famous and held in such high regard.

Given that the invention of "Dorothea" occurred well after Dolley's death, the question remains: Why did either Dolley tell Mary that her name was "Dorothy" or did Mary invent this appellation? Mary's motivation may have been similar to that of her biographers: she wanted a more refined name, one that she could connect to her Virginia family. "Dolley" seemed more like a nickname; moreover, "dolly" was a slang term for a lower-class, sexually suspect woman or a courtesan. It may seem absurd that, by the end of her life, Dolley Madison felt the need to underscore a respectable reputation, but in the early years of her political career, there had been much press around alleged sexual politicking engaged in by Dolley and her sister Anna. Such "revelations," no matter how ludicrous, must have hurt, and it is not unrealistic to think that Dolley might have still felt the taint. Note that the source for Dolley's reputation in Orange County mentioned in Shulman's essay, the historian and local W. W. Scott, used quotations marks rather pointedly: "the Madison kith and kin did not like 'Dolly.'" Another explanation may lie in her Quaker background. For all of the above reasons, Society of Friends members may have referred to Dolley as "Dorothy," as reflected in a letter from Quaker preacher, Rebecca Hubbs, in 1814, which addressed her as "dear Dorothy."[29]

27. CM I, 89. For the best summation of this historical confusion, see Ethel Stephens Arnett, *Mrs. James Madison: The Incomparable Dolley* (Greensboro, N.C.: Piedmont Press, 1972), 9–12.

28. Maud Wilder Goodwin, *Dolly Madison* (New York: Charles Scribner's Sons, 1896), 3; Allen C. Clark, *Life and Letters of Dolly Madison* (Washington, D.C.: W. F. Roberts, 1914), 9–10.

29. Rebecca Crispin Hubbs to DPTM, 13 July 1813, DMDE.

Dolley's mother, Mary Coles, is also pressed into service to establish Dolley's indisputable "Virginia-ness." Young Mary was "a belle and a beauty, and is said to have had many lovers" (the more Victorian Lucia crossed that out, substituting "admirers"), among whom was the ultimate Virginian, Thomas Jefferson! In spite of friends urging his suit, citing Jefferson's "promising talents," Mary Coles "preferred Mr. Payne," who possessed a favorable "personal appearance."[30] All existing historical evidence suggests that this was invention.

Mary skips over the rather unfortunate North Carolina episode; indeed, she establishes John Payne as a settled planter in North Carolina before he married Mary Coles: "soon after his marriage he purchased an estate in Hanover County, Virginia, twenty miles from Coles Hill the residence of Williams Coles." She also refers to him as a "resident of North Carolina," as well as a captain in the Revolutionary War; both statements are untrue. The Paynes' new home was called Scotchtown. "Late in life," Dolley reminisced about her first Virginia home and is quoted as saying, "I can just remember the mantel peices, they were of black marble supported by white figures, there were twenty rooms on a floor, every one had marble hearths and mantels." In Virginia, even real estate has a bloodline—Dolley's "first" homestead "was built by an English nobleman" who lived like feudal lord, surrounded by Scots emigrants and small brick houses attached to the main building.[31]

Dolley's reminiscences of her childhood home are problematic. John Payne probably purchased or rented Scotchtown in 1769 or 1770, but any paperwork around the sale has been lost, probably during one of the many fires that burned official buildings and their records during the Civil War. In 1771, Patrick Henry bought Scotchtown, according to local lore, from John Payne for the bargain price of £600. From then on, all other owners of the estate are documented, and John Payne is not one of them.

So if Dolley lived at the 960-acre estate, she must have done so only from the age of two until three years old. She could not have remembered the architectural details; most probably Dolley saw them on a later visit.[32] But in her reminiscences she either deliberately or unconsciously made her stay at Scotchtown into a long one, stretching through her childhood. Such a desire for a memory of stability is not hard to understand—if she

30. CM I, 89. 31. Ibid.
32. Arnett, *Incomparable*, 17–18.

left Scotchtown at three, Dolley would have moved twice in the first three years of her life.

Again, according to local knowledge, the Paynes built a house on Mary Payne's family plantation, Coles Hill. In 1771, William Coles deeded to his daughter 176 acres, where the Paynes settled.[33] That William Coles deeded this land to Mary and not her husband might be an expression of Quaker ideals. It was not uncommon, however, for men of the gentry class and all religious affiliations to deed land or other resources to their married daughters. Though a married woman had no separate legal identity, and could not therefore own anything, the law recognized the right of fathers to protect their inheritances, either from less-than-sterling sons-in-law or simply to preserve assets for their grandchildren and descendants. One cannot know the reason behind Williams Coles's use of this protective device—perhaps this is another ripple of discord around the reputation of John Payne.

According to Mary's account, Dolley's Virginia girlhood was an ideal (and an idealized) one, "tranquil," inspiring the "happiest reminiscences."[34] To cover this period of Dolley's life, Mary included several charming stories that have become a part of the Dolley legend, but they serve larger purposes than merely to present Dolley in a favorable light. Rather, they aid Mary in her dual missions—to hold Dolley Madison up as an exemplar of womanhood during a time when that definition was undergoing massive change and to demonstrate her historical significance.

Quaker Controversies

Dolley Payne had been raised a Quaker, a controversial sect in the late eighteenth century. In discussing her early life, the hardest contradiction that Mary Cutts had to handle was Dolley's abandonment (seemingly without a backward glance) of her Quaker religion upon her marriage to James Madison. Mary goes a long way to depict John and Mary Payne's Quakerism as a good thing—making them "pure minded parents" and, when Dolley was about fifteen, leading John to renounce slavery and free his slaves, a decision that had an even more resonant meaning in midcentury.[35] Dolley even dutifully marries the Quaker man her father has chosen for her. What, then, does it mean that as soon as she remarries to the rich, slave-

33. Ibid., 19–20.   34. CM I, 89.   35. Ibid.

holding, political, and therefore worldly James Madison, she discards her Quaker dress and plain ways with a vengeance?

Proper wifely obedience partly excuses her. As Mary Cutts explained, Dolley's position as the wife of a leading statesman demanded that Dolley dress well and drop the Quaker "restraints." Mary was careful to stress, however, that she "retained for many years the name, and *always* the fundamental principles," of the Society of Friends, specifically "love of truth, abhorrence of vice, and universal benevolence of character, which had been so deeply implanted by her parents."[36]

Still, an implied criticism of the Quakers as harsh and unnatural runs throughout the account from the start. Mary described both Payne parents as "strict members of 'the Society of Friends.'" Though Mary describes Dolley's childhood home as "tranquil" and her childhood as "the happiest," the bare facts of that time hint at deep discord.[37] Circumstances were hard on the young family, as their poverty and peripatetic life demonstrated. In addition, even in this heavily sanitized account, her father, John Payne, emerges as a cramped and crabbed individual, an oppressive parent, the kind of person whose strength comes from inflexibility.

Even his most courageous act contains some ambivalence. According to the memoir, John Payne was "one of the first who of his Sect in Virginia who became doubtful and afterwards concientiously scrupulous" about slavery. John eventually freed his slaves, an act that doomed him and his family to poverty. While this was a heroic act, it does not follow that heroes are easy people to live with. Indeed, the gritty qualities that drive heroes do not necessarily make them good parents. His neighbors thought him "a fanatic," a label that may not just reflect the dramatic decision to free his slaves, but also serve as a comment on a certain flintiness of character.[38]

Mary Cutts does not openly criticize John, but she makes some interesting associations in the text. After freeing their slaves, the Paynes could not make a living in agriculture, so in 1786, they went to Philadelphia, the center of American Quakerism. Mary characterized the move as motivated by "one aim, the support of his religious belief." Even in that ultra-Quaker atmosphere, John Payne made an impression. "He was an elder," reports Mary, and "spoke in meetings and was called a 'Quaker Preacher.'" One wonders what earned him this appellation, since Quakers do not generally have "preachers" in the way most Christian religions understand the term. Rather, Quakers testify when moved by the spirit; Mary's misapprehension

36. Ibid., 99.   37. Ibid., 89.   38. Ibid., 90.

might suggest that John Payne made his mark by testifying more regularly or more dramatically than others.[39]

Mary segues, within a discussion of Dolley's father, to the "early 'friends'" of whom he was a part. They "were very strict and allowed no ornaments, not even in their houses." With her own eyes, Mary "saw recently in Phila an ancient clock in the house of 'a Friend'—which had been stripped of its ornamental work by the ruthless hands of 'a deputation from meeting.'" Mary's next sentence goes back to John: "Mr. Payne was very exact with his children and brought them up in that religion which has utility for its basis, and which forbids the acquirement of those graceful and ornamental accomplishments which are too generally considered the most important parts of a female education."[40]

Mary tries to put this in the best light possible, tying the Quaker rejection of ornamentation to the contemporary, mid-nineteenth-century preference for the practical in female education. Still, the idea of a deputation coming into the house of someone with whom they are supposed to be in community in order to strip a clock seems far beyond a desire for "utility"; it seems, well, fanatical. And this was the meeting in which John was a leading character. Interestingly, it was Mary Coles Payne, Dolley's mother, who was born and raised in the Quaker faith; John was a convert. Perhaps he felt the extra zeal of the converted; perhaps moving to the seat of Quakerism brought out the zealot in him. From what is known of Mary Coles's behavior later in life (her willingness to marry all of her children out of her sect, for instance), it seems likely that John was the more extreme, a fact that Mary Cutts, perhaps when she was conscious of her bias, tries to correct. At one point in Mary's manuscript, Mary writes that Dolley's father implanted Quaker principles into her. She then crosses "father" out and substitutes "parents."[41]

In trying to puzzle out the relationship among Dolley, the Society of Friends, and her father, perhaps the most important perspective is the future, how Dolley chose to live her life. In 1805, a full adult and married to James Madison, Dolley found herself virtually trapped in Philadelphia by illness. She confided to Anna that, stimulated by a visit to her sickbed from the Friends, the memories of her girlhood among the Quakers gave her "terror[s]."[42] Even if wifely duty can excuse her being read out of meeting, surely it is significant that Dolley reacted to this exclusion by becoming the

39. Ibid., 90.   40. Ibid., 90–91.   41. Ibid., 99.
42. DPTM to Anna Payne Cutts, 19 Aug. [1805], DMDE.

most worldly, famous, and ornamental woman in America, at the center of the very kind of coercive power that Quakers abhorred. Dolley Madison lived not just in the world, but she was also indubitably of it.

After the move to Philadelphia, life with Father only got harder, in circumstances that would try hardier souls. As Mary so delicately puts it, "After a few years Mr. Payne, unaccustomed to city life and the management of money matters," found himself needing employment. He went into business as a starch merchant. Perhaps most symbolic of his family's fall from grace, John was forced to draft his son Walter into the business, though he had sent him to Europe to receive a gentleman's education. But this venture failed, too, as had his North Carolina enterprise. The fault was put at the door of the falling value of "Revolutionary money," but the reaction of the Society of Friends contradicts Mary's depiction of John as a hapless victim, felled by patriotism.[43] As Shulman has demonstrated, the Quakers' problem with John Payne had less to do with his debt, though indebted and defaulting he was, than with the shady business practices that accompanied it. He was read out of meeting. Maybe the best proof of the rigidity and inflexibility behind John Payne's strength is that after this final failure he had a breakdown, never raising his head or leaving his room until he died a short time later.

Before he died, he insisted on Dolley's marriage to John Todd, an eminently suitable Virginia lawyer, who was also a member of the Society of Friends. At this point in the narrative, given the amount of energy Mary has expended to construct a tale of peace and harmony and of parents wise and good, what untold stormy story lies behind this sentence: "Young Mr. Todd had long been a suitor of Dolley's, who did not incline to relinquish her girl hood, but this was a match that pleased her father in every way. . . ."?[44] In other words, Dolley knew John Todd and had refused him previously, precluding the possibility that Dolley either loved him before her father's involvement or that she fell in love at first sight with her father's choice.

At points in the memoir, Mary Cutts calls upon the conventions of the sentimental novel to cover uncomfortable moments. Nowhere is that more evident than in the scene of Dolley's acquiescence, which takes place at her father's "deathbed," where he "told her how much happiness it would give him in his last moments to know that she was married to so estimable a person and in her own Society." Again, the understatement speaks volumes:

43. CM I, 91.   44. Ibid., 92.

"We have heard her say, she did not wish to marry, it was a hard struggle, but she never for one instant thought of disobeying her father's wishes." But of course she did, or why the struggle? Apparently, after the struggle, Dolley found herself "amply repaid by receiving the joyful blessing of her dying father!" John Payne's decline was a long one. Dolley Payne and John Todd married in November 1791, and John Payne died October 24, 1792, not "[a] few months afterwards," as stated in the memoir by Mary. He did so, one must assume, still hidden in his room.[45]

Mary's treatment of this event reflects her own milieu. Though people of her time (and ours!) might disapprove of John Payne's use of emotional blackmail to manipulate his daughter into marriage, his concerns and actions were not only typical of an eighteenth-century paterfamilias, they were exemplary. Love was not a primary consideration when it came to marriage, and John Payne, possibly knowing he was about to die and that his family was in bad financial straits, may have wanted to ensure that Dolley was taken care of and not an additional burden on her natal family. It may seem cold-blooded that John Todd's chief qualification was his Quakerhood and his earning potential. But John Payne had failed at the two jobs his culture demanded of him—to protect and provide. By insisting on Dolley's marriage, John Payne could see her married back into respectability, with a financial security that he never gave her. Or perhaps this assessment gives his insistence too much credit and his decree was a controlling man's final act of control.

Mary Cutts, and certainly, Lucia, wrote from within a culture that valued romantic love in marriage, one that would have judged a marriage commanded by a father for mercenary or social reasons as almost barbaric. Mary's first tack excuses John Payne on the grounds of "other times, other manners": "Implicit obedience was then the order of the day," but then one of the women crosses it out. Mary then redeems this union during her discussion of the yellow fever epidemic of 1793 by presenting the Todds not merely as a loving couple, but as though they were characters in a romantic novel.

When the epidemic began, John Todd took his family out of the city; Dolley, still weak from delivering her second baby, "implored him not to return" to the disease-filled town. But John felt keenly his duty to family and friends left behind. He promised he would go only to see to them and to his business and then return—"he would never again leave her." Sadly,

45. Ibid.

by the time John Todd returned to Gray's Ferry, where he had sequestered his family, it was too late. "[T]he fever is in my veins!" he exclaimed to Dolley's mother. Knowing he was dying, he begged, "'let me behold her once more!' Mrs. Madison, said, at the sound of his voice, she heeded not her mother, but left her couch and throwing herself in his arms welcomed him affectionately as usual and would gladly have returned with him to Philadelphia, but was not allowed either by her husband or mother."[46] In a few hours, he was dead. A few days later, Dolley's newborn son followed his father to the grave. If Dolley was an obedient eighteenth-century daughter when she married, she became (with Mary's pen) a nineteenth-century sentimental tragic heroine.

Dolley as "True Woman"

As an eighteenth-century person, Dolley lived in a world where women were seen as lesser versions of men, not as smart, not as strong, not as virtuous. This formulation resulted in "facts" about women that would go on to be reversed or transformed in the nineteenth century. By the time Mary Cutts was creating her historical Dolley, the gender prescription for womanhood had undergone a massive change. For instance, it stood to reason for hundreds of years that, as the weaker vessel, women would be more prone to vices, especially sexual. By the mid-nineteenth century, however, received wisdom understood women to be "passionless," morally obliged to guard both men and women from the consequences of male lust.

Similarly, women of Dolley's cohort were not restricted to homes, sheltered from a public sphere. Rather, for women of the elite, home was a place of business, where families participated in building political, economic, and social networks. For them, privacy was not a value or even a possibility. In contrast, by the mid-1800s, a "private sphere" of middle-class homes, distinct from the public worlds of business and politics had emerged, if only as an ideal. Such homes became refuges for middle-class white men, weary of the marketplace, and sites where women proved their femininity by their devotion to domesticity and their abhorrence of the public.

With a new science that rendered femininity and masculinity biological facts, women saw their nature as one of passivity, dependence, and morality and their roles restricted to homes where they were to be "angels of the hearth." Mary wanted to present Dolley not just as historically significant,

46. Ibid., 93.

but also as an exemplar to American women struggling to fit into prevailing models. To borrow the categories from Barbara Welter's landmark article, Mary wanted her Aunt Dolley to appear as a "true woman"—pious, pure, submissive, and domestic.[47] But Mary had to acknowledge that Dolley had other traits that made her extraordinary and more visible than the garden-variety angel; for instance, Dolley's incredible charisma and the power (some political) it had over people, and her sense of style, expressed through decor, elaborate clothing, and jewelry that passed the bounds of middle-class taste.

An important measure of a "true woman" lay in the quality of her heart. Throughout the memoir, Mary illustrates Dolley's "warm heart" in action. Dolley's love radiated to all. Children followed her like puppies, and she even inspired a band of young boys to declare themselves "Mrs. Madison's guard." Her charm transcended species—"even the favorite cattle on the lawn, whom she had carressed and stroked with her hand, would give a sound of recognition and walk after her, so she was always sure of company."[48]

In a slaveholding society, the surest demonstration of a superior heart is one that can overcome even the oppression of slavery, and several times the reader is assured of the mutual love between Dolley and enslaved people. Sometimes these lesser folks appear in coded terms, as in "the high and the low" born. Sometimes they are identified, as is Dolley's nurse, "Mother Amy," who refused her freedom, traveled with the Paynes from Virginia to Philadelphia, and remained close to Dolley all her own life. As a final testimony of an affection that overcomes tyranny, in her will, Amy left her former mistress a much-needed five hundred dollars.[49]

Dolley's behavior and generosity did not change when she reached high office, according to Mary. Her "servants," including the enslaved African Americans Joe Bolen and Paul Jennings, as well as the white "French John" Sioussat, the White House doorman, "were singularly attached to her." Working for free (as women did) demonstrated the most disinterested love, as when Mother Amy did so for the Paynes; at one point, John Sioussat did so as well. Paul Jennings, in Mary's version of his life, so valued his "home of ease" that once free he longed to return to the Madisons' service. Later, when he was once "again enamoured with freedom," Dolley allowed him to

47. Barbara Welter, "The Cult of True Womanhood, 1820–1860," *American Quarterly* 18 (1966): 151–74.

48. CM I, 114, 116.   49. Ibid., 91.

purchase it "for a very small Sum."[50] Writing in the 1850s, Mary was conscious that the American reading public was a dual one. The southerners in Mary's audience would appreciate her reinforcement of the "benevolent mistress model" that excused slavery. Her northern readers would approve of Dolley's abolitionist impulses. Both of these characterizations, as Shulman discusses, were more complicated.

For Mary, the invocation of affection seems also to serve as further proof of Dolley's properly apolitical nature. It is as though personal warmth obviates the capacity to calculate. As a consequence, every incident or situation (especially if it was political) is second to a pure and loving heart, as Mary (or Dolley through Mary) reassures—"Her early advantages were few in the way of high intellectual culture, but with her pure minded parents the affections of her heart were well developed and these twelve years of childhood had an effect upon her after life!"[51] Surely such tutelage could not produce a dangerous political woman!

Making her case for the quality of Dolley's loving heart is one thing—a trickier issue was that of Dolley's charm and her strong effect on people. While "charming" is usually considered a compliment when said to one's face, it can carry the odor of hypocrisy, of dissembling and manipulating for one's personal ends. In a political context, it would be too easy to turn that gift into hard political currency, as Dolley herself did. Mary Cutts had to work hard to squelch this notion. She makes sure her readers know that Dolley exhibited charm and exercised her sway over people from her earliest years, so it was obviously a God-given gift, not a learned skill or a conscious art. In Mary's relation of Dolley's childhood, she was "a favorite with all," a status she held so graciously, that, even as a tot, Dolley awakened no envy in her playmates.[52] It was as though they recognized her as a force of nature or one blessed by Providence.

From the start, the gifted girl never used her influence for selfish ends. As she "grew in grace and beauty," so did her charm, and young Dolley Payne attracted "numerous suitors." In the extant copy of Mary's fair version, Lucia crossed out the sentence that follows this assessment—"her powers of fascination were wonderful!" Perhaps its proximity to the lines about suitors was too sexually suggestive. Reinforcing the notion that her

50. Ibid., 115. It should be noted that Mary's version of Paul Jennings's story does not match reality. For a historically accurate treatment of his life, see Elizabeth Dowling Taylor, *A Slave in the White House: Paul Jennings and the Madisons* (New York: Palgrave Macmillan, 2012).

51. CM I, 90.   52. Ibid., 89.

"powers of fascination" sprang not from vanity or a desire to manipulate but were instead a manifestation of her noble spirit, Mary claims that, again, for all of Dolley's popularity, no one ever resented her preeminence.[53]

As a young woman, according to Dolley's two oldest girlfriends, she had influence over the hearts of all, and she "disarmed envy. A word or look caused all to love her as they did themselves." According to Mary, Dolley did not lose this capacity. Mary bore witness to how, in her final years, beset with grievous financial problems, Dolley inspired "high and the low [to] take from themselves to give to her and think themselves well repaid by the affectionate glance of this otherwise powerless lady."[54]

In Mary's depiction, Dolley's charm can be understood by its cause—it flowed from her spirit—and its effect—it brought out the best in people. But whatever the perspective, the two points that Mary emphasizes are that Dolley's charm was as natural and abundant as a healing spring and as indiscriminate. It seems highly unlikely that Dolley operated on an unconscious level at all times and that she did not make any enemies. Dolley's charm and kindness to others, her enjoyment of people, and her power to empathize were important parts of her personality. But the fact that she possessed these traits "naturally" did not preclude her from using them as an intelligent adult, a loving wife, or as a participant in a high-stakes, uncertain political world. In the Madison marriage and political partnership, personality became a tool of policy.

With charm safely contained, Mary had to also grapple with another suspect issue in Dolley's past. As an adult, Dolley became famous for her extravagant ensembles. The semi-regal nature of her outfits always garnered remarks, either approving or horrified. For good or ill, people saw them as political statements, sending messages of both democracy and aristocracy. Recently, scholars such as Linzy Brekke and Holly C. Shulman have taken a page from European historians, who have always considered clothing, especially court clothing, seriously as a measure of power and cultural formation.[55] In many ways, scholars of the early republic are just catching up with their subjects. The new Americans discussed clothing,

53. Ibid., 91.

54. Ibid. If legend is correct, the "high" would include Henry Clay, who often sent over groceries to the house in Lafayette Square. The "low" could indicate the freed slave Paul Jennings, who gave Dolley money during the late Washington years.

55. Catherine Allgor, *A Perfect Union: Dolley Madison and the Creation of the American Nation* (New York: Henry Holt, 2006), 235–40; Linzy Brekke, "Fashioning America: Clothing and the Politics of America, 1783–1845" (Ph.D. diss., Harvard Uni-

bearing, and personality as a form of political analysis, using men such as George Washington and women such as Dolley Madison to measure the legitimacy and viability of an administration, a leader or leading family, or even the republic itself.

But Mary cannot allow these clothes to function either as political weapons, expressions of personal vanity, or assertions of aristocratic privilege. Her concern may have been how the story of Dolley's spending ended—with a financial failure rivaling any of John Payne's debacles. During the White House years, the acquisition of these outfits, the accessories and accoutrements, drove James Madison into severe debt. Dolley knew she was spending too much—on more than one occasion, she went to some pains to hide her expenditures from her husband.[56]

By the 1850s, the consequences of the Madison lifestyle were clear in ways that they would not have been in Dolley's early-nineteenth-century heyday. When James Madison died, he left his widow with little but Montpelier, which Dolley had to sell in 1844. The former "Queen of Washington City" lived her last years in genteel poverty (at one point accepting handouts from her Lafayette Square neighbors and a former slave, Paul Jennings), and everyone knew of her profligate son who had bilked thousands of dollars from his mother and stepfather.

Mary obliquely handles these issues of sartorial excess with an emblematic story, one that functions on several levels. "Give me the child at seven, and I will show you the man," goes the old saying, and, according to Aunt Dolley, when she was just about that age, "[h]er grandmother [Payne] testified her affection by constant presents of her old fashioned jewelry, for which it must be confessed Dolley ever had a woman's fondness." Not wanting to offend her strict Quaker parents, young Dolley hid the jewelry in a bag tied around her neck. On her way to school one day, the tie loosened, and Dolley lost her secret treasure in the woods. This, again according to Dolley via Mary, was the first grief of her life.[57]

Given the inaccuracies of the narrative as a whole, it may be this story is created, though there is something so particular about that bag—it has the ring of truth. Another reason for supposing the story true is that in relating this tale, Mary prefaces the conclusion with, "we have heard her say. . . ." This indication of the source occurs only a few times in the manuscript.

versity, 2007); Shulman, "The Politics of War, 1809–1817," in DPM, *Selected Letters*, 93–94.

56. Allgor, *Perfect Union*, 235.   57. CM I, 89–90.

Even if this rather sweet story of childish greed and grief is true, Dolley's remembrance and privileging of it in this account shows that it functions in a deeply symbolic way. The story of the secret jewelry and its loss plays its part in laying the groundwork for Dolley's eventual rejection of Quaker-hood and its stern, unnatural strictures. Making this admission of vanity in the context of childhood robs it of much of its stigma. By asserting that such a love of finery was a natural weakness, not only does Mary provide a rationalization for Dolley's later spending, but Dolley also is affirmed in her own status as a "natural woman." Mary does not have to account for the meaning of Dolley's later fetish for clothes and jewelry, neither the purposes they served nor the costs they demanded.[58]

"Queen" Dolley as Lady

As other biographers would after her, Mary dealt with these issues handily, subsuming them all under the category of "personal qualities for personal uses." She did the same thing with Dolley's legendary sociability. For Mary Cutts, Dolley entertained regularly and rigorously, first as the wife of the secretary of state and then as First Lady, merely because she loved people and parties. And there the analysis ends. As Mary does not openly acknowledge that Dolley put her charm or her sense of fashion to political uses, she also refuses to see that Dolley won supporters for her husband, reconciled or defused his enemies and rivals, gathered and disseminated information, facilitated patronage and engaged in nation-building at her parties, most notably at her famous weekly drawing rooms.

As a historian and biographer, Mary Cutts faced a paradoxical task (as would all subsequent biographers of Dolley who would rely on Mary's account). She had to establish Dolley Madison's historical significance within a culture that measured such import by proximity to state power, while also presenting her as a perfect, and therefore apolitical and private, lady. This was not a new dilemma. Queens and saints aside, few female historical subjects were lauded for their political work. Writing about a highly placed woman who played politics successfully in the mid-nineteenth century, moreover, was particularly fraught.

Women had been considered "a disorder in the polity" since Aristotle's time. Closer to Dolley's era, men such as Thomas Jefferson worried about the influence of women on the new republic and took pains to exclude

58. Ibid., 90.

them; indeed, Jefferson's almost obsessive abhorrence of political women seemed pathological. Recent research, however, demonstrates that Thomas Jefferson may have had ample evidence that women were threatening to break through political barricades. Colonial women had been politicized by the American Revolution, and in the days before voting became the sine qua non of political participation, women participated freely in politics out-of-doors, petitioning, and other political activities. Elite women even became known as "politicians," that is, women knowledgeable and vocal about politics. As Rosemarie Zagarri has persuasively demonstrated, women's growing political capacities were abruptly curtailed as a way of defusing the bitter partisanship engendered by the new two-party system. Contemporaries worried that such discord would rend the fabric of the new nation; sending women back into the home seemed a way to guarantee that at least half the population would preserve social harmony. Cultural custom was made into law as, during the early decades of the 1800s, state after state made maleness a requisite for voting.

Dolley Madison, however, had lived and worked under the old system. Like other political women of her era, she borrowed from court systems to create new networks of power for the United States government. This strategy allowed women to assume public visibility and personal display and to indulge in monarchical practices, such as patronage. For the most part, Dolley's culture approved her actions, seeing them as not only patriotic but an also as the exemplary actions of a devoted wife.

But when Mary wrote her paean to Dolley, such behavior was seen as dangerous, an anathema to a democracy. In the latter half of the nineteenth century and beginning of the twentieth, "woman" guarded the portals of the private sphere, and her political involvement was limited to a "concurrent patriotism." "Unwomanly conduct" would be the least of the crimes laid at Dolley's door should she be identified as "political."[59] Even decades after their heydays, the ghosts of Mary Wollstonecraft, Frances Wright, and Victoria Woodhull, with their threats to the sexual order and the family, would haunt any discussion of an American political woman.

Mary Cutts tackled the contradictory task of presenting this totally feminine, apolitical woman as a historically significant figure in several ways, all of them involving a certain amount of coded language. As noted above, she often employed the "significance by association" technique,

59. Not to mention the abuse an author who made such a claim would receive from an indignant public (Rosemarie Zagarri, "Petticoat Politicians and Concurrent Patriots," presentation, American Antiquarian Society, Nov. 1996). See also Zagarri, *Backlash*.

wherein Dolley could remain a passive, unconscious object, her influence made manifest not by anything she *did*, but just by being herself. In this formulation, her love of people, parties, and clothes might have helped James, but only as an unexpected consequence.

In writing about one of the most well-known women in the United States, Mary also relied on the idea that her aunt's fame was self-evident. In addition, Mary larded her accounts of Dolley's life with gobs of "history"— tales of elections, battles in the War of 1812, and the like. These "side trips" are fairly straightforward accounts, not offering anything beyond a text-book recounting; Mary offers no insider access to the "real story." As with her digression about Patrick Henry, the heavy emphasis on official male characters and seemingly female-free political events was not a departure from her discussion of Dolley. Rather, by juxtaposing personal accounts of Dolley with the Big Men and Big Events of her time and place, but not including her in them, Mary neatly sidesteps any unfeminine involvement, while subtly signaling that Dolley's mere presence on the scene gives her historical import.

The energy Mary Cutts expends to contain this dangerous part of "Aunt Dolley" surely reveals more than she intended. She feels it important to mention that the "citizens of Washington," though they could not vote in a presidential election, took "peculiar interest" in who occupied the White House. Their concerns centered around "social position" and "political preferences." "What wonder then, that an event which placed Mrs. Madison in the 'White House' should give such general satisfaction and plea-sure!" The citizens of Washington City may have been pleased, but they could have hardly been surprised. Rather than merely being "placed" at the head of society by a kind fate, Dolley had assiduously worked for nine years to win friends and supporters for her husband. Instead, Mary attributes the approval of citizenry to the fact that Dolley "had endeared herself to all classes."[60]

To illustrate this point, Mary inadvertently shows Dolley working the hustings like a pro, exercising the diplomacy and self-control needed by the politician—even as Mary endeavors to subsume these activities under the category "personal virtue." She does not acknowledge there could be any political use to the fact that Dolley appealed "to all classes; the poor-est beggar could come to her with confidence, and confide his or her cares and wants, sure of an attentive and sympathizing audience if possible, she

60. CM I, 108.

would send them on their way rejoicing—if not, she gave them comfort and advice, causing them to feel they had in her—a friend."[61]

Any inadvertent political successes Dolley enjoyed came about because she was a "foe to dullness, wherever She went she promoted gaity and happiness, she returned all visits that were made her by ladies, and it gave her pleasure to do so. Her 'dove parties' composed of the ladies of the Cabinet and foreign ministers, when their lords were engaged in formal Diplomatic dinners, were exceeding popular."[62] Little would the reader know that, far from being a pleasure, Dolley's calling was onerous. She became well known for calling on every individual and family—local, government official, or visitor—in Washington City. She complained rarely, but the freely voiced outrage by Louisa Catherine Johnson Adams, a later secretary of state's wife who tried to imitate Dolley, gives a sense of the task's toll. Scholars have noted a movement in the mid-nineteenth century to "naturalize" female labor as a way to convince women that their place was in the home. In her own way, Mary tried to naturalize the onerous tasks of calling and diplomatic entertaining in the most American of all homes— the White House.

One particular political strategy Mary Cutts categorizes as a personal quirk, not only to avoid the charge of "petticoat politicking," but also to excuse Dolley from base hypocrisy. "To the powerful and arrogant, she would accord all their vanity exacted," Mary relayed. "She would say, it was not her place to treat them otherwise. One of her peculiarities was, never to contradict—." Originally, Mary added "any one" to this sentence; perhaps she took out this specifier to make the practice more a politeness and less a kowtowing to the rich and powerful.[63]

Such an attitude and behavior is typical of a professional politician, and even as Mary shies away from the obvious conclusions, she gives herself away. In praising her aunt, Mary declares: "[A]ll parties appeared [at Dolley's drawing rooms], knowing that they should all share her kind welcome and benignant smile, she felt that i[t] was her duty to pour oil on the waters of discord, and draw malcontents into the fold of her husband, and successful she was for few would oppose the partner of such a wife!"[64]

Nor does Mary acknowledge the raw power that Dolley wielded. Stating that "So harmonious was her disposition, she never argued a point, if friends or relations indulged in satire or wit, in her presence, which might

61. Ibid., 108.   62. Ibid., 110.   63. Ibid., 108.
64. Ibid., 110–11.

wound the feelings of others, she would quickly leave" makes Dolley sound almost saintlike. Mary does not draw any inferences from the fact that if people were "indulg[ing] in satire or wit," Dolley's mere presence would make them stop: "when the peculiar and welcome returning sound of her high heeled shoes gave token of her approach all ill feeling would be forgotten or suppressed and the topic changed, so well known was her dislike to contention; for she always said 'I would rather fight with my hands than my tongue.'"[65] Or, in this case, her feet, which had the power to change the conversation.

Dolley was popularly known as the "Queen of Washington City"; she was also the "Queen of Patronage." She, like many political women, could influence-peddle where the officially virtuous husbands could not. Dolley was a master at patronage. In her memoir, Mary actually alludes to this source of Dolley's power and renown, though from her description, it seems more like a trip down the garden path than a descent into the dirty world of politics. The key words and phrases are "reciprocate," "friends," and "making friends," which were all political code words in this era. "Friends" were political supporters; "reciprocity" blurred the transactional quality of quid pro quo. Mary states: "Receiving so many congratulations she could not but reciprocate the pleasure it gave her friends to have her in this exalted position, she saw nothing but flowers in her path, from the thorns she turned aside. Her countenance, beaming with inward happiness made friends wherever it glanced!"[66]

Continuing with nature images—petitions shower like rain—Mary makes it clear what she meant. Amazingly, even though it means acknowledging Dolley's involvement with politics, Mary proudly declares Dolley's "unbounded" influence on James: "It delighted her to do good: petitions from afar and near were showered upon her; she was never annoyed, and always answered them favorably, if possible; as her influence over her husband was unbounded and seldom exerted in vain." Fear of accusations of meddling kept Dolley, like other political women, from making her efforts public, but Mary attributes this less to discretion and more to modesty and loyalty: "Many, whom the world little knows, are indebted to Mrs. Madison for independence and position in society—she never said so, for she never betrayed a confidence, but grateful letters have proved it."[67]

65. Ibid., 115–16.   66. Ibid., 108–9.   67. Ibid., 109.

A Language of Love

When Mary Cutts framed Dolley's political work in personal, feminine, and domestic ways, it must have seemed as natural as breathing. By the 1850s, when Mary was working on her manuscript, such "sentimental" language had been in use for decades. It was a technique for women to talk about politics and social change in acceptable ways; male and female reformers, too, found a language of love and family a handy way to "naturalize" issues such as abolition and equal rights. And 1852 would see perhaps the apotheosis of the use of this female argot, with the publication of Harriet Beecher Stowe's *Uncle Tom's Cabin*. With a home in its very title, Stowe's story of family and domesticity remains one of the most powerfully articulated answers to pro-slavery apologists.

Historians have noted the beginnings of this language of sentimentality around the late 1820s and 1830s, linking it to the rise of capitalism, the abolition movement, and the modern public/private distinction, with its emphasis on true womanhood.[68] But its development began earlier and was nurtured by political, rather than social, necessity.

68. For more on this sentimental language, see G. J. Barker-Benfield, *Abigail and John Adams: The Americanization of Sensibility* (Chicago: University of Chicago Press, 2010), 188–206; Anne M. Boylan, *Origins of Women's Activism: New York and Boston, 1797–1840* (Chapel Hill: University of North Carolina Press, 2002), 54, 76–84; Bruce Dorsey, *Reforming Men and Women: Gender in the Antebellum City* (Ithaca: Cornell University Press, 2002), 38–39, 88, 134; Lori D. Ginzberg, *Women and Work of Benevolence: Morality, Politics, and Class in the Nineteenth-Century United States* (New Haven: Yale University Press, 1990), 11–16, 25–35, 59–60, 96–97; Philip Gould, "Civil Society and the Public Woman, *Journal of the Early Republic* 28, no. 1 (Spring 2008): 38; Julie Roy Jeffrey, *The Great Silent Army of Abolitionism: Ordinary Women in the Antislavery Movement* (Chapel Hill: University of North Carolina Press, 1998), 36–41, 67–68, 130–33; Mary Kelley, *Learning to Stand and Speak: Women, Education, and Public Life* (Chapel Hill: University of North Carolina Press, 2006), 29, 53–54; Carol Lasser, "Voyeuristic Abolitionism: Sex, Gender, and the Transformation of Antislavery Rhetoric," *Journal of the Early Republic* 28, no. 1 (Spring 2008): 94–95, 112; Beth Salerno, *Sister Societies: Women's Antislavery Organizations in Antebellum America* (DeKalb: University of Illinois Press, 2005), 75–76, 83; Jean Fagan Yellin, *Women and Sisters: The Antislavery Feminists in American Culture* (New Haven: Yale University Press, 1989), 63–65, 92–93; and Susan Zaeske, *Signatures of Citizenship: Petitioning, Antislavery, and Women's Political Identity* (Chapel Hill: University of North Carolina Press, 2003), 157–60. In discussing the Revolutionary and post-Revolutionary era, before the emergence of an antebellum language of sentimental reform, Dorsey shows how women operated within a political world of masculinity,

Ironically, the language of sentimentality and domesticity that proved so handy for Mary Cutts was put into place by her subject and her cohort of political elite women. In the face of a prevailing antipolitical culture of republicanism, political women in the early decades of the federal government "covered" the exercise of political power in many ways. Even as the federal government was struggling to amass and organize the political power it would need to become a two-party democracy and a nation-state with a strong executive, women used patronage, connection making, and lobbying to foster the federal government's structure. But they contained these blatantly power-building activities under feminine rubrics, in order to preserve their own (and their culture's) sense of female propriety. Mary Cutts paid unconscious tribute to Dolley and her generation as she used domestic terms and analytic constructs that they themselves would have understood and approved.

The Rosewood Box Revisited

Sadly, Mary Cutts was doomed by circumstances and by her culture to remain outside what was rapidly becoming a credentialed profession—that of "historian"—that excluded her. Even her story of the first First Lady would not be published until long after her death. The publishers of her time regarded the story of a woman, even a woman as renowned as "Mrs. Madison," doubtfully. Aside from the occasional Joan of Arc or Elizabeth I, women could not be the topic of "real history," or so Mary was informed.

As we have seen, fragmentary evidence exists that Mary Cutts tried to get her "memoir" published, and, when discouraged, may have rewritten her first draft to be more "marketable." Or perhaps, as scholars now surmise, added parts to an existing manuscript. As far as evaluating the writing itself, the prose is perfectly correct, but until the second half of the second memoir, only occasionally does emotion or originality break through the writing conventions. When Mary begins her narration of the Madisons' retirement years at Monticello, however, descriptions and impressions leap out with specificity and color. No wonder; unlike most of the events

---

using masculine symbols and language, and in some cases, adopting "a masculine persona, to assert an authoritative public role" (Dorsey, *Reforming*, 29–39, 30). Amy Kaplan argues that domesticity also provided a language for imperialism and racialized "othering" (see Kaplan, *The Anarchy of Empire in the Making of U. S. Culture* [Cambridge: Harvard University Press, 2005], chap. 1).

The rosewood box. (Cutts-Madison Collection, Massachusetts Historical Society)

of the memoir, the retirement years were experienced by Mary firsthand. Her time there, as well as her relationship with both her aunt and uncle, remained vivid for Mary. Her remembrances of the place and the personalities of Montpelier are so powerful that scholars of the Madisons and the staff at James Madison's Montpelier, now a historic home and museum, regularly use them. But Mary's claim on this material was not as a gifted writer. Instead, Mary asserts the power of familial authority that Shulman describes. In her final extant letter about her work, she avers: "Every thing, throughout the narrative is true, dear Mr. Gilpin, and there is very little I cannot prove." So hopeful was Mary that publication was imminent that she even suggested illustrations.[69]

Mary's publishing attempt was thwarted by her early death. Her own niece Lucia B. Cutts would freely excerpt from the memoir, accepting Mary's editorial hand at face value and adding one of her own, informed by more Victorian sensibilities. This had the effect of further sanitizing Dolley's political work. It is Lucia's account that would go on to become the primary source for all writings about Dolley, fact or fiction.

In the end, the little box stands alone, a mute tribute to the woman who tried to make history. Surely, the most moving aspect of this little collection is that, before the relics found their home in the handsome rosewood casket, Mary wrapped her hair collection in torn bits of used paper. Like women before and after her, most notably Emily Dickinson, Mary used scrap paper to contain her life's work. The ephemera of paper, compared to

69. Mary Crowninshield Silsbee Sparks to MEEC, 10 June 1856; MEEC to Henry D. Gilpin, n.d., Cutts-Madison Papers, Massachusetts Historical Society.

the solidity of wood and brass, the whiff of the thrifty housewife, recycling waste paper—it would all be unbearably poignant. But even in this seemingly most self-abnegating act, Mary may have unconsciously sent a signal to "History," ensuring that her efforts would live on. The papers in which she wrapped her souvenirs were her father's letters.

History, Memory, and Dolley Madison

Notes from a Documentary Editor

HOLLY COWAN SHULMAN

When Mary Estelle Elizabeth Cutts began writing her memoir of the life of her aunt, Dolley Payne Todd Madison, Mary tucked into its introductory pages a hint of why she was undertaking this labor and provided an indication of her understanding of the role of evidence in the writing of history. She wanted her aunt remembered as a great American wife and woman. And she believed that she, a favorite niece, was the repository of family memories.

Mary started the first of her two accounts of Dolley with her genealogy: grandfather, grandmother, father, and mother. But she quickly passed through these direct ancestors in favor of a discussion of one distant relative, Patrick Henry. Of him, she wrote, "we cannot forebear a few passing remarks," which became no fewer than six paragraphs, more than anything she wrote about Dolley's parents or numerous siblings. These "remarks" were later deleted, most probably by Lucia Cutts. While we cannot know much about who later deleted the section on Henry or why, we can pause a few moments to consider what impulse prompted Mary Cutts to write at length about Patrick Henry in the first place.

Mary described Henry as a great patriot and orator who was both modest and unselfish, a man not dazzled by power but compelled by patriotism. He "seemed to spring into existance as a meteor when most needed by his country and who by the power of truth led them on to assert their rights." As Catherine Allgor insightfully notes in her essay in this volume, Mary used Henry as a "mirror" to cast "luster" onto the Payne family. Patrick Henry was not only Dolley's most famous relative (after James himself), but also a legend of Virginia history, a model for how Mary wanted her aunt to be remembered. But in addition to this straightforward association between her subject and a famous American patriot who was her relative, Mary left us another clue in the deleted Henry section when she noted, "[a] very pleasing sketch of this Orator is found in the *Homes of American Statesmen.*" In the margin opposite this text, she noted the initials of its author, "E.J.," for Edward William Johnston.

Like Mary, Johnston was related to the subject of his biographical essay. Patrick Henry was his great-uncle, and thus Johnston, a now-obscure writer cum librarian and schoolmaster who was in his day a prominent journalist, was probably moved to offer his sketch of Henry out of a general regard for his famous relative, but also, and perhaps especially, by what he considered to be flagrant mistakes in William Wirt's biography of Henry. Johnston argued that Wirt had tarnished the great orator's reputation for the simple reason that Wirt had not talked to the surviving women of the Henry family "for any particulars of his early life, which of course none knew so well as they . . . we may have cause to know the astonishment with which they viewed this written account of his [Henry's] early years and his breeding."[1]

The evidentiary principle that Edward Johnston asserted in his biography was that of personal knowledge and individual witness. Mary Cutts, writing in her own role as historian, would surely have agreed with this principle, and she affirmed her claim to be an expert witness on Dolley Madison's life. In the absence of a biographer, she would record her first-hand testimony to her aunt's life. As relative, participant, and witness, she would provide the most authentic literary deposition possible.

In the twenty-first century, we understand the problematic nature of evidence. As one historiographer has written, we "are periodically aware that memory is among the most fragile and capricious of our faculties."[2] We assume that history is a process of construction and reconstruction, that

1. Edward William Johnston, *Homes of American Statesmen* (New York: Putnam, 1854), 165. It is perhaps also worth noting what Johnston wrote of Dolley in his chapter biography of James Madison in the same publication: "There were few houses in Virginia that gave a larger welcome, or made it more agreeable than that over which Queen Dolley—the most gracious and beloved of all our female sovereigns—reigned; and, wielding as skillfully the domestic, as she had done worthily and popularly the public, scepter, every thing that came beneath her immediate personal sway—the care and entertainment of visitors, the government of the menials, the whole policy of the interior, was admirably managed, with an equal grace and efficiency" (189).

2. Yoseph Hayim Yerushalmi, *Zakhor: Jewish History and Jewish Memory* (Seattle: University of Washington Press, 1982), 5.

we create and revise our understanding of the past, and that in the process we may challenge personal memory. We know that memory reflects the forgetfulness of aging, the self-fashioning of individuals, and the selective shaping of societies. But Mary Cutts was writing her memoir/biography before the nineteenth-century scientific study of history had begun and prior to the development of the research protocols of our academic profession. She could assume, and implicitly assert, the unquestionable reliability of personal testimony. Mary, through her use of Patrick Henry, was announcing to her audience that her memory—and therefore her memoir—should become the source for all future biographies of Dolley Madison.[3]

Mary, of course, was not writing in an intellectual vacuum. By the 1840s, there were women writing about women on both sides of the Atlantic. In the United States, Elizabeth Fries Ellet, Lydia Maria Child, and others were establishing the critical role of American women in the founding of our nation.[4] These women were, as Mary Kelley has written, looking "to the past to substantiate their claims to intellectual equality in the

3. It is possible that the six paragraphs on Patrick Henry were deleted as part of a larger shaping of Dolley's family genealogy. Originally the first paragraph began with John Payne, Dolley's grandfather. Few editorial changes were made to that paragraph; only three words—Virginia James River—were crossed out. The second paragraph initially introduced Dolley's maternal line. Most of that was deleted. Those edits may not have eliminated Patrick Henry at first, although dating and order of editorial changes are impossible to ascertain as the manuscript presently stands. The second paragraph as edited would simply have read: "His son John Payne, the father of Mrs. Madison, was a planter and settled in North Carolina. He married Mary Coles, the daughter of Williams Coles, a native of Enniscorthy in Ireland. Her mother whose maiden name was Winston was an aunt of Patrick Henry, the celebrated orator." Eliminated from that paragraph, however, was (following "Enniscorthy in Ireland"): "whose mother's maiden name was Philpot. Williams Coles married the widow of Benjamin Dabney, by whom she had several children. Isaac Winston, the father of Lucy was one of three brothers who came to Virginia, from Essex by England. He had three sons and three daughters. Mary, married John Coles, Lucy first Williams Coles, and Dorothy, who married first John Syme of New Castle Virginia, and afterward John Henry, by whom she had several children." The third paragraph introduced Patrick Henry as "this gifted son of Virginia." Dolley's relationship to Patrick Henry was through her mother's side, and the manuscript as redacted emphasized the Payne family and minimized Dolley's maternal genealogy. Lucia Beverly Cutts retained this strategy. Perhaps Henry went the way of Dolley's mother's family, deleted, after Mary decided to highlight the paternal side of the family and ignore the maternal side.

4. See Elizabeth Ellet, *The Women of the American Revolution* (New York: Haskell House, 1969); Mary Kelley, "Designing a Past for the Present: Women Writing

present," and to insist upon women's "contributions to the struggle for independence."[5] Dolley had claimed her own role here as the heroine of the War of 1812, and Mary reinforced that image. By setting Mary's stories against the documentary record, we learn both about what Mary—and probably Dolley—wished us to believe, and what we, as historians, may now conclude.

As we will see in this essay, Mary misleads. Personal testimony, after all, can be used for many purposes. As professional historians, we need to dig into the written record to excavate a fuller portrait of Dolley Madison.

This essay looks at three relationships in Dolley's life: with her parents and siblings, with her Madison in-laws, and with her slaves. It uses Mary's memoirs not only as personal narrative but also as evidentiary foil, contrasting Mary's text with our own historical research, and in the process deepening our understanding of Dolley Payne Todd Madison.

First there were the Paynes: father, mother, and Dolley's eight siblings.[6] We have little information about Dolley's father, John Payne. The genealogy records we turn up online agree with Mary E. E. Cutts's lineage: Dolley's grandfather was John (or Josias) Payne, sometimes spelled Paine (1705–1785). Her grandmother was Anna Flemming, both from Goochland County, Virginia. If this record is correct, Dolley's father, John Payne, was the eighth and youngest child of this couple.[7] He married a Quaker named Mary Winston Coles in 1761, and on 12 October 1765 he applied for membership in the Cedar Creek Meeting. That May, both John and his wife, Mary (who had probably been disowned by the Quakers when she first married John Payne) were admitted to the meeting. She was twenty

Women's History in Nineteenth-Century America," *Proceedings of the American Antiquarian Society* 105, no. 2 (1995): 339.

5. Kelley, "Designing," 323, 339.

6. Mary E. E. Cutts states that there were six siblings, but this is not true. Dolley Payne had four brothers, who, in order of birth, were Walter, William Temple, Isaac, and John Coles Payne. She had three sisters who lived to maturity, who, in order of birth, were Lucy, Anna, and Mary, and a fourth sister, Philadelphia, who died in infancy in 1787. For Philadelphia's death and burial, see Philadelphia Monthly Meetings Southern District Burials, 1733–1806, Box 410, 20 July 1787, Friends Historical Library of Swarthmore College.

7. www.hickmanresearch.com/genealogy/payne/wpayne.htm.

years old, he about twenty-five.[8] They soon went to North Carolina, but returned in 1769, where we can trace them as they are readmitted to the Cedar Creek Meeting.

The family remained in Virginia until 1783, when Dolley's father freed his slaves. Mary Cutts never enumerated the slaves her grandfather owned; she may not have known. The count is important, however, in light of the claims Mary makes. According to the Virginia census, at the point of manumitting his slaves, "John Payne (Quaker)" of Hanover County, Virginia, had a household of nine whites and five blacks.[9] Mary states that he was "one of the earliest of his sect in Virginia who became doubtful and afterwards conscientiously scrupulous about the rights of holding slaves as property," and then that he "persisted in setting his plantation and giving freedom to his slaves." The word "plantation" is critical. The ownership of five slaves places his farm on the cusp between a small and middling operation, but it would not be considered a plantation. Whatever he forfeited for his beliefs—whether by selling property in Virginia or losing the investment value of his slaves—it was not the financial sacrifice Mary Cutts implied in her memoir.[10]

In 1783, the family moved to Philadelphia. There they joined the Northern District Meeting, and engaged as active members of their religious confession. For five years we simply know they are in the city, the older children friends with the family of Elizabeth Drinker, who mentions them in her diary.[11] In 1786, they moved from the Northern District to the Southern District Quaker Meeting, by which time John and Mary had nine children,

8. Ethel Stephens Arnett, *Mrs. James Madison: The Incomparable Dolley* (Greensboro, N.C.: Piedmont Press, 1972), 16–17; Cedar Creek Monthly Meeting Men's Minutes 1739–1773, Box B-95, 12 Oct. 1765, and 11 May 1765.

9. The one slave about whom Mary provided any details was a woman named Amy. Mary tells us that Amy went to Philadelphia with the Paynes as she did not want to leave her "master" and his family. This was probably true, as there are eight mentions of an "Amy" or "Old Amey" sprinkled in Dolley's correspondence between 1797 and 1808. In each one, Amy has no last name, which indicates that she was a former slave who remained in Philadelphia and kept her "familial" status. Moreover, at all times Dolley referred to Amy with great affection. For references to Amy, see DMDE. For more on John Payne and slavery, see DPM, *Selected Letters*, 11–12.

10. *Heads of Families at the First Census of the United States Taken in the Year 1790: Records of the State Enumerations: 1782 to 1785: Virginia* (Baltimore: Genealogical Publishing, 1970), 28.

11. Elaine Forman Crane, *The Diary of Elizabeth Drinker*, vols. 1–3 (Boston: Northeastern University Press, 1991).

of whom all but the eldest, Walter, went with them: William Temple, Dolley, Isaac, Lucy, Anna, Mary, John, and Philadelphia.[12] But all cannot have
been placid, for there is a note in the Quaker records of 22 July 1783 indi-
cating that the community was already concerned about the Payne family's
behavior. The minutes read:

> The arrival of this Family among us having produced a care and tender concern
> on their Account, and particularly respecting the Children: who if not especially
> guarded and watched over may be exposed to various temptations in this City
> where vanity and many Evils are sorrowfully prevalent—a lively sense of the
> dangers which these young people and others who came amongst us may be
> drawn into having spread in their Meeting.[13]

Some of those good Quaker youths we read about in Elizabeth Drinker's
diary were socializing with the Paynes, in the hope that they would "visit
with the Family and impart such caution and counsel as the occasion may
call for."

Slowly, however, we witness the three older Payne boys get into difficulty.
Let us begin with the oldest, Walter. He may have been going back and
forth between Philadelphia and Hanover County, Virginia, as early as 1779.
We know he was there in 1783, seeing if it would be wise for his parents to
resettle there, and that in 1784 he sailed for England, where we find him in
1785 attending the Grace Church Street Meeting, and in 1786, at the Dev-
onshire House Meeting.[14] Walter, however, had returned to Philadelphia by
1787 and by the end of 1788 was in trouble, having "absented himself from
his usual Place of abode & not . . . given up Property in his possession, that
is judged he should surrender for the Benefit of his Creditors." A month
later, the Arch Street Quaker Monthly Meeting declared that he had left
"without doing what was in his Power toward the discharge of his Debts,"
and assigned members to investigate the case. A year and a month later,
he was disowned. The tone of these Quaker decisions could be austere and

12. William Wade Hinshaw, *Encyclopedia of American Quaker Genealogy*, vol. 2,
Pennsylvania and New Jersey (Baltimore: Genealogical Publishing, 1994), 617; Phila-
delphia Monthly Meeting Southern District Men's Minutes 1781–1793, Box PH-425, 27
Dec. 1786, Friends Historical Library of Swarthmore College.

13. Philadelphia Monthly Minutes, Northern District, Men's Minutes 1782–1789
Box PH-411, 22 July 1783, Friends Historical Library of Swarthmore College.

14. For another account of Walter Payne in London, see Jacob Downing to Walter
Payne, 2 Mar. 1785, Cutts Microfilm, DLC; and Drinker, *Diary*, 1:431.

magisterial, but here perhaps even a note of anger seeped in, as the meeting decreed:

> Walter Payne, who was Educated and made from profession with us the People called Quakers, left this City some time since in Order to transact Business in Virginia; and having obtained considerable property of divers persons on Credit instead of complying with their just demand for payment agreeable to Contract, hath absconded from his usual place of abode without satisfying his Creditors, or giving them the necessary information respecting his Effects by which they are in danger of suffering great loss—We therefore think it incumbent on us to Testify against such dishonest proceedings, and disown him the said Walter Payne from being a Member of our religious Society, until from a due sense of his evil Conduct he condemns the same to the satisfaction of the Meeting—which is our desire.[15]

Walter Payne abused his creditors, embezzled their money, and fled to Virginia, where he could avoid the worst of the consequences of his behavior.

The other two older Payne boys further degraded the family reputation. William Temple, like Dolley, was born in North Carolina, three years her senior. As we have seen, he was still living with his parents and siblings (except Walter) in 1786. Six years later, in April 1792, he joined the U.S. Army, appointed, according to a contemporary newspaper, as an ensign—formerly of North Carolina—serving under Anthony Wayne as a soldier in the Army Expeditionary Forces fighting the Indians in the Northwest Territory. That November, General Wayne wrote Henry Knox that Payne had been "cashiered by the sentence of a Genl. Court Martial upon the enclosed charges." We no longer have the charges, but William Temple was allowed to resign to maintain his honor.[16] Nevertheless the Philadelphia Southern District Meeting disowned him, stating:

> William Temple Payne who had a right of membership amongst us the people called Quakers, but not duly attending to the precepts of the Gospel and our religious profession, has accepted a Commission in the Army, and set off on a

15. See Philadelphia Monthly Meeting (Arch Street) Men's Minutes 1782–1789, Box PH-385, 26 Dec. 1788, 30 Jan. 1789, and 27 Feb. 1789.

16. *Gazette of the United States,* 25 Apr. 1792, America's Historical Newspapers (website). Anthony Wayne to Henry Knox, Anthony Wayne Letterbooks, Clements Library, University of Michigan, as found in Papers of the War Department: 1784–1800. Enclosure not found. http://wardepartmentpapers.org/docimage.php?id=7593

warlike expedition to the Western Country: for this deviation from our religious principles & practice he has been tenderly treated with in order to convince him of the nature of our peacable testimony, but our labours proving unsuccessful, We disown him the said William Temple Payne from membership with us, until from a due sense of his error, he is through Divine favour enabled to make a satisfactory condemnation thereof, which is our desire for him.[17]

The third of the Payne sons, Isaac, also shifted to Virginia. In 1789, he also was read out of his Philadelphia Monthly Meeting for "resorting to houses of ill fame and gaming; for all of which he has been tenderly treated with in order for his reformation but our Labour not having the desired effect, We therefore testify our disunion with his reproachful conduct, and that we do not esteem him a member of our Religious Society."[18] He was presumably an alcoholic and a wastrel who died around 1795.[19] According to Elizabeth Drinker, he had "offended a man in Virginia, who some time afterward shot him with a pistol, of which wound he died."[20] Mary never mentioned Walter by name, and she excised William Temple and Isaac from her text.

John Payne is usually portrayed by legend as an honest man, a planter who failed in business after he moved to Philadelphia, a merchant disowned by his meeting for debts. We know that the Paynes moved to Philadelphia in 1783, and we have a record of their participating in Philadelphia Quaker business in the years following their migration. The Quaker local leaders were sufficiently concerned by John's finances to start an investigation of him in 1788. The records of the Philadelphia Southern District Monthly Meeting state:

We are informed that the case of John Payne has claimed the attention of the Overseers for a considerable time past, divers complaints having been made to

---

&docColID=8247&page=138. See also "General Wayne's Orderly Book," introduction by C. M. Burton, Michigan Pioneer and Historical Society, Michigan State Historical Society (Lansing, 1905), 34:405.

17. Philadelphia Monthly Meeting, Southern District Men's Minutes, 1781–1793, Box PH-425, Friends Historical Library of Swarthmore College.

18. Philadelphia Monthly Meeting, Southern District Men's Minutes, 1781–1793, Box PH-425, Friends Historical Library of Swarthmore College.

19. Philadelphia Monthly Meeting, Southern District Men's Minutes, 1781–1793, Box PH-423, Friends Historical Library of Swarthmore College.

20. Drinker, Diary, 638.

them of his failure in complying with Contracts, which induced them to fear his Circumstances were much embarrassed, on which account Labour & Care was repeatedly extended; but it has lately become manifest that he has contracted Debts to a large amount beyond his ability to pay whereby his Creditors (some of whom from his plain appearance having placed confidence in him) are likely to become great sufferers, and the reputation of our Religious Profession is subjected to reproach through his culpable inattention, mismanagement and unjustifiable Conduct in transacting his temporal affairs.[21]

The leaders of John's meeting were concerned not only that Dolley's father had acquired debt—the Quakers did not necessarily punish their members for debt in and of itself. Many of them, after all, were businessmen. What seems to have troubled them was John's financial and personal behavior. They saw him as using his status as a Quaker to gain a reputation that he would otherwise not have had; of taking on a greater debt load than he could sensibly have seen himself paying off; and putting himself in the position where repaying his creditors would become impossible. All of this, in their eyes, was a stain on the larger Quaker community. It was John Payne's sense of irresponsibility and lack of good faith with his fellow communicants that troubled them most.

A year later, the Quakers produced a report on John Payne, noting that "this Case has been very exercising and much Reproach occasioned by his Conduct."[22] And then they disowned him, implying in his report that he had "made profession among us, but not duly attending to the dictates of Truth which would have preserved . . . him in a conduct consistent therewith." He had not only overextended himself, but had done so in a way they labeled a "misconduct" that disgraced the Quakers.[23] He died in 1792. Deeply depressed, he had taken to bed and turned his face to the wall. He was a Quaker who was not only bankrupt but shunned by his community for dishonest behavior, a father whose three elder sons had also been excommunicated for financial and social misbehavior.

Within three years, his older sons were all dead. The second-oldest girl, Lucy, was disowned in 1793 for marrying outside the faith. The following

21. Philadelphia Monthly Meeting, Southern District Men's Minutes, 1781–1793, Box PH-425, 24 Feb. 1788, Friends Historical Library of Swarthmore College.

22. Philadelphia Monthly Meeting Southern District Men's Minutes 1781–1793, Box PH-425, 28 Jan. 1789, Friends Historical Library of Swarthmore College.

23. Philadelphia Monthly Meeting Southern District Men's Minutes 1781–1793, Box PH-425, 21 Feb. 1789, Friends Historical Library of Swarthmore College.

year Dolley married James Madison, and she, too, was expelled. Dolley's mother, Mary Winston Coles Payne, left the Southern District Monthly Meeting with two of her children still in tow, the youngest surviving of her brood, Mary Payne Jackson and John Coles Payne, while Anna Payne Cutts remained in Philadelphia with Dolley.[24]

Thus we see that by 1800, four out of five of the men in Dolley's immediate family had failed to make a living, become respectable Quakers, or establish a secure life. The fifth, her youngest brother, John Coles Payne, as an adult became an alcoholic. In 1806, the Madisons sent him to Tripoli, North Africa, as an aide to the U.S. consul, hoping a new environment and professional responsibilities would cure him of drink and waste, but he returned in 1811 in worse shape than when he had departed. Dolley settled him on a farm near Montpelier, and in the 1820s and 1830s, by then married with children, he dried out, even helping with editorial tasks on James Madison's papers. But after his brother-in-law died, John Coles Payne again lost his bearing, moved his family to Illinois, and failed, losing his family, his sobriety, and his health.

Mary E. E. Cutts could not excise Dolley's son, an alcoholic and a gambler, from historical memory. As the stepson of the fourth American president, his life was too well documented. But she could reshape the memory of Dolley's natal family, especially her father and brothers. And she could remake her aunt's relationship with the Society of Friends, about which Dolley had once penned, "our Society used to controle me entirely & debar me from so many advantages & pleasures." She clearly had bad memories.[25]

In large measure, Mary E. E. Cutts accomplished her goal. While Dolley's brothers Walter, William Temple, and Isaac have been recovered to some extent in the historical literature, they are present only as shadowy figures. And while historians and biographers consistently recount that Dolley's father was disowned by his Quaker meeting for debts, Mary ex-

24. In 1797, Mary Payne with her children Mary and John were again registered as members of the Cedar Creek Monthly Meeting in Hanover County.

25. On 19 August 1805, while staying in Philadelphia for medical treatment, Dolley wrote her sister Anna, "I had a visit last night from Nancy Miflin & Sally Zane, who remonstrated with me—on seeing so much company—they said that it was reported that half the City of Phila had made me visits—this lecture made me recollect the times when our Society used to controle me entirely & debar me from so many advantages & pleasures—& tho so entirely from their clutches, I really felt my ancient terror of them revive to disiagreeable degree" (DPTM to Anna Cutts, 19 Aug. 1805, DMDE). Nancy Mifflin and Sarah Zane were both zealous Quakers who were much consumed by the problem of religious purity.

cuses John Payne for whatever trespasses he made by the exigencies of post-Revolutionary inflation and the financial burden of southern hospitality. Mary's memoir erased the Payne family about whom the Philadelphia Society of Friends had fretted in 1783. Nowhere do we read about these Paynes: men who overextended their credit without concern for their creditors; who took advantage of their reputation as Friends to defraud the public; who joined the American military and were then court-martialed out; and who were accused by their fellow Quakers of resorting to houses of ill-fame and gaming.

We may choose to take these accusations with a grain of salt. It seems reasonable to assume that the more zealous Friends populated the committees that made these decisions. But we cannot dismiss them. It is not credible that the Quaker leaders made up these charges out of whole cloth or special malice for the Paynes. Yet our historical memory of Dolley Madison's family is of fine Quakers of upper-class Virginia lineage. They are a family redeemed by Dolley's marriages, first to an upstanding young Quaker named John Todd, and then to the great American leader James Madison. In her account, Mary affirmed and furthered this redemption.

Mary Cutts's Aunt Dolley is a woman of kindness, generosity of spirit, and warmth. As Mary writes in her first memoir, Dolley retained the Quaker "principles of that religion that love of truth, abhorrence of vice, and universal benevolence of character which had been so deeply implanted by her parents." Her grace extended to all, or, as Mary states, her aunt

> endeared herself to all classes; the poorest beggar could come to her with confidence, and confide his or her cares and wants, sure of an attentive and sympathizing audience if possible, she would send them on their way rejoicing—if not, she gave them comfort and advice, causing them to feel they had in her—a friend. To the powerful and arrogant, she would accord all their vanity exacted.— She would say, it was not her place to treat them otherwise. . . . Her countenance, beaming with inward happiness made friends wherever it glanced! It delighted her to do good: petitions from afar and near were showered upon her; she was never annoyed, and always answered them favorably, if possible; as her influence over her husband was unbounded and seldom exerted in vain. Many, whom the world little knows, are indebted to Mr: Madison for independence and position in society—she never said so, for she never betrayed a confidence,

but grateful letters have proved it and recorded thoughts and facts, which outlive the spoken word!

Accordingly, the First Lady could "pour oil on the waters of discord, and
draw malcontents into the fold of her husband, and successful she was for
few would oppose the partner of such a wife!"[26]

Well before Mary wrote her memoir, Dolley Madison had achieved her
reputation as a woman of grace who could win the hearts (if not always
the minds) of those who opposed her husband. Margaret Bayard Smith
portrayed her in 1836 as a woman whose "greatest charm consisted in the
warm heart, that leant its glow to her cheek and sparkle to her eye."[27] A
Boston monthly, the *American Magazine of Useful Knowledge,* published
a biographical essay in 1837 applauding "the softening influences of her
conciliatory disposition, of her frank and gracious manner." Not only, said
the anonymous author of this essay, was she the greatest Washington hostess of the first two decades of the nineteenth century, in Virginia as well
she was "neighborly and companionable . . . as if she had never lived in a
city."[28] In this regard, then, Mary was echoing what previous biographers
had said. This description of Dolley appeared again and again in letters
about her and in contemporary descriptions of her. It must have captured
something real, powerful, and profound about her character. But Mary's
voice had a special resonance; she was the great lady's niece who knew
her intimately and could portray her with the greatest verisimilitude. As
Edward Johnston said of the legacy of Patrick Henry, only those who had
known the historical figure could portray him—or her—with accuracy.
Mary's memory was special; it carried evidentiary weight.

Yet as we examine the documentary record of Dolley's relationships
with the Madison family, we shift perspectives and see a different side of
her character. In her private life, Dolley failed to bring her much-lauded

26. CM I, 108–9, 111.
27. Margaret Bayard Smith, "Mrs. Madison," in *The National Portrait Gallery of
Distinguished Americans,* ed. James Barton Longacre and James Herring (New York:
Monson Bancroft, 1970), 3:17.
28. "Mrs. James Madison," *Virginia Free Press* (Charleston, WV), 17 Aug. 1837,
19th Century U.S. Newspapers, http://infotrac.galegroup.com/itw/infomark/
756/230/134620531w16/purl=rc1_NCNP_0_GT3008138793&dyn=3!xrn_15_0_
GT3008138793&hst_1?sw_aep=viva_uva. For the original, see http://books
.google.com/books?id=UB0_AAAAYAAJ&pg=PA488&source=gbs_toc_r&cad
=4#v=onepage&q=Madison&f=false.

political talents of conciliation and consensus to family issues and even her personal reputation. In order to explain these impressions, however, we must begin with Dolley and her family: her sisters, her only surviving brother, and her son. Dolley cherished all three of her sisters: Mary, Lucy, and Anna. Mary Payne Jackson, wife of the Virginia congressman John George Jackson, died in 1807, still in her twenties. Although Dolley remained in loving contact with Jackson until he died in 1825, and Mary's one surviving child, Mary Jackson Allen, throughout her life, those relationships became increasingly attenuated. Although they continued to correspond and seek news of each other, by 1847 Mary Allen was writing her aunt that she had "not received a letter from you for many years, but I hope you have not entirely forgotten me."[29]

Dolley also had her sister Lucy, who was married twice, first to George Steptoe Washington and then to Supreme Court Associate Justice Thomas Todd. Unlike Mary, Lucy lived to an old age, dying in 1846. After her first husband died in 1809, she spent much of the next several years living with the Madisons in the White House, and in 1812 she married for a second time, in the first wedding ever held in the White House. Soon thereafter, however, the couple returned to Thomas Todd's home in Kentucky. Thereafter, Dolley did not see Lucy again until 1840.

But summer after summer, during the sixteen years the Madisons lived in Washington and used Montpelier as their vacation home, Anna's family, the Cuttses, were there for weeks and even months. When James's second presidential term ended, and the Madisons retired permanently to Virginia, the Cuttses were often to be found there. Dolley called Anna her daughter as well as sister, as Anna had lived with Dolley as a child. It was to Anna—on Anna's honeymoon—that Dolley reported that she had "shut myself up from the Morg you entered the stage . . . all our acquaintance call'd in to see me on the different mornings those few I saw seemed all to sympathise with me in your loss."[30] When Richard Cutts went bankrupt after the War of 1812 and found himself faced with forfeiting his house for debt, it was James who purchased the residence so that Anna and her family would not be homeless. When Anna died in 1832, Dolley was bereft. We can hear her pain as we read her letter to a young friend, written soon after Anna's death. "It is, as you observe my dear Miss Vail," Dolley wrote, "that religion and time, can alone reconcile us to bereavments—like that I feel,

29. Mary Elizabeth Payne Jackson Allen to DPTM, 6 Jan. 1847, Papers of Dolley Madison DLC.

30. DPTM to Anna Payne Cutts, 26 Apr. 1804, DMDE.

in the death of a most beloved Sister!"[31] In her mourning, Dolley reached out to her brother-in-law, from whom she had long been estranged, telling him, "the heart of your miserable Sister mourns with you," and "with your precious daughters, with your Sons! Come to us as soon as you can, & bring them with you."[32] A few weeks after Anna's death, Richard traveled to Montpelier with his two daughters, Dolley Cutts and Mary E. E. Cutts, to do what they could to soothe each other and share their grief. When Dolley Cutts died in 1838, Mary Cutts, the author of our memoir, became ever more like the daughter Dolley never had. When it came to the women of her kin circle, Dolley enjoyed warm, reciprocal relations. Politicians and political observers had long lauded Dolley's "heart"; when it came to the women of the family, Dolley's love and devotion were well placed.

Dolley's emotional and psychological attributes, however, did not help her to deal with her menfolk; indeed, her nurturing instincts and avoidance of conflict most probably exacerbated their worse traits. Dolley and James also took care of her only surviving brother, who, like his older brother Isaac, was an alcoholic. The Madisons sent him to North Africa as an American diplomat, but in 1811 he returned in a hopeless condition.[33] Dolley, and presumably James, then persuaded John to apply for an army commission, which he received in May of 1813 and was honorably discharged two years later.[34] In 1816, he married Clara Wilcox and began farming, first in Louisa County, Virginia, and then, when financial difficulties ensued, moved to a farm adjacent to Montpelier. It was there, living as a farmer and in continuous contact with James and Dolley, that her brother stabilized his life. After John Coles Payne moved to Illinois in 1837, one of his daughters, Anna Payne Causten, joined the loving female circle Dolley had cultivated. She stayed behind as Dolley's companion, in which role she remained throughout the rest of Dolley's life.

Dolley had one surviving son from her first marriage, John Payne Todd. He failed in his education, disappointed his stepfather by not attending

31. DPTM to Eliza Vail Longueville, 24 Aug. 1832, DMDE.

32. DPTM to Richard Cutts, 6 Aug. 1832, DMDE.

33. See DPTM to John Coles Payne, 21 Sept. 1809, DMDE; DPTM to Anna Payne Cutts, 19 Aug. [1811], DMDE; DPTM to Anna Payne Cutts, 15 July [1811], DMDE; DPTM to Anna Payne Cutts, 22 Dec. [1811], DMDE; and James Madison to Richard Cutts, 16 July 1811, in *Papers of James Madison, Presidential Series*, ed. J. C. A. Stagg et al. (Charlottesville: University of Virginia Press, 1996), 3:342.

34. Francis B. Heitman, *Historical Register and Dictionary of the United States Army* (Baltimore: Genealogical Publishing, 1994), 1:777. Payne was both a captain and an assistant quartermaster.

Princeton, and was sent by his parents to Europe as part of the diplomatic mission for a treaty to end the War of 1812. In Europe, his hosts behaved toward him as if he were a prince, and further spoiled him. Payne Todd was an alcoholic and a gambler. But Dolley doted upon him, playing the role we would today describe as enabler. When he stopped traveling in pursuit of his habit, he embarked on a series of misadventures in Orange County. In the 1830s, Payne explored establishing a gold mine. A few years later, in 1840, Payne was "much engrossed by a marble quarry."[35] After that failed, he disavowed the extractive industries and began, as Mary E. E. Cutts notes in her memoir, to build his own plantation house. He called it Toddsberthe, the central structure of which was a "large round tower-like building." And throughout all he incurred debt after debt. In 1829, he was thrown into prison in Philadelphia for his obligations. After James died, Dolley must have countersigned some of Payne's debt, for by the 1840s she, too, was not only paying for her son's financial disasters, but was being dragged into court to make sure she paid them. On 29 June 1844, the assistant clerk of the Orange County Court House wrote out an order that "Dolly P. Madison if she be found within your bailiwick," appear "at the clerk's offices of the Circuit Superior Court of Law and Chancery for the County of Orange" to answer to a William Smith for the debt of $2,600 John Payne Todd owed him.[36] It is worth noting here that the assistant clerk who signed the order was Philip S. Fry, a member of the local elite whose mother belonged to the Slaughter family, who had married into the extended Madison family, while the clerk was Reynolds Chapman, a son-in-law of William Madison, who had also married into the extended Madison family.[37] Her Madison kin, as officers of the law, hauled her into court to pay for her son's profligacy.

If Dolley's widely hailed "powers of fascination" succeeded in Washington circles, they apparently failed within the Madison family and the local Orange County community. The Madison family, and their neighbors, un-

35. DPTM to Edward Coles, 20 Oct. 1840, DMDE. For mention of the mine, see DPTM to Anna Payne Cutts, ca. 15 May 1832, DMDE.

36. "The Commonwealth of Virginia, To the Sheriff of Orange County, Greetings," 29 June 1844, Circuit Superior Court of Law and Chancery, Library of Virginia. With thanks to Lisa Timmerman of Montpelier, who collected and scanned these documents.

37. On Reynolds Chapman, see the DMDE; on Philip S. Fry, see Frederick Johnston, *Memorials of Old Virginia Clerks* (Lynchburg, Va.: J. P. Bell, 1888), 271–72. Chapman served as clerk from 1801 to 1844, Fry from 1844 to 1859.

doubtedly gossiped about Dolley's family over the decades. We have no written record, and can only imagine that James's nieces and nephews, and in turn their children, felt that Dolley's family had displaced theirs in James's regard, or feared that Dolley and her family would receive the whole of the Montpelier estate that James had inherited as eldest son. We can be certain that neither the Madisons nor their neighbors had any use for John Coles Payne. They would have seen him as a failure and a sycophant. They never appointed him to any local office or county militia position—emoluments a man of his position should have had.

Worst of all was John Payne Todd, whose behavior had clear consequences for how James's relatives saw Dolley. We hear that voice most clearly in the 1919 memoir of an Orange County resident and historian, W. W. Scott.[38] Scott was not only a local historian; he grew up on a neighboring plantation to Montpelier. He was born four years before Dolley died, and went on to become a Virginia state librarian and a member of the Virginia Historical Society who served for ten years as the state law librarian. And, perhaps most critically, he was the son-in-law of Nelly Madison Willis's son, Col. John Willis. Scott's grandmother-in-law was thus James Madison's favorite niece.

"As a youth," Scott wrote, "the writer was often in the company of two of the nieces of the President, and in mature life was in intimate relations with many of his nearest relatives—a good many of whom still reside in Orange." Those he knew were guarded in their replies to his questions about the former president and his wife; some chose complete silence on the topic. It eventually became clear to Scott that his Orange County neighbors had unpleasant memories of Dolley Madison: "It was manifest that her indulgence of her spendthrift son, Payne Todd, and her permitting him to waste the estate of her husband, had left a sting in their memories— if they had ever admired her; which is doubtful."[39] And more brutally, he commented:

[T]he Madison kith and kin did not like "Dolly." They heard too much of her "low neck and short sleeves," of her "turban" and her gay life in Washington society; and especially distasteful to them were her renewed appeals to Congress

38. W. W. Scott, "Memoir," Montpelier Memorial Foundation. William Wallace Scott lived from 1845 to 1929. Additional information on Scott is from Ann Miller and Thomas Chapman, to whom I extend many thanks.
39. Ibid.

for appropriations to buy his manuscripts. She had plenty, and "frugality" in the administration of the government was deemed a public virtue. It humiliated them that the widow of this great kinsman should be continually knocking at the door of the public treasury, and they resented it.[40]

Madison family anxiety and contentiousness were not limited to their feelings about Dolley. At least some of James's siblings and their children fought with each other as well. James's youngest sister, Frances, married a local doctor, Robert Rose. Nelly Willis, the daughter of James's brother Ambrose and James's favorite niece, wrote Dolley in 1812 that she, Nelly, would not visit her grandmother "on account of Dr Rose & his family being there," adding that it was "extremely painful to me to be in company with Aunt Fanny."[41] The Roses were soon locked into a bitter dispute with James's brother William over James Madison Sr.'s will. William was a man of malice who generated trouble as a matter of convenience. It was William who blocked Fanny Rose's claims. It was William who believed that he most of all had been cheated by the execution of James Madison Sr.'s will. After James's death, it was William who took Dolley to court and declared to his brother-in-law Thomas Macon that "he [William] would sue the [James's] estate for every dol. that he could obtain because he expected his brother owed his father to half its amount."[42]

The Madison family had its share of fault lines, grievance, and meanness. But what interests us is not why or how they quarreled, but how Dolley handled these conflicts. They are, if you will, a kind of test case of Dolley's ability to—or perhaps desire to—convert enemy to friend through kindness, generosity of spirit, and warmth, or play the role of hostess who brought together opposing factions as she had done in Washington, D.C. All evidence indicates that Dolley failed that test, unable, it seems, to ameliorate conflict or contention among her in-laws. Nor did her larger-than-life image carry the same messages of legitimacy and reassurance to the locals as it did to the Washington community. She was never able to exercise the social power or judgment in Orange County as she did in Washington. She could neither conceal her preference for her own family nor successfully woo her Madison kin. Perhaps as a consequence, Mary

40. Ibid.
41. Nelly Conway Madison Willis to DPTM, 24 June 1812, DMDE.
42. "Statement by DPTM Regarding Thomas Macon's Remarks Relating to General William Madison's Suit for Funds from James Madison's Estate," DMDE

may have penned her memoir precisely to lead future biographers away from family unpleasantness, while framing her prose in the conventional hagiography of her day.[43]

In her second memoir, Mary Cutts described Montpelier. There, alongside depiction of the interior of the house, the fields, and the trees, she talked about the life of the slaves. In her recounting, the Madison slave community was a happy one, where the masters provided an enviable carefree state of living for their "people." She wrote little about the slave children, the field hands, or even the house servants. Mary restricted her most personal encomia to the elderly. "None but an eye witness can know of the peace and ease of these sable sons of toil!" she wrote. They retired "with health and not a care for the morrow and surrounded by their progeny, on those plantations which remain in the same family for over a century!" In another passage, Mary recalled General Lafayette visiting in 1825 and remarking on the family of a slave "104 years of age, whose daughter and granddaughter, the youngest nearly 70, were all at rest retired from their labors, living happily together; their patch of ground cultivated for them; their food and raiment supplied by 'Mass Jimmy and Miss Dolly.'"[44] It is hard to read these phrases without wondering whether Mary—and perhaps Dolley—contrasted the unlikely leisure state of slave retirement with Dolley's own poverty as a widow. Mary also may have emphasized how long the Madisons had owned Montpelier and the Montpelier slaves, in order to excuse Dolley for selling first slaves, then pieces of Montpelier, and finally the whole plantation in 1844.[45]

Mary's attitudes mirrored those of her time and class. Hers is the view reflected in such southern novels as John Pendleton Kennedy's *Swallow Barn*, a book Mary may well have read in James Madison's library, and which became known as the archetypal sentimental portrayal of rural life in Virginia before the Civil War. Of the plantation master, Kennedy wrote, "although he owns many slaves, they hold him in profound reverence, and

43. Alison Booth, *How to Make It as a Woman: Collective Biographical History from Victoria to the Present* (Chicago: University of Chicago Press, 2004), 4, 25–47.

44. Lafayette made two trips to Montpelier. The first was in November 1824, and the second in August 1825.

45. Here I would like especially to thank Julie Doxsey, a former student at the University of Virginia, who in 2008 did much of the research for this section of the essay.

are very happy under his dominion."[46] As William R. Taylor pointed out in his now classic book on the antebellum South, *Cavalier and Yankee,* "the image of sunshine and happiness around the old plantation home could . . . win the sympathies of many" who might otherwise question the wisdom of the peculiar institution.[47] Mary simply followed the staple narrative of southern self-depiction.

James Kirke Paulding, a close friend of James and Dolley's and a northerner whose book would also have been in the Madison library, reinforced Kennedy's portrait of happy slaves when he wrote in *Slavery in the United States* that, "of all the varieties of the human race and of our human condition that have ever fallen under our observation, the African slave of the South best realizes the ideal of happiness," for "he is . . . the most lighthearted, sportive, dancing, laughing being in the world."[48] Mary wrote of "the [Montpelier] Negroes, [who] like the birds of their woods, have their sweet wild notes, filled with melody—but their songs and dances need no encomium!"

Dolley never wrote down her views on the institution of slavery, and Mary added nothing to elucidate her aunt's thoughts. Historians have assumed that as the daughter of a Quaker who freed his slaves, and as a girl growing up in the Quaker, northern, and antislavery city of Philadelphia, Dolley Madison—if not antislavery—was not entirely sanguine about the peculiar institution. Consequently, they have often presented her as a "good mistress." Her own background, coupled with her marriage to the architect of the U.S. Constitution who was a staunch supporter of the American Colonization Society, joined with the fact that so many of her biographies were written during the era of Jim Crow, when it was not required that historians and biographers grapple with their subjects' relationships with

46. John Pendleton Kennedy sent a copy of *Swallow Barn* to James Madison on 28 July 1834 (see John P. Kennedy to James Madison, 28 July 1834, Papers of James Madison, DLC, American Memory, http://hdl.loc.gov/loc.mss/mjm.24_0543_0543). In 1838, Kennedy sent Dolley, now a widow, a copy of his newest novel, *Rob of the Bowl* (see DPTM to John Pendleton Kennedy, 28 Dec. 1838, DMDE). For *Swallow Barn,* see http://docsouth.unc.edu/southlit/kennedyswallowbarn1/kennedyswallowbarn1.html, p. 28.

47. William R. Taylor, *Cavalier and Yankee: The Old South and American National Character* (New York: Oxford University Press, 1993), 300.

48. James Kirke Paulding, *Slavery in the United States* (New York: Harper and Brothers, 1836), 143, 171, 176.

slavery, has allowed historians to leave this question largely unasked.[49] But closer investigation casts doubt on these assumptions.

She must have hated the economic dislocation that was attendant on the Payne family's move to Philadelphia, and associated that experience with both leaving Virginia and her father freeing his slaves. And she was probably delighted to return to Virginia through her marriage to James Madison because she wanted always to be thought of as a Virginian—a member of the Virginia planter class. This wish governed her reporting of her ancestry both to Margaret Bayard Smith in the mid-1830s and Mary E. E. Cutts in the 1830s and 1840s. Mary Cutts thus wrote in her first memoir that John Payne (Dolley's father) was "highly connected and nearly related to many of the Virginia gentry."[50]

Dolley wanted to establish her historic memory as a member of the planter class, whose family owned slaves who worked the fields and tended the house. We never glimpse a Dolley who jibbed at owning slaves, or had any reservation about the system that kept her in comfort. It is doubtful that Dolley ever let the desires or feelings of a slave interfere with what she, herself, desired. We can explore her possible thoughts on the issue more fully in three ways: by examining the thoughts of her beloved brother John Coles Payne, by looking at slave statements, and by examining some of the comments that Dolley made over the years in her correspondence.

Soon after James Madison died, Dolley's brother John Coles Payne decided to move west. His main objective was to find a way to live as a white southerner without slaves. He had decided to abandon his home, he wrote his cousin Edward Coles, because "those who like myself neither possess nor have means of obtaining it [slaves] here, find our own labour in the field of agriculture reduced to their scale of profit while our expenditures are increased to the style of living indulged in by their masters." He wanted to find somewhere without "the annoyance of insects and free-blacks," for "the southern prejudice is strong with us all in regard to the social position of these people."[51] Once in Illinois, it was clear that he desired to locate, as he wrote Edward Coles on 28 February 1837, "north of the dividing line which separates the descendants of Europe & of Africa."[52]

49. For a discussion of Dolley and slavery, see Catherine Allgor, *A Perfect Union: Dolley Madison and the Creation of the American Nation* (New York: Henry Holt, 2006).

50. CM I, 91.

51. John Coles Payne to Edward Coles, 15 Mar. 1837, DMDE.

52. John Coles Payne to Edward Coles, 28 Feb. 1837, DMDE.

We cannot affirm that Dolley and her brother John held the same deep-seated racial views. We know that James Madison greatly worried about the impact of the institution of slavery on American society and economy. But it seems reasonable, knowing what John Coles Payne believed, to wonder if his sister did not share his prejudices, sentiments that certainly were not unique to him in the American South in the 1830s and 1840s.

Let us turn to slave comments. Madison Hemings, a son of Sally Hemings, likely child of Thomas Jefferson, and a member of the Monticello slave community, dictated memoirs published in an Ohio newspaper in 1873. He recalled:

> I was named Madison by the wife of James Madison, who was afterwards President of the United States. Mrs. Madison happened to be at Monticello at the time of my birth, and begged the privilege of naming me, promising my mother a fine present for the honor. She consented, and Mrs. Madison dubbed me by the name I now acknowledge, but like many promises of white folks to the slaves she never gave my mother anything.[53]

Hemings need not have said anything about Dolley Madison, but he went out of his way to do so. Historians have questioned the veracity of this story, but the specific dates of birth and presence of Dolley Madison in the actual accusation itself are not the critical issues here. Rather, it is the voice of a Monticello slave determined to find a way to criticize Dolley Madison. As we will see below, the only Montpelier slave to write his autobiography, Paul Jennings, echoed Hemings. As a scrap of evidence, Hemings's report proves little, but as an indication of sensibility, it shades our portrait of Dolley.

Dolley did talk about specific slaves in some of her letters, and we know that their lives—those of both slaves and masters—were intimately intertwined, as in the case of a slave named Sukey. In February 1833, we hear Dolley reporting to her brother-in-law Richard Cutts that Sukey "lies very ill with bilious fever," although no one else was ill.[54] In that same letter, Dolley described Sukey as her "most efficient House servant." Sukey, in other words, was both an integral part of the Madison household and an important component of Dolley's well-being. But we get closest to

---

53. Madison Hemings's memoir was originally published (as told to S. F. Wetmore) in Ohio's *Pike County Republican* in 1873. Text taken here from PBS online: www.pbs .org/wgbh/pages/frontline/shows/jefferson/cron/1873march.html.

54. DPTM to Richard Cutts, 11 Aug. 1833, DMDE.

Dolley's feelings about Sukey—and slaves with whom she has the nearest relationships—in a letter to her sister Anna in July 1818:

> Sucky has made so many depridations on every thing, in every part of the house that, I sent her to black Meadow [a Madison satellite farm] last week but find it terribly inconvenient to do without her, & suppose I shall take her again, as I feel too old to undertake to bring up another—so I must even let her steal from me, to keep from labour myself—more than my strength will permit— I would buy a maid but good ones are rare & as high as 8 & 900$— I should like to know what you gave for yours.[55]

It is a familiar story in the annals of slavery: masters who descry the theft of their servants, but who cannot do without them. Allgor noted in her biography of Dolley, "she exhibited that curious mixture of familiarity and distance common to people of her culture," and concluded, "celebrated as she was for her good heart and warm personality, Dolley seems to have been quite cold on this particular subject."[56]

Historians—including both Allgor and myself—have generally closed the book on the story of the Montpelier slaves in 1844, when Dolley sold the plantation to Henry Moncure. But looking more carefully, it was a more complex narrative. In 1844, Dolley gave Sukey to her son, rather than sell her to Moncure along with most of the Montpelier slave community.[57] How Sukey experienced that transaction we can only guess, but being sold to Payne Todd must have felt like being dropped into a dark pit. The whole of the Montpelier slave community knew not only how deeply in debt Payne Todd was, but that he was being called into court to pay off his loans, and that they, his slaves, were his primary source of ready cash. We witness this in November 1844, when Payne Todd asked his mother to "get out of Sukey who was the father secretely of Becca for it may be of an advantage in the Sale."[58]

It is in this context that we need consider the fact that during her lifetime, Dolley was attacked as proslavery in the abolitionist press, and we are left to wonder if this, too, was a part of her aunt's life that Mary E. E. Cutts chose to excise from her memoirs, including only recollections of contented slaves. Dolley was a perfect target for the radical wing of the

55. DPTM to Anna Payne Cutts, [ca. 23 July 1818], DMDE.
56. Allgor, *Perfect Union*, 215.
57. Deed to John Payne Todd, in DPM, *Selected Letters*, 372.
58. John Payne Todd to DPTM, in DPM, *Selected Letters*, 379.

abolitionist movement. She was the slaveholding widow of James Madison, and she was an important figure in the city of Washington who had sold slaves. While by and large her iconic status brought her comfort—it made her an honored member of the highest levels of Washington society—in matters relating to slavery it proved a burden.

Although we must assume that Dolley knew that some of James's friends, especially his younger acolytes, were disappointed that James had not freed his slaves, we first encounter in her correspondence this attitude as a public one in 1839.[59] In March of that year, she heard from Lewis Tappan, merchant and abolitionist, who had once supported the American Colonization Society but had gone on to help found the American Anti-slavery Society. At the request of a British reformer, George Stringer Bull, Tappan asked Dolley for a copy of James's will. On 3 April, she wrote him back declining the request. Five days later, Tappan forwarded to her Bull's letter, and while we do not have it, it must have been persuasive as on 11 April, she acceded to the request. Two months later, an anonymous essay appeared in the *Emancipator*, furnishing the details of James's will: that he had bequeathed his slaves to his wife, and given $2,000 to the American Colonization Society. Tappan, presumably the author, pasted a copy of the article into his diary. In part, it said:

> Why did not Madison, who was President of the Colonization Society, when he made his will, manumit his slaves that they might go to Liberia? Was he opposed to manumitting for such a purpose? Did he wish that only those born free, or who had purchased their freedom, should be sent to Africa? Was he merely in favor of the Colonization society because, by expatriating the free colored people, slaves were made more quiet and more valuable?[60]

As James Madison's widow, Dolley faced expectations that her actions should conform to the public belief that James had been—at least in some

59. She must, for example, have known what her cousin Edward Coles thought. We hear Coles's voice in a letter to his sister Sally Coles dated 28 July 1836, a month after James's death. Coles began his letter: "His [James's] Slaves not emancipated. . . . I cannot divest myself of the belief that he has made a secret Will, by which his slaves will be free at the death of his Wife" (Edward Coles to Sarah [Sally] Coles Stevenson, 28 July 1836, DMDE).

60. DPTM to Lewis Tappan, 3 Apr. 1839, DMDE; Lewis Tappan to DPTM, 8 Apr. 1839, DMDE; DPTM to Lewis Tappan, 11 Apr. 1839, DMDE. See also Drew McCoy, *The Last of the Fathers: James Madison and the Republican Legacy* (Cambridge: Cambridge University Press, 1989).

mild form—an antislavery man. Tappan's accusations, especially when publicly expressed in the *Emancipator,* must have grieved Dolley as the protectress of her husband's memory.

The most sustained attack on Dolley, however, took place in 1848. Anti-slavery rhetoric and activity were increasing. That February, France experienced a revolution that produced the Second Republic. "In Washington especially the event was joyously acclaimed," observed one historian.[61] There were public meetings, citizens decorated the city with flags and bunting, and the president had the White House trimmed.

Meanwhile, political debate about the spread of slavery and the slave trade in the District of Columbia heated up after the end of the Mexican-American War and the expansion of American territory. The manifestations included increasing attacks on slavery and the creation of the Free Soil Party. The political atmosphere inside the capital city was fractious and tempestuous. As agitation increased, tempers became brittle, and the antislavery press began including Dolley as one of their targets. On 31 March 1848, William Lloyd Garrison's newspaper, the *Liberator,* blasted Dolley for selling slaves, stating:

> The actor is the *widow of James Madison, the fourth President of the United States—the confidential friend of Washington, and writer of the principal papers which bear his signature—whose memory, by the universal consent of all parties at this time, is cherished with the deepest reverence.* This thing is not done, let it be noted, in the darkness of the Alabama cotton-field, or of the Louisiana cane-brake, but at the heart of the Federal City—in the midst of genteel, fashionable life.[62]

The incident of the *Pearl,* a ship that attempted to transport slaves to freedom, took place in mid-April. Reports about Dolley and her slaves began appearing at least as early as March. As James Madison's widow, Dolley was a lightning rod for the part of the antislavery movement that condemned the U.S. Constitution as a proslavery document, as was the case with Garrison and his paper—they also attacked her as a slave owner. It seems reasonable to guess that these newspaper reports were part of the lead-up to the actual attempted slave escape. On 15 April 1848, seventy-

61. John H. Paynter, "The Fugitives of the *Pearl*," *Journal of Negro History* 1, no. 3 (June 1916): 244–45.

62. "Mrs. Madison's Slaves Again," *Liberator,* 31 Mar. 1851, 19th Century American Newspapers (website).

seven slaves boarded the *Pearl* in order to sail out of the city, up the Potomac River, and through the Chesapeake Bay. The winds, however, turned against them, and the venture failed. The captain of the ship, a Daniel Drayton, was captured along with his two white assistants, Edward Sayres, the pilot, and Chester English, the cook, and tried in court. English was released, but Drayton and Sayres were convicted and jailed. Many of the slaves were sold south.[63]

The antislavery press subsequently excoriated Dolley as a slave owner. Horace Greeley's *New York Tribune* included an article that proclaimed that "the widow of the illustrious Madison" was a woman "whom we would like on his account to respect, but on her own we cannot." The government had paid her ample funds, the paper pointed out, for James's papers, but once again she was without money, "though she has sold off sundry 'sable sisters' meantime into the Louisiana cane-brakes," and was once again trying to sell more of his papers for cash.[64]

One of Dolley Madison's slaves, Ellen Steward, attempted to escape from her mistress in the hull of the *Pearl*, and when she failed, Dolley sold Ellen to a slave dealer. Dolley was rebuked in the antislavery newspapers, and most assuredly criticized in certain drawing rooms, among some politicians, and in selected Washington streets. She must have also sensed a shift in attitude from her own servants. For a woman dependent upon her remaining slaves for such daily chores as lighting her fire in the winter, bringing her tea in the morning, and cooking her meals at all times of the day, she would henceforth experience a bitterness as the mistress who had sold their comrade. This was a part of Dolley's widowhood that Mary E. E. Cutts would certainly not want to have included in any future writings about her aunt, and Mary certainly did not write about it.

There is an additional layer to this story: the role played by James's former valet, Paul Jennings.[65] In 1848, Jennings was a free black citizen of Washington, a leader in his community, and one of the three African

63. Drayton went on to write his memoirs, and in 1916, John Paynter told the story from the slave's point of view through his connection with the largest, and perhaps most prominent, African American family on board, the Edmondsons. The *Pearl* episode partially inspired Harriet Beecher Stowe to write *Uncle Tom's Cabin* and, in 1850, boosted support in Washington, D.C., for ending the slave trade.

64. "Meanness and Revolutionary Papers," *New York Herald*," 25 May 1848, 19th Century U.S. Newspapers (website).

65. For more on Jennings, see Elizabeth Dowling Taylor, *A Slave in the White House: Paul Jennings and the Madisons* (New York: Palgrave Macmillan, 2012).

Americans involved in the planning of the *Pearl* incident.[66] He was a former Madison slave whom Dolley had sold in 1846 to a man named Pollard Webb, who in turn sold Jennings to Daniel Webster, from whom Jennings purchased his freedom.[67] A mulatto whose father was an English trader, Jennings had been James's faithful valet and house slave and had expected to be able to buy his freedom from Dolley after James died.

Ellen Steward was also a house slave, and she may well have been the daughter of the Sarah Steward, who had written Dolley in 1844, asking Dolley to take care of her slaves in the face of imminent sale of the estate and the slave pickers lurking around the property.[68] Ellen belonged to the upper stratum of the Montpelier slave community, a young woman most assuredly close to Paul Jennings. In fact, it is tempting to wonder if Jennings was not instrumental in Ellen Steward's attempted flight. The story in the newspapers was that Dolley sent Ellen to fetch water from the pump, where the slave picker could observe her. Ellen, knowing of Dolley's plan, escaped, and hid. Paul Jennings may have made the arrangements.

In March 1848, before the incident of the *Pearl*, the antislavery newspaper the *Albany Patriot* published a story about Jennings and Dolley. "Gentlemen," it read, "You have readily admitted to your columns my account of the manner in which Mrs. Madison deals with her people, called slaves." But "I have a correction or two, which I wish to make." "Mrs. Madison promised to set the man [Paul Jennings] free, as she knew was the wish and expectation of Mr. Madison."[69] Instead, she sold him. Internal evidence suggests that Jennings became an abolitionist and a source of news for the antislavery papers.

Jennings must have been angry at and resentful of his former mistress. Although we have no letter or other document explicitly stating that case, we do have Jennings's memoir, *A Colored Man's Reminiscences of James*

66. This is according to John H. Paynter in his fictionalized account of the *Pearl* (see Paynter, *Fugitives of the* Pearl [Washington, D.C.: Associated Publishers, 1930]).

67. See G. Franklin Edward and Michael R. Winston, "Commentary: The Washington of Paul Jennings," *White House History* 1 (1983): 46–63. See also Paynter, *Pearl;* and Patricia Lynn Hunt, "A Story Not to Be Told: The Depiction of Slavery in American Novels, 1875–2000" (Ph.D. diss., University of Maryland, College Park, 2007). It is important to remember here that Paynter had talked to members of the Edmondson family, and therefore carried on the oral traditions in the black community. Paynter was not only African American, but also a descendant of the Brent and Edmondson families.

68. Sarah Steward to DPTM, 5 July 1844, in DPM, *Selected Letters*, 372–73.

69. As quoted in the *Liberator*, 31 Mar. 1848, America's Historical Newspapers.

Madison.[70] In it, he went out of his way to describe Dolley as a "remarkably fine woman [who was] beloved by every body in Washington, white and colored."[71] But read in context, this statement seems a public cover for his true feelings, for on the previous page Jennings had written:

> It has often been stated in print, that when Mrs. Madison escaped from the White House she cut out from the frame the large portrait of Washington (now in one of the parlors there), and carried it off. This is totally false. She had no time for doing it. It would have required a ladder to get it down. All she carried off was the silver in her reticule, as the British were thought to be but a few squares off, and were expected every moment.

Jennings knew how greatly Dolley cared about her role in saving George Washington's portrait and the state, or cabinet, papers—and the extent to which she had gone to preserve that reputation. Indeed, we may argue that her determination to be remembered as the heroine of the war shaped the way in which she had Margaret Bayard Smith write her first biography. We need only remember her correspondence with Robert DePeyster in February 1848 in which she took great effort to see that DePeyster and his 1814 comrade Jacob Barker put their—and her—version of the story into the public press to combat the version being bruited by Daniel Carroll, who had taken it upon himself to rob Dolley of her reputation as the heroine of the war. Jennings must have known how much this meant to his former mistress.[72]

Jennings, moreover, would have witnessed John Payne Todd burn through money and seen Dolley dote upon her son and pay off all his debts—not the least with money she had gained through the sale of a slave.[73] It seems likely that it was not random that the *Albany Patriot* reported Dolley's attempted sale of Ellen Steward well before the *Pearl*'s attempted

70. Paul Jennings, *A Colored Man's Reminiscences of James Madison* in Documenting the American South, http://docsouth.unc.edu/neh/jennings/jennings.html.

71. Jennings, *Colored Man*, 14.

72. See Robert G. L. DePeyster to DPTM, 5 Feb. 1848; DePeyster to DPTM, 25 Feb. 1848; and DePeyster to DPTM, 29 May 1848, all in Papers of Dolley Madison, DLC.

73. There is a letter dated 13 July 1848 from a Benjamin Steward, who may have been another relative of Sarah's and Ellen's. This Steward asked Dolley to "buy me so that I might come back to Virginia." Eager to return to his own family, he offered to "be a dutiful and Faithful Servant as long as you may live Which I hope Will be many years yet" (Benjamin F. Stewart to DPTM, 13 July 1848, Papers of Dolley Madison, DLC).

escape, and that the *Rochester Evening Star* stated that as Mrs. Madison was a mother, she should have had heart not to sell "another's child away into Southern bondage."

What Paul Jennings wanted to say, and what abolitionists were eager to write about Dolley, soon melted away. In her memoir, Mary avoided all mention of slavery in Washington, or the antislavery attacks on Dolley. As with Dolley's difficult brothers, there remained no historical memory of Dolley and slavery in the revolutionary year of 1848. Mary's memoir undoubtedly played an important role in this collective amnesia.

Dolley is not remembered as a plantation mistress, or as the child of a dysfunctional family, or as the widow left fighting her combative Madison family. We recollect her in two ways: the great hostess of the national capital during the early republic, and the heroine of the War of 1812. This was as Dolley, and then Mary, wanted it. This is why Dolley instructed Margaret Bayard Smith to tell the story of saving the portrait of George Washington, and why Dolley fought hard throughout her life to support that memory.

Dolley and James burned many of their letters, leaving us with a strikingly impersonal record of the most famous First Lady of the nineteenth century. It was as Gamaliel Bradford, a popular biographer writing in the early twentieth century, said when he wrote in his journal that he had "spent a whole morning in the hope of finding some touch that might make Dolly Madison stand out a little more vividly." And why he stated in frustration, "it is hardly fair to infer that the woman had no inner life because we hear nothing of it."[74] We read Mary's memoir in the hope of finding that inner, personal Dolley, and experience a combination of frustration and sadness when we do not find her. As a documentary editor, it is my conclusion that we must "look" at Dolley as well as "listen" to her—or her niece. It is why the Dolley Madison Digital Edition decided to include nonepistolary materials such as land sales and court records. We need always to remember what is *not* said, and do our best to watch as well as listen. It is with these episodes in mind that we can begin to reevaluate Dolley Madison's personal and inner life.

74. As quoted in DPM, *Selected Letters*, 1–2.

Miss Cutts

ELIZABETH DOWLING TAYLOR

Mary Cutts was born into a city smoldering from war, edgy with foreboding, and facing a crossroads. The fires in Washington City in September 1814 were out but not over. The aunt who would play such a major role in this girl's life, and who was known for her gaiety, positive outlook, and adaptability, was fearful and despondent. Would Washington continue as the nation's capital? Would the Madison administration recover from the shame of abandoning the federal city to British torches less than a month before? Would Dolley Madison resume her role of admired leading lady of the land?

Yes. Yes. And Yes. Mary Cutts's life would always be shaded in political colors. Her father's career and the family's financial well-being ebbed and flowed with the embargo, the War of 1812, the patronage of his brother-in-law President Madison, and the boot from later chief executive Andrew Jackson. Unmarried, Mary was part of her father's household until his death, and would always rely for nurture and sociability on her relationships with immediate and extended family members. Here she was bestowed with a fortunate foundation. Her mother, Anna, was the much younger sister of Dolley Madison, who had raised her as a daughter from early adolescence. Aunt Dolley had just one child of her own, who was a great heartache and took without giving, so she relished her relationships with this favorite sister and her sons and daughters where there was warm reciprocity.

Anna Payne married Richard Cutts in 1804, a festive occasion in the new capital of Washington, a planned city that, indeed, existed largely in

I am grateful to Catherine Allgor for the invitation to contribute to this book, and I thank her and Holly Cowan Shulman for their helpful discussions on my essay.

plan. Bride and groom were both connected with the federal government. She was the secretary of state's sister-in-law, and he a congressman from Maine (then a district of Massachusetts). By the time James Madison became president in 1809, the Cutts family had grown to five with the births of three sons; they lived in the President's House on Pennsylvania Avenue for some months and then took a house on nearby F Street, an enclave of townhouses of the well-connected. During this period, Richard Cutts was James Madison's confidential companion and daily recounted to the president the proceedings of Congress and other news over a glass of wine. That sisters Dolley and Anna were intimates went without saying; though they formed an especially well-knitted pair, there were other Payne siblings, sisters Lucy and Mary and brother John, who, along with their spouses and children, made for a large kin circle. As the Madison biographer Ralph Ketcham has it, many of these connections were "closer to Madison than his own relatives."[1]

Mary Estelle Elizabeth Cutts was born on 16 September 1814. She would always relate most closely to the two siblings that flanked her in birth order, her sole sister, Dolley, and only younger brother, Richard. Richard was born in 1817, the same year that their father became the second comptroller of the United States Treasury and that the Madisons retired to their Virginia plantation, Montpelier, after a two-term administration. It had been a tough eight years, yet when they were over, an air of proud nationalism settled on the country's citizens. England had now twice proved unable to beat them at war. Even curmudgeonly John Adams had to admit that, "notwithstanding a thousand Faults and blunders," James Madison's tenure "acquired more glory, and established more Union than all his three Predecessors." The Cutts siblings shared an active correspondence with their Aunt Dolley and Uncle James for most of the year; summers they spent, along with their mother, at their aunt and uncle's country estate. Mary Cutts later described the view from the mansion's front portico: "The Blue Ridge [Mountains] . . . extend as far as the eye can reach, forming successions of landscapes varied at every turn, from the wildest to the most cultivated, immense waving fields of grain, tobacco, &c." While a "harbor of hospitality" for Madison friends and extended family, Montpelier was also workplace and residence to more than one hundred enslaved men,

1. Minnie Clare Yarborough, ed., *The Reminiscences of William C. Preston* (Chapel Hill: University of North Carolina Press, 1933), 8; Ralph Ketcham, *James Madison: A Biography* (Charlottesville: University of Virginia Press, 1990), 617.

women, and children. Mary writes of this community in the paternalistic vein common to her class, employing terms that minimize and misrepresent the oppression and exploitation of the enslaved.[2]

Dolley Madison's son, Payne Todd, born in 1792, was a pampered boy whose continued indulgence led to his dissipation and alcoholism. He wandered from city to city along the Eastern Seaboard, drinking, gambling, and trying to stay a step ahead of his creditors. Though he never lost his mother's love, she salved the hurt he caused her with the loving attentions of nieces and nephews. By the time Mary Cutts was ten, her aunt was addressing her as "my sweetest of daughters." The next year she engaged the young girl in a philosophical exchange on the relative merits of the personal quality of "decision." "'Decision' my darling Mary is an excellent trait of character," she advised, "provided it is not blended with too much obduracy." It was in a later letter to Mary that she revealed the oft-quoted "secret" she had discovered: that all have "a great hand in the formation of our own destiny." Such musings were interspersed with requests for gossip, for Aunt Dolley missed city life, "where variety reigns," and where she had kept abreast of—and often set—the day's social and fashion trends. "I hope you will soon be at the parties and will give me a detail of what is going forward, amidst the various characters in Washington," Dolley wrote her niece.[3] Besides news and gossip, Mary and her sister exchanged books and ladies' magazines, patterns and fabrics, and a medley of gifts with their aunt.

In one letter to her young namesake, Aunt Dolley mentioned an illness of Mary's: "I expect Madame Serurier has been very kind in her sickness as she seemed to love her while here." Madame Serurier was the French minister's wife, and the reference is just one indication of the many opportunities that came the Cutts sisters' way at Montpelier and in Washington to make the acquaintance of individuals of note and influence. Their aunt coached them in social graces and pitfalls. One Washingtonian, she cautioned Mary, has it "in her power to be kind and perhaps useful to you,

2. Quoted in Ketcham, *James Madison*, 611; CM II, 154. On Mary Cutts's misrepresentation of Montpelier slave life, one example will suffice: "None but an eye witness can know of the peace and ease of these sable sons of toil! to retire with health and not a care for the morrow and surrounded by their progeny" (CM II, 157).

3. DPTM to MEEC, 22 Jan. 1825, DMDE; DPTM to MEEC, 15 Aug. 1826, DMDE; DPTM to MEEC, 1 Aug. 1833, DMDE; DPTM to Dolley Cutts, Dec. 1831, DMDE.

but if she is ever offended in any way she is *bitter*." Dolley also warned her younger relatives of the evils of tobacco. It was too late for her: she was addicted to the weed, and her constant accoutrement, the snuffbox, was as well known as her signature turbans.

In 1820, Mary's father had a new house built for his family on Lafayette Square, just a block from the White House. The two-story dwelling with garret and cellar levels and a garden in the back was one of the earliest houses facing the public square and sat catercorner to St. John's Church, the Episcopal "Church of Presidents." Life was pleasant and privileged for the Cutts family throughout most of this decade. They enjoyed the company and the entertainments of their neighbors, who, as Dolley Madison put it, "keep up the fashion of dissipation." Richard Cutts's roots were in Saco, Maine, and often while his wife and children were visiting with the Madisons in Virginia, he would return to his home state when his government position allowed it. Occasionally the entire family gathered at Cutts Island in the Saco River. "The Saco falls were just opposite, and could be heard for two miles distant," Mary recalled, "their descent is very rapid and the scenery altogether wild and romantic."[4] Her father's shipping and other commercial concerns had suffered earlier due to the embargo that preceded the War of 1812. His financial recovery proved to be short-lived, however, and in 1828 Richard Cutts found himself insolvent, which led to his being briefly jailed. This embarrassing situation was resolved by brother-in-law James Madison stepping in and purchasing the Cutts house so that the family would not be evicted. The next year Richard Cutts faced more bad news when, under the Jacksonian spoils system, he lost his government position in the Treasury Department.

By this time, when Mary visited Montpelier, she found her cousin Annie Payne, John's daughter, in permanent residence. Annie would remain Dolley Madison's live-in companion through the close of "Auntie's" life. All indications are that Mary and Annie—five years apart in age—were close and compatible cousins. One letter to Mary, written in tag-team fashion by Aunt Dolley and Cousin Annie, described caring for the ex-president in his infirmity. "Aunt D . . . [is] incessantly engaged as Uncle's deputy morning,

4. DPTM to Dolley Cutts, Dec. 1831, DMDE; DPTM to MEEC, 10 March 1833, DMDE; DPTM to Anna Payne Cutts, [June] 1804, DMDE; DPTM to Sarah Coles Stevenson, ca. Feb. 1820, in DPM, *Selected Letters*, 239; Henry Burrage, "Richard Cutts," in *Collections and Proceedings of the Maine Historical Society*, 2nd ser., 8 (1897); CM II, 143.

noon and night," wrote Annie, and Aunt D. herself added, "Your Uncle is now so feeble as to be just and hardly able to walk from his bed to the little chamber." James Madison suffered from a painful and diffusive rheumatism, but nevertheless kept up a good-natured correspondence with the Cutts siblings through the end of his days. When they came to visit, they took turns reading aloud to him in the "little chamber," his study or sitting room. Mary left him a memento in 1831: "Your uncle Madison still wears the bead ring you placed on his finger," wrote Aunt Dolley, "I see him look at it every now and then."

On 4 August 1832, Anna Payne Cutts died. Just two days before, her sister Dolley had written from Montpelier, "Strive to be . . . well . . . what should we do without you!" In another letter, she referred to "your precious daughters, whom I shall ever consider and feel are my own children." Certainly Anna died comforted that her sons and daughters would not want for motherly love. Yet, as one of Dolley's city friends informed her later that month, "Poor Mr. Cutts seems to be incosolable as well as Doly and Mary who feel they have made an irreparable loss." This correspondent referred to brothers Madison and Richard, too; the former, she said, had never left his mother's bedside during the last part of her illness while "little Richard shows much feeling for one of his age."[5]

Mary and her sister, by the former's own account, had not been sent to school. Their mother "would never allow [her daughters] to leave her for boarding school, tho' every inducement was offered—she had them taught her own favorite accomplishments, and instilled in their minds a taste for poetry, [and] the clasics." Mary Cutts also cultivated an inclination to draw, and produced pencil sketches of her Aunt Dolley and others. The sisters' home schooling was complete enough that their aunt characterized them in 1834 as "well educated and sensible girls," going on to describe their well-roundedness by adding "full of gaiety & fashion."[6]

Dolley Madison began 1836 in characteristic cheerfulness, writing to nieces Mary and Dolley the day after New Year's, "I embrace you both, beloved daughters, with a thousand wishes for your happiness and prosperity on every and many Christmas days to come!" But her beloved husband would be gone before the first half of the year was over. When Mary

5. Anna Coles Payne Causten to MEEC, 18 Apr. 1836, Cutts Family Papers, DLC; DPTM to MEEC, 16 Sept. 1831, DMDE; DPTM to Anna Payne Cutts, ca. 4 Aug. 1832, DMDE; Eliza Vail Longueville to DPTM, 12 Aug. 1832, DMDE.

6. CM II, 171; DPTM to Mary Payne Jackson Allen, 25 Feb. 1834, DMDE.

received the news of her uncle's death, she rushed from Washington to be at her aunt's side. During his nineteen-year retirement, James Madison had worked, with the assistance of various family members, on organizing and copying the papers of his life's work, especially those concerned with the Constitution. Mary Cutts was one of the "inexpert aids" to whom her uncle John Payne referred in a letter written shortly after the great man's death enlisted to complete the task.[7]

The passing of Anna Cutts and James Madison tightened the bonds among Mary, Dolley, and their aunt. The paired sisters were the "Misses Cutts" and enjoyed society. At a fancy ball in Washington in the 1830s, "the nieces of Mrs. Madison, the Misses Cutts, appeared as Night and Morning." During the same period, the noted geologist George Featherstonhaugh referred to a dinner party in Georgetown where he had "the pleasure of seeing our valued young friends the Misses Cutts." As the sisters reached the age where girls were expected to turn their thoughts toward marriage, Aunt Dolley prodded them with advice and suggestions on potential mates. In 1833, she urged Mary to "sett your Cap or Curls" on a Washington diplomat who was a European baron.[8] But both Cutts nieces remained single. This was a serious matter in the society of the day: women might have been restrained as spouses, but as "spinsters" their options for fashioning a mode of living that was both satisfying and acceptable were severely restricted.

For Mary Cutts, the germ of the idea of becoming an authoress, or at least compiling her famous aunt's life story, may have been planted in 1834. In that year, the writer Margaret Bayard Smith asked Dolley Madison if she would forward material for a short biographical sketch she wanted to construct of her famous friend. In her reply, Dolley mentioned that niece Mary was at Montpelier, so the younger woman was aware of this biographical effort from the start. A subsequent letter revealed that Mary was employed as courier to "lend [some of her aunt's letters] to Mrs. Smith for

7. DPTM to MEEC and Dolley Cutts, 2 Jan. 1836, DMDE; Martha Jefferson Randolph to DPTM, 6 July 1836, DMDE. See also Anna Coles Payne Causten to Frances Lear, 16 July 1836 DMDE; CM II, 180; and John C. Payne to Edward Coles, 18 July 1836, DMDE.

8. Samuel Busey, *Pictures of the City of Washington in the Past* (Washington, D.C.: William Ballantyne and Sons, 1898), 360; George Featherstonhaugh to James Madison, 15 July 1835, Founders Early Access, University of Virginia Press, http://rotunda .upress.virginia.edu/founders/FOEA.html; DPTM to MEEC, 13 March 1833, DMDE.

her perusal." Smith was not the only possible inspiration to whom Mary was exposed when it came to female authors. Others, single women, and for that reason alone more audacious than the conventionally married Smith, included Anne Royall, Frances Wright, and Harriet Martineau. These independent women crossed Mary's circle of acquaintances on their treks to the nation's capital. Wright and Martineau visited at Montpelier as well. After the visit of the latter, Dolley wrote her niece admiringly of Martineau's "enlightened conversation." Ironically, in this same letter wherein she expressed approval of Harriet Martineau, one of those females who had to contend with the ridicule aimed at learned women, Dolley responded thusly to Mary's apparent comment on a risqué new dance: "I have no idea of the new dance or its motions but approve of your declining to learn it, if disapproved of by society.—*Our sex* are ever loosers, when they stem the torrent of public opinion." Mary claimed that her mother trained her "to listen to 'the still small voice within.'" The complication came when multiple voices beckoned.[9]

The widowed Dolley Madison was far from rich. Her husband had hoped she would be able to sell his political papers. With difficulty, she eventually did, in two lots, but they fetched only half of what James Madison had predicted. She sold family slaves; her husband had left her to deal with the fact that they owned more slaves than the Montpelier farmland could sustain. Dolley informed Richard Cutts that, as owner of the Lafayette Square house, she now intended to take it over, and the Cutts family good-naturedly set about finding a new place to live and helping Dolley in the transition. Sisters Mary and Dolley were concerned that their aunt be comfortable in the house and that general knowledge of her financial difficulties be minimized. Initially, the widow Madison planned to alternate between her country and city houses according to season, and began the pattern of summers at Montpelier and winters in Washington in 1837, renting the city house in her absence.

When Aunt Dolley was in Washington along with niece and live-in companion Annie Payne, they joined with Mary and Dolley Cutts to form a coterie of four. The Washington social chronicler Sarah Vedder recollected seeing Mrs. Madison at her Lafayette Square house "dozens of times . . . sitting on her front steps, surrounded by young girls, laughing and talking,

9. DPTM to Margaret Bayard Smith, 31 Aug. 1834, DMDE; DPTM to MEEC, Oct. 1834, DMDE; DPTM to MEEC, 10 March 1835 DMDE; CM II, 171.

for she was fond of young company." Then they were three when they lost young Dolley to pleurisy in 1838. The surviving sister was bereft: Mary's bosom companion was gone, and she could not be consoled.[10]

Dolley Madison was unable to keep up the expense of maintaining two residences and sold Montpelier in 1844, though even this did not allow her to live in financial ease for the remainder of her days. Payne Todd pressured his mother unconscionably into passing on her financial resources to him until finally, pathetically, she informed him that she had nothing left to convey. Nevertheless, she was happy to be in the vibrant capital, and its citizens were happy to have her. She was always in social demand and became a treasured living icon of the age of the Founders.

Mary Cutts lived with her father and favorite brother, Richard, in a small house on Fourteenth Street, not far from Lafayette Square. The fourth member of their household was a free black woman. According to the terms of Dolley Madison's 1841 will, Mary stood to acquire an enslaved girl at her aunt's death. "I give to my niece Mary E. E. Cutts one negro Girl of ten or twelve years of age, as [a] Mark of my affection," the document read; no such term, however, was included in later wills that superseded this document.[11] Former president John Quincy Adams and his wife, Louisa Catherine, lived around the corner on F Street, and Mary was a frequent visitor there, dropping in for tea and conversation. "Miss Cutts dined and spent the evening here," reads one of many entries that mention her in the ex-president's incredibly thorough diary. When, in 1848, John Quincy Adams, now serving as a congressman, collapsed with a stroke on the floor of the House of Representatives, Mary accompanied Louisa Catherine as she rushed to his side. They found him just losing consciousness. "I was at the Capitol most of the time he was laying there ill," Mary informed a friend in England, but President Adams, her kindly neighbor, never regained consciousness.

It was an interesting life, and it would seem that Mary used the character trait of "decision" to make it so. In the spring of 1842, Dolley Madison, along with nieces Mary and Annie and one of her nephews (probably Richard), traveled to New York City. On their way north they made a leisurely

10. Dolley Cutts to MEEC, 9 Sept. 1837, Cutts Family Papers, DLC; Sarah E. Vedder, *Reminiscences of the District of Columbia* (St. Louis, Mo.: A .R. Fleming, 1909), 5; DPTM to Caroline Hite, 19 Dec. 1838, DMDE.

11. DPTM to John Payne Todd, 24 Sept. 1847, in DPM, *Selected Letters,* 386; will of DPTM, in DPM, *Selected Letters,* 356.

stop in Philadelphia to visit old friends. Once in New York, they checked into the Astor House. Aunt Dolley met with the ultrawealthy John Jacob Astor, to whom she arranged to mortgage her house, and—still in quest of a publisher for her husband's official papers—with editors at Harper Brothers. Presumably, the foursome also made time to take in the sights of the nation's most populated city.[12]

In 1845, Mary Cutts's father died. The loss of his fortune, position, and wife proved too much for him. He had lived out the last part of his life in quiet despondency, his "energies paralyzed," in his daughter's description. This same year Mary's brother Richard married a member of the extended Jefferson family, Martha Jefferson Hackley. Her brother Madison had taken a wife a dozen years earlier, so Mary now had sisters-in-law she cared about, and, as they came along, nieces and nephews of her own on whom to focus attention. Her brother Madison's daughter Adele, born in 1835, was a lively girl who would blossom into a popular belle. Adele cultivated a different lifestyle from that of her aunt; though Mary Cutts was sociable, she never aspired to be a socialite like Adele. Adele could be seen each evening promenading along Pennsylvania Avenue, first escorted by her father and later by any of a host of beaus, among whom was her future husband, Stephen A. Douglas, best remembered in the history books as Abraham Lincoln's opponent in a series of debates and a run for the presidency.[13]

On 12 July 1849, Dolley Madison died. The nation's capital honored her with the largest state funeral to date. During her last year, Mary recalled, "Her memory was buisy with the past, she caused old letters to be reread to her." Mary wrote a correspondent of her aunt's final days: "She sank into a quiet sleep Sunday afternoon while I was by her . . . nothing was thought of it until it was prolonged until the next morning when she woke—smiling sweetly at those round her . . . she lingered until Thursday." Her aunt's death, "like her life," Mary pronounced, "was calm & beautiful."

Mary Cutts, who turned thirty-five that September, spent what would turn out to be the last seven years of her life attending to her famous aunt's papers. She aspired to be a biographer, to write a "Life of Mrs. Madison." Even if, as has been suggested, the impetus for this went back to 1834,

12. John Quincy Adams, Diary, 13 Apr. 1841, Adams Family Papers, Massachusetts Historical Society; MEEC to a friend visiting England, 12 Apr. and 10 May 1848, www .liveauctioneers.com/item/4214232; CM II, 187; Allen C. Clark, *Life and Letters of Dolly Madison* (Washington, D.C.: W. F. Roberts, 1914), 312.

13. CM II, 171; Virginia Miller, "Dr. Thomas Miller and His Times," *Records of the Columbia Historical Society of Washington, DC* 3 (1900): 307.

when Margaret Bayard Smith wrote a biographical entry on Dolley Madison for an anthology of prominent Americans, she may not have seriously engaged in the effort until her aunt's demise. After she "untied the faded ribbons, from [her aunt's] letters," and completed two overlapping drafts of a memoir, Mary concluded, "We lay down the pen *dissatisfied*! —feeling how inadequately we have performed the duty assigned to us—totally unaccustomed to composition of any kind." She claimed that the effort had been undertaken "sadly and mournfully" and only for the sake of producing a tribute to the First Lady's memory.[14] But one might detect some false modesty in Mary's assessments of both her talent and ambition as a writer. It seems that she did make attempts to have her manuscripts reviewed with an eye to publication, and may have tried her hand at prose or verse beyond the "Life of Mrs. Madison."

It is not clear where Mary Cutts's home base was during her last years. At the time of the 1840 federal census, she was living with the Richards, father and brother, on Fourteenth Street. In 1844, when her brother was planning to marry, he expressed concern that any future arrangements be "conducive to the happiness of Mary," and he envisioned Martha, his wife-to-be, joining their family group "under Mary's management," citing his sister's "taste and skill" in this role. He believed that Mary wanted "a house companion" and felt "sure that Martha will be loved by all." But additional changes were afoot; by the end of 1845, not only was her brother married, but their father had passed on, and it seems that Mary accepted, and perhaps even embraced, living independently. She stayed with Richard and Martha at times but did not become a permanent member of their household. They lived in Maryland over part of this period while Mary Cutts identified her place of residence as Washington (though she does not show up there or anywhere in the 1850 federal census).[15]

Mary Cutts lost the constant companionship of Annie Payne when she married in 1851, then lost her altogether when she died in 1852. Mary pressed on with the determination to lead an *interesting* life. Taking advantage of famous connections, she went to Massachusetts in the fall of 1852 to spend time with the Adamses in Quincy—"my true hearted Yankee friends"—and to visit Boston. She was having a fine time by the tone of her note to a financial advisor calling for more funds: "Flying about as I have

14. CM II, 191; MEEC to a correspondent named "Annie," 29 Aug. 1849, www.secondstorybooks.com/details.php?record=1141499&URLPAIR; CM II, 194–95.

15. Richard D. Cutts to DPTM, 27 Oct. 1844, and Richard D. Cutts to DPTM, 1 Nov. 1844, Dolley Madison Papers, DLC.

the last two months I find my money takes wings also."[16] Her many friends and correspondents included several of Thomas Jefferson's granddaughters as well as international acquaintances.

In July 1856, Mary Cutts took what turned out to be her last trip, a visit to the Allen family, relatives in southwestern Virginia. Mary's mother and Mary Jackson Allen's mother, Mary Payne Jackson, were sisters. Mary Jackson Allen had lived most of her life in Clarksburg, Kentucky, and the two Marys, though first cousins, were not close. Mary certainly would not have embarked on this journey had she known what a serious illness was about to overtake her. By this year, the Allen family lived in Botetourt County, Virginia. Letters among the Allens reveal that Mary Cutts arrived at their home via Lexington, Virginia. She rendezvoused there with her cousin's son Robert. Not feeling at all well, she waited for him to attend a Fourth of July oration before the two set out for Beaverdam, as the Allen place was called. She was "Miss Cutts . . . Ma's cousin" to Robert. Later, when his father, who was out of town, heard that his wife's kin had arrived at his doorstep with consumption, he was "provoked." His son should have known better than to introduce this contagious disease into their house. Excessively weak, Mary Cutts never rose after she lay down on Sunday, July 6. Eight mornings later, "she commenced sinking and before the doctor arrived breathed her last." Spinster Mary Cutts, forty-one, died of consumption on July 14 in a bed in the household of extended kin, the head of which resented her presence. Her brother Madison came to retrieve her body.[17] Mary Cutts wished to be buried alongside her sister and parents. The remains of all four rest today in Georgetown's Oak Hill Cemetery.

Four years before her death, Mary Cutts had prepared a will. Given that she was well-heeled at her death, she must have been a skillful manager of her resources. Mary bequeathed many handsome gifts to various relatives. In addition to land, bonds, cash, silver, furniture, and jewelry, her will mentions books and drawings. But it makes no note of any papers or manuscripts.[18] Though the name of her famous aunt does not appear in the will, Mary Cutts's great gift to her, and to posterity, were the unpublished manuscripts on the "Life of Mrs. Madison." These were taken up, in turn as

16. MEEC to Richard Smith, 27 Oct. 1852, original unlocated.

17. Henry C. Allen to John J. Allen, 19 July 1856, and Mary Payne Jackson Allen to son John Allen, 9 July 1856, Papers of the Allen family, University of Virginia Special Collections.

18. Will of MEEC, Aug. 1852, Box 24, Wills, United States National Archives and Records Administration, Washington, D.C.

it were, by her own unmarried niece, her brother Richard's daughter Lucia (who was just five when her Aunt Mary died). Rather sadly, Lucia Cutts chose not to acknowledge her aunt's work in the book based on Mary's manuscripts that was published in 1886, but then Lucia Cutts herself, editor of the volume, was not identified by name in the original edition.

Texts

Editorial Note

Now to the documents themselves. The goal of the transcription team was to give Mary Cutts's writing as scholarly and professional a treatment as possible, using the standards and methods utilized by presidential paper projects, while at the same time making reading easy for everyone. This meant finding ways to preserve all markings, additions, insertions, and deletions for the serious scholar, but presenting them in unobtrusive ways for the general reader.

Thus, an illegible word is represented with "[. . .]." Conjectural reading of an illegible word is followed by a question mark and presented in square brackets, e.g., "[misbehaved?]." Underscored words are set in italic. The material here is lightly annotated, so as not to disrupt the reading flow. There are "x" marks scattered throughout the original manuscript; we conjecture that they were editorial marks, likely denoting where Mary wanted to insert material and sometimes (though not always) marking the material to be inserted. These marks have been set as asterisks (and bracketed, if the placement wasn't clear in the original manuscript); where there was associated text, this appears at the foot of the page, marked by an asterisk and preceding the editor's notes. The various elements of letters included in the texts—such as date lines, addresses, salutations, valedictions, and signatures—have been set consistently for readability.

Keep in mind that these two pieces are the manuscripts of a writer. Unlike other historical documents the reader may have encountered, these do not have the polished, professional look of a published work, such as a pamphlet or Declaration. Nor does the writing here resemble that of a diary or personal letter, written freely, with no editing. Rather, these are "books in progress" that show process, and highlighting that construction is crucial, reminding us that these accounts are not sources of unmediated information. Complicating the picture are the two sets of editorial marks on the pages: Mary Cutts crossed out and added material, and so did Lucia B. Cutts.

Thus, text added after the initial time of writing is presented in square brackets beginning with the initials of the author, e.g., "[LC: however]." All cancelled text was struck out by Mary unless otherwise noted. To make these deletions easier to read, cancelled text is printed with a tint rather than in solid black. Cancelled text with a double strike-through is printed with a tint and a single strike-through. Text cancelled by Lucia is followed by "[LC]." When an LC addition follows cancelled text, the strikeout is read as Lucia's, e.g., "first who [LC: earliest]." When Mary and Lucia cross out adjacent words or phrases, an "[MC]" is provided for clarity.

In her conception of this book, Mary followed a "Life and Letters" model that was popular in her day, interspersing her own prose with transcribed letters. Some of the letters Mary wrote into the text still exist in their original form; they have already been transcribed professionally in the Dolley Madison Digital Edition (DMDE) and in *The Papers of James Madison, Presidential Series*. In other cases, the originals that Mary used have been lost, and her transcriptions are the only sources extant. Since both kinds of letters are found in the Dolley Madison Digital Edition, we debated whether or not to include Mary's versions here. In the end, the letters that Mary chose were so important to her vision of the book as a whole that we decided to include them. But, in all cases, the DMDE is the final word.

Cutts Memoir I

Transcribed by LEE LANGSTON-HARRISON,
CATHERINE ALLGOR, *and* JAMES T. CONNOLLY

"So brief our existance, a glimpse at the most,
Is all we can have of the friends we hold dear;
And oft even joy is unheeded and lost,
For want of some heart that could echo it near.
Oh! well may we hope, when this short life is gone,
To meet in some world of more permanent bliss,
For a smile, or a grasp of the hand hastening on,
Is all we enjoy of each other in this."
—by THOMAS MOORE.

John Payne the grand father of M^rs: Madison was an English gentleman of wealth and education, he [LC: who] emigrated to this country and settled in Goochland, County, Virginia [MC] James River [LC], Virginia. he married Anna Fleming, grand daughter of Sir Thomas Fleming, second son of the Earl of Wigd[LC: t]en of Scotland, who married Miss Tarleton of Wales, and came to this country in 1616, landed at James Town and afterwards settled in [LC: the county of] New Kent, Cy. Va. [LC: in Virginia] where he lived and died.*

His son John Payne, the father of M^rs: Madison, was a planter and settled in North Carolina—he married Mary Coles, the daughter of Williams Coles, a native of Enniscorthy in Ireland whose mother's maiden name was Philpot. [LC: Her mother whose]

Williams Coles married the widow of Benjamin Dabney, by whom she had several children. Her maiden name was Lucy Winston. Isaac Winston, the father of Lucy was one of three brothers who came to Virginia, from Essex Cy. England. He had three sons and three daughters.— Mary—married John Coles—Lucy first Williams Coles—and Dorothy, who mar-

ried first John Syme of New Castle Virginia, and afterwards John Henry—
by whom **she had several children [LC: was an aunt of] Patrick Henry, the
celebrated orator,** was one.

As this gifted son of Virginia, was a near relative of M⁗ Madison's,
and one of whom she might well be proud, in a Democratic Republican
Country, where inborn genius, such as his, constitute the **[MC: its]** true
aristocracy—we cannot forbear a few passing remarks, though we are well
[MC: aware] that no words of ours could add **[MC: more than 'words']** to
the enthousiastic descriptions already given by those who had the good
fortune to know him personally. Reared under similar auspices in Hanover
County, afterwards meeting in Philadelphia, in public life, for a short time
the opponent of her hus Mʳ Madison, pub socially, they always maintained
an affectionate intercourse.

A very pleasing sketch of this Orator is found in the "Homes of American Statesmen—". It is in some respects better than those of his previous biographists, because the **[MC: writer]** has taken the pains to seek for
information, from the fountain head, his own family. To make his success
and career more brilliant, his early advantages and associations have been
depreciated.

History furnishes but few examples of such patriotism, with the power of
swaying the minds of men, of carrying them away witho him by the power
of eloquence, and the might of right! which he so powerfully depicted,
and with so modest and unselfish a nature, withal!— How many spirited
youths, animated by reciting from his patriotic and soul stirring speeches,
have exclaimed, "oh, that I had lived in the days of Patrick Henry"!

He refused all public appointments, except from his own State—even
the nomination for the Presidency, when the Federalists proposed him as
the successor of General Washington. He was dazzled by neither power,
nor dignity. "He had served his state only in perilous times, when to be
highest was only to be exposed foremost to the bolt of the dreaded enemy,
or at some conjuncture of civil danger, but when peace and ease had come
and ambition, was the only lure to office, he would not have it." E. J.

Virginia is proud of this son, who seemed to spring into existance as a
meteor when most needed by his country and who by the power of truth
led them on to assert their rights and shake off the trammels with which
England would bind her Colonies more tightly to herself!

After the lapse of years a statue has been erected to his memory in the
city of Richmond. (Sepr: 1855) extract from a public journal "The colossal
bronze statues of Jefferson and Henry were elevated to their temporary

pedestals on the lower pediment of the Capitol Steps—Jefferson is in perfect contrast with Henry; the latter is all action, Jefferson is calm, majestic and in repose, representing the deep thought and composure of the master Statesman. While the statue of Henry represents the fire and impetuosity of the impassioned orator." [LC]

Mary Coles was doubtless [LC: herself] a belle and a beauty, she had many lovers [LC: and is said to have had many admirers] and among them Thomas Jefferson [LC: who was favored] her friends, who appreciated his promising talents, urged his being accepted, but she preferred Mʳ: Payne, whose [LC: however was preferred and his] personal appearance was [LC: certainly] in his favor.

John Payne was a [LC: He was] [MC: a Capⁿ· in the Revolutionary War and] resident of North Carolina, where his father had given him a plantation, but soon after his marriage to Mary Coles he purchased an estate in Hanover Cy [LC: County] Virginia, twenty miles from Coles Hill the residence of Williams Coles, late in life Mʳˢ· Madison was asked to describe this homestead she said "I can just remember the mantel peices, they were of black marble supported by white figures, there were twenty rooms on a floor, every one had marble hearths and mantels—it [LC: the house] was built by an English nobleman [LC: (?)] and was called Scotch town because of the emigrants, and was surrounded with small brick houses attached to the main building." It was purchased by her father from Peter Randalph—or Randolph as he afterwards spelt his name— Mʳ: Randolph was a wealthy Virginian fond of gaity, and of its excess, so common at that period—in a frolic, he unfortunately killed a man in humble circumstances, was imprisoned, [LC: and] tried and [LC: but finally] acquitted by the wealth of his friends and his own means of his wealth and that of his relations [LC].

Mʳ: Payne had six children, of whom the second, the subject of this memoir was born [MC: the 20ᵗʰ· of May 1772], while [LC: while her parents were] on a visit to his relations in [LC] North Carolina and was named Dorothy in compliment to her [MC: mother's] Aunt Mʳˢ· John Henry— As she grew up the name was getting [LC: growing] out of fashion, and she ever afterwards wrote it Dolley and so she was called— Her parents were both strict members of "the Society of Friends"—her childhood was passed in this [LC: their] tranquil [MC: country] home.—of which she had the happiest reminiscences, She was the [LC: as being a] favorite with all, and what was [MC: then] more remarkable, her companions never envied her— who [MC: Her grandmother] testified her affection by constant presents of her old fashioned jewelry, for which it must be confessed she [MC: Dolley] [LC: her grand child] ever had a woman's fondness—tho', child as she was, she dared not offend her parents by wearing them in [LC: their] sight, but they were [LC: however] put in a bag and tied round her neck—and we have heard her say, that the first [MC: true [LC]] grief she ever had [LC: of her childhood] was when she discovered, in her country school, that the string had become unfastened, in her ramble through the woods—and her treasures were gone! she cried heartily! [LC] Her early advantages were few in the way of high culture intellectual culture, but we must think that [LC] with her pure minded parents the affections of her heart were well developed and these twelve years of childhood had an effect upon her after life!—she used to say that in summer her white sun bonnet was always sewn on, while going backwards and forwards to school she wore long gloves and sometimes even a white linen mask[1]—so particular were the old fashioned ladies about the complexion—these and other childish tales [MC: of her childhood] she often told her neices, for the [LC: sixty?] seventy years afterwards. [LC: P]

Mʳ Payne was one of the first who [LC: earliest] of his Sect [MC: in Virginia] who became doubtful and afterwards concientiously scrupulous about the rights of the Slave of holding slaves as property. he was called a fanatic, but persisted in setting his plantation and setting giving freedom to his own [LC: slaves], whom he took with him to Philadelphia— One [LC: of them, always] faithful and true, deserves to be mentioned, mother Amy, the nourse of Mʳˢ Madison, She did not wish her freedom, but remained with the family, while [MC: lived in Philᵃ] they lasted.

she was tall and stately in her appearance, always dressing as a quakeress. a most excellent likeness was taken of her [   ] and recopied of late years for her sisters Mʳˢ Madison and her sisters, she died, leaving 500 dollars to her former mistress.

In the year 1786 Mʳ Payne removed to Philadelphia, seemingly with but one aim, the support [LC: maintenance] of his religious belief— He was an elder, spoke in [LC: the] meetings and was called a "Quaker Preacher"— the early "friends" were very strict and allowed no ornaments, not even in their houses. We saw recently in Philᵃ an ancient clock in the house of "a

1. In the original document, this passage has small superscript numbers: "she used to say that in summer her ²white sun bonnet was ²always sewn on, while going backwards¹ and forwards to school." The editors believe that these numbers, along with some corresponding lines that Mary drew, were reordering the phrases, showing Mary's editorial mind at work.

Friend"—which had been stripped of its ornamental work by the ruthless hands of "a deputation from [LC: the] meeting" of that [LC: early] period. Mᴿ Payne was very exact with his children and brought them up in that religion which has utility for its basis, and which forbids the acquirement of those graceful and [LC] ornamental accomplishments which are too generally considered the most important parts of female education.

Highly connected and nearly related to many of the Virginia gentry, his house was one of the principal resorts of the gay Southerners. His eldest son was sent to England for a year [MC: to complete his education] So strong was the prepossession for "the old country." Dolley—the second had grown child grew in grace and beauty, [LC: and soon] She [LC] had numerous suitors; her powers of fascination were wonderful! [LC] A few still lingering [LC] on the earth who knew her in [MC: at] that day [MC: time], (among them two of her bridal attendants—Mʳˢ R. B. Lee and Mʳˢ Anthony Morris)[2] [LC: they] bear testimony to her influence on the hearts of all. She disarmed envy. A word or look caused all to love her as they did themselves. We who only knew her as an aged lady [MC: when passed the meridian of life] have seen the high and the low take from themselves to give to her and think themselves well repaid by the affectionate glance of this otherwise powerless lady. The old fashioned slanting roofed house where John Payne had lived was pointed out to us a few years since, standing in its lowliness, surrounded by new and handsome buildings, respected for its former owner, especially by the Society of Friends—then and still among the most respectable in Philadelphia— The names of the Pembertons, the Morrises, the Shippens, the Gilpins, the Drinkers the Roberts, the Fishers, the Baches, the Mifflins, the Physics and hosts of others are still [LC: yet] familiar [LC: and belonging to that Society] Ere this, possibly, this relic house may have been removed for the [LC: on account of the increased] value of its lot [LC: the ground on which it was built.]

After a few years Mᴿ Payne, unaccustomed to city life and the management of money matters found it necessary to go into business, and on his son's return from Europe associated took him into partnership. Much of his capital was in Revolutionary money, [MC: &] as that suddenly [MC: gradually] depreciated in value, he failed and his family, were [LC: became] reduced to poverty [MC: in their circumstances]— He felt his failure deeply [LC: deeply his misfortune] and [MC: Mʳˢ M. said] [LC: used to say he never] afterwards raised his head nor [LC] left his room but to be [LC: until

---

2. Eliza Collins Lee and Mary Smith Pemberton Morris.

he was] carried to his last resting place. M^rs: Payne was persuaded by her cousen a prominent Isaac Coles, a prominent member of the first Congress, to take himself and two or three gentlemen of his selection to board [LC: with her] which she did.

Most prominently useful and kind to M^r: Payne at this juncture in his affairs was John Todd, a young lawyer of promising talents [LC: also] belonging to the society of "Friends["] as was [MC: did] his father and [*page torn*] who was a citizen of ability and wealth. Young M^r: Todd had long been a suitor of Dolley's, who did not incline to relinquish her girl hood, but [LC: as] this was a match that pleased her father in every way, so [LC] he called his daughter to his bedside and told her how much happiness it would give him in his last moments to know that she was married to so estimable a person as and [LC: one] in her own Society. Implicit obedience was then the order of the day. We have heard her say, she did not wish to marry, it was a hard struggle, but she never for one instant thought of disobeying her father's wishes,—and was amply repaid [LC: for her obedience] by receiving the joyful blessing of her dying father! She was married to M^r: Todd in 1791. [LC: A few months afterwards her father died.]

The following year her younger sister [MC: Lucy Payne], a sprightly girl of fifteen was united to George [MC: Steptoe] Washington, a nephew of the General's [LC: Washington]. he was rich in lands, owning a large plantation in Jefferson County, Virginia (called by M^r: Jefferson, the garden spot of Virginia [LC: that State]) It was inherited from his father Samuel Washington—a younger brother of Genl Washington [LC: the General], this place [MC: was] called Harewood. This estate was Harewood, still in possession of his grandson George Lafayette Washington, a youth every way worthy of his name.

Samuel Washington was a gay hunting Virginian who thought much of his horses, dogs and wine and wives—if we may judge from legends and having seen "the banquetting room" built at the end of a large old fashioned English Garden, where the gentleman would retire after dinner. It is now used as a receptacle for lumber and garden implements. "*Wives*" of whom [LC: he was certainly fond of, for] he had five, whose graves are side by side in the old family burying ground.

On the walls at Harewood still hang his own portrait and that of his wife in powdered wig, long coat and waistcoat, with laced ruffles, with that of his wife Anne Steptoe, from whom descended the present "George of Harewood". She also is represented in the costume of that day, with cush-

ioned hair and [LC: in] blue brocade trimmed with point lace, still bearing
the impress of a beautiful girl of sixteen, in stately robes, who would rather
be at sport than sitting for her portrait.

To return to Mʳˢ: Todd, the third year of her marriage, the dreadful yellow
fever, broke which ravaged so many dwellings, broke out in Philadelphia—
her husband, filled with alarm, caused her and two children, one an infant
of three weeks old, to be removed to Grey's ferry on a litter— He then returned to Philadelphia and witnessed the death of his parents by the fell
disease and on coming to his wife a few days afterwards, she implored him
not to return he said he must [MC: it was necessary,], for there was still
another member of his family, who required his presence and he must close
his office, then he would never again leave her— he went, this relation died
as well as a Law Student who was in his house— once more he returned, he
asked for his mother in law, Mʳˢ: Payne—and exclaimed, "the fever is in my
veins! let me behold her once more"! Mʳˢ: Madison, [ ] said, at the sound
of his voice, she heeded not her mother, but left her couch and throwing
herself in his arms welcomed him affectionately as usual and would gladly
have returned with him to Philadelphia, but was not allowed either by her
husband or mother.— He reached his house and died in a few hours, so
rapid was the plague!*

[LC: On] The 11ᵗʰ: of September of 1793 Mʳ: Jefferson wrote to Mʳ: Morris
We print the following note addressed to Mary Payne from a cherished
friend in Philᵃ:

Respected Friend,

Philadelphia 28ᵗʰ October 1793
I received thy favor by the nurse from the Ferry and most sincerely sympathize with thee and thy amiable daughter in your present affliction—
having myself drank of the cup, I know the bitterness of yʳ· draught but
resignation to the Divine Will is our duty; and I hope with patience, Peace
and Comfort will yet be afforded.

Nurse Amy informs me you wish to purchase a small light waggon. I
fear just now, it will be difficult, as few or none are left in town; the number of inhabitants that hath fled to the Country to avoid the Fever having

---

* A trench was dug to bury the dead, where they were thrown in by cartloads.
Washington Square is laid out on the spot.

occupied nearly all the carriages that could be procured— I will however enquire and if I find one for sale, I will mention it as soon as an opportunity occurs.

Nurse also desired me to apply at the Post Office for any letters that may be there—which I would cheerfully do; but by a late regulation of the Post Master, the Person to whom letters are addressed or *their executors*, must apply themselves or give a *written* order for them, otherwise none will be delivered. I am yet very weak and unable to use much exercise, but will, agreeably to thy request meet thee at the lower ferry any *clear* day (about noon) that thee may appoint—and shall esteem myself happy if by any advice or assistance, in my power to offer, I can at all mitigate thine or thy good daughter's afflictions.

> With best wishes for her and your happiness,
> I remain respectfully thy friend,
> Thomas Parke.

"An infect[LC: i]ous and mortal fever is [LC: has] broke[LC: n] out in this place. The deaths under it [LC: during] the week before last were about forty, the last week about fifty, this week they will probably be about two hundred and it is increasing, every one is getting out of the city who can. Col Hamilton[3] is ill of the fever, but is on the recovery. The President according to an arrangement of [LC: made] some time ago, set out for Mount Vernon on [LC] yesterday. The Secretary of War is setting out on a visit to Massachusetts. I shall go in a few days to Virginia. When we shall reassemble again may depend on the course of this malady, and on that may depend the date of my next letter."

Mrs: Todd [LC: herself was felled with the disease. She] was very ill!— her infant son died and she was left with but one child, John Payne.— As soon as all danger had Subsided her mother returned with her to her residence in Philadelphia. I [MC: We] should have mentioned previously that her father died a few months after her marriage.* [LC]

Mr: Todd left a handsome fortune, she [LC: His widow] was still young, just twenty two, with beauty, loveliness of character and perfect freedom from vanity, she [LC: soon] became celebrated. Her height was five inches feet, seven inches and three quarters, well proportioned, her features [LC: pleasing though] not remarkable [LC: in form] excepting her mouth which was beautiful in shape and expression—her hair was jet black and eyes

3. Alexander Hamilton, then secretary of the treasury.

blue, forming a contrast admired by many, her complexion was perfect, white as the driven snow and so it remained until her death. In speaking she had no action, when seated she was in perfect repose, in moving [LC: always] graceful. A [LC: Her] contemporary and bridesmaid [LC: Mrs Lee] now M^rs· Richard B. Lee of Washington, formerly Miss E. Collins of Philadelphia and one [LC] to whom we have previously [LC: already] referred says [LC: has told us that] "gentlemen when they heard of her being in the street would station themselves in stores to [LC: where they could] see her pass. Every body loved her, she had no vanity, In walking with her, she [LC: her friend,] would say "really Dolley, thee [LC: thou] must hide thy face!—["] M^rs· Todd would laugh heartily and obediently put up both hands— [LC: It was on one of these occasions that] M^r· Madison, was [LC] walking with Col I. Coles and [LC] for the first time saw her and was struck with her charms. M^rs· Lee says, she sent her sister Anna to me one evening with a strip of paper on which was written "Thou must come to me, Aaron Burr says that the great, little Madison has asked him to bring him to see me this evening"— She went—M^rs· Madison Todd [LC: has told me us that] at M^rs· Paynes request she [. . .] on the evening M^r· Madison was introduced to her. She] was dressed in a mulberry colored sateen, with a thule[4] silk kerchief over her (afterwards so celebrated) [LC: fair] white neck relieved by a string of yellow glass beads, so, was this regulation evaded [LC: Her] [LC: "Friends" were not allowed to wear jewelry, so, was this regulation evaded) [LC: on her head] an exquisite cap, from which an occasional uncropped curl would escape— So In this first interview, at her own house, she conquered the recluse bookworm Madison, who "was considered an old batchelor". M^r· Madison [LC: He] was [LC: then] rather more than twenty years her senior. The lady from whom we had have this narration[5] now nearly four score years and ten, exclaimed [LC: as she repeated it to us] "speak no more of her. it crazes me [LC: makes me too sad] to think I shall see her not more [LC: again] on this earth!["]

We hope it will not be amiss to say one word, and but one in favor of the repudiated Aaron Burr, who figured so conspicuously in that day and for several years afterwards. He is said to have been a man destitute of feeling, his devotion to his only daughter Theodosia, and grief at her mysterious death, was unsurpassed! He was full of genius, fond of literature, and one who spared no pains to inculcate the cultivation of taste [MC: among] the

4. Probably means toile, a printed cotton.
5. Eliza Collins Lee.

young—almost all were Friends in that city of Penn, so music, painting, poetry and dancing were denounced as they still are in that Seat—he did his best to counteract their rules by presenting a box of colors with palette and drawing books to one, an English Guitar with music to another, standard writings to another one third and so on, and then, when all these gifts were imported from England—their possession was doubly precious to those who could not afford their purchase—in after years many of those young girls who married "out of meeting" [MC: had cause to] remember with gratitude the name of Aaron Burr! [LC]

Neither pianos nor the Spanish Guitar had been then introduced, the Spinnet and English Guitar with its wire cords were their substitutes—and we have heard of *Spinning* Wheels at that time now only read up of in Cowper.[6] The Spectator and Tatler[7] were the text books, and reverenced as law givers—while the writings of the wits of Queen Anne's day were favorites and read as freely and with as much pleasure as the light literature of the present, there was then but little opportunity for high cultivation in the sciences and the many studies in which youth are now instructed—but our grandparents had *their own classics* and *poetry,* as they had learned and loved them in their British Homes. Much attention was paid to penmanship and composition—the beautiful Italian hand, has almost disappeared to give place to one more runing and rapid.

The rumor of this conquest [LC: engagement] of Mrs: Todd created quite a sensation in Philadelphia; when it reached the Presidential Mansion both General and Mrs: Washington felt expressed great interest and were desirous it should take pla not be mere rumor. The mutual esteem and confidence, existing until General Washington's death, between Mr: Madison and himself, is an historical fact, too well known for comment. Mrs: Washington impatient to know how true was the report, sent for Mrs: Todd, who not knowing the wherefore, [LC: the cause of this at once] obeyed the summons the lady presidentess [LC: when Mrs Washington] asked her "Dolley is it true, thou art engaged to James Madison?" the conscience stricken widow hung her head and answered stammeringly "No, Madam"—Mrs: Washington said, "do not If it is so, do not be ashamed to confess it, rather be proud, he will make thee a good husband, all the better for being so much older, we both advocate it."

6. William Cowper (1731–1800), an English poet and hymnodist.

7. Richard Steele founded the *Tatler,* an English journal of news, gossip, and commentary, which ran from 1709 to 1711. Steele then founded a similar publication, the *Spectator,* which ran from 1711 to 1712, with Joseph Addison; it was revived by Addison in 1714.

M^{rs:} Washington's drawing rooms began [MC: were in high fashion] at that time and were brilliant with beauties, which were who would [MC: have been] preeminent at any Court—these are ably noticed in "the Republican Court." We have heard that the pretty "friends" longed most ardently to attend, 'tho even the desire was naughty, but by dint of persuasion and logic we know not of, many of them did go once and it was an epoch in the lives. We [LC: but we] do not think M^{rs:} Todd had the good fortune to attend any before her second marriage, owing the to the extreme rigidity of her sectarian parents [LC: the rules of the Society of Friends which she belonged].

In the month of September 1794—M^{rs:} Todd in an open barouche left Philadelphia, to visit her sister M^{rs:} George S. Washington, the publick conveyances were few and far between, so the gentry usually travelled in their own coaches. [LC] She was accompanied by her sister Anna, a child of twelve years and whom she had adopted, her little son nearly four, her maid and several friends who were delighted to enjoy her society; amongst them was James Madison, her accepted lover. This gay cavalcade pass'd nearly a week on the journey—and "had beautiful sunny weather" as well as the sunshine of happy hearts. Shortly after arriving at Harewood she was united to M^{r:} Madison by M^{r:} Belmaire, an Episcopal Clergyman, established in Winchester, Virginia—whose sister was the wife of M^{r:} Howard a near and highly respected neighbor of M^{r:} Madison's—Among the guests were Frances Madison, his sister, who afterwards married M^{r:} R. Rose, Harriot Washington sister of George, and a ward of the President's (afterwards M^{rs:} Park) and most of the neighbors for many miles round, all related, for it was (and still is) a settlement of Washingtons. and a merry party it was! Virginia weddings are far famed We heard one of the number say that the girls vowed they would have a remembrance of the evening—and cut the Mechlin lace from M^{r:} Madison's shirt ruffles. When the frolic was over M^{r:} Madison took the bride and her party to his father's residence in Orange County Va —It was named Montpelier from its resemblance to that [LC: the county of that name] in the South of France.

Owing to the kindness of M^{r:} E. Coles, who has allowed us to make some extracts from his note book, we are enabled to give a slight sketch of the forefathers of M^{r:} Madison, [LC: and the incidents of his life] feeling confident of its interest to many of our readers.

"In the year 1653 John Madison took out a Patent for Land situated between 'North and York Rivers' on the shores of the Chesapeake Bay—He was the father of John Madison, who was the father of Ambrose Madison—who married Frances Taylor August 30^{th:} 1700—and lived at Montpelier in Orange County Va. and was the father of James Madison, who [MC: who married Elenor Conway[8] and] was the father of [LC: President] James Madison the ex- [LC: afterwards] president of the United States—who [LC: This gentleman] was born at the house of his grand mother at Port Conway, on the Rhappahanoc[9] —[LC: on the 16th of] March 16th 1751. He was educated by M[r:] Robertson a Scotchman, who taught him Greek, Latin, French, [LC: and] Italian and cetera. [LC] He graduated at Princeton, New Jersey in 1771 and there remained under D[r] a year afterwards studying Hebrew and other languages under D[r:] Witherspoon[10]—at this period his health was very bad, otherwise he would have entered the Army

In the spring of 1776, he was elected by the people of Orange Cy a member of the General Assembly of Va—in 1779 and 1780 he was elected by the General Assembly, a member of the Continental Congress of which body he remained a member until the autumn of 1783—he was elected a member of the General Assembly of Virginia, in 1784 and 5—he was elected by the General Assembly a member of Congress in 1786 and also in 1787 to the Philadelphia Convention—which made [LC: formed] the present Constitution of the United States—he was elected by the people of his county in 1788 a member of the Virginia Convention which ratified that Constitution. he remained in Congress from 1786 to March 1797—the end of Gen[l:] Washington's Administration. In 1801 he was appointed Secretary of State by M[r:] Jefferson which office he held 8 years—in 1809—he was elected President of the United States, reellected in 1813—in March 1817 he retired to Montpelier [MC: and] only leaving [LC: afterwards left it] to attend the Meeting of the Agricultural Society, of which he was long President, as a Visitor and Rector of the University of Virginia, and as a member of the State Convention to amend the Constitution of Va. to which the people of his County elected him in 1829.["]

Mr: Madison [MC: jr] had three brothers [MC: and three daughters] Ambrose who was older than himself died early [MC: he married the daughter of Major J. Hancock Lee and] leaving left one daughter [MC: who was] ever a favorite neice, and we think a resident in his family [MC: still living]—William who was in the War of 1812. Frank married a daughter of Captain Throgmorton of the English Army Frank, married Miss Bell, Mary, married Major Kite, Sally, Thomas Macon, a brother, we believe,

8. Nelly Conway Madison. She was never Elenor or Eleanor Rose, as determined by her signature on her own will.

9. The Rappahannock River.

10. John Witherspoon (1723–1794) a signatory of the Declaration of Independence and president of the College of New Jersey, later Princeton University.

of Nathaniel Macon of North Carolina. Frances, the youngest—D⁛ Robert
Rose of Virginia. [LC]

The residence at Montpelier was not very large, it had a large [MC:
wide] hall, in the centre and [LC: a] dark carved staircase, the walls were
painted in Fresco; wherever with flowers and landscapes, wherever they
were not wainscoted, this was done by an English Artist, called a Pre[LC:
Red-]emptionist[11] (according to a custom of that day), who was bound for a
certain number of years, until his passage was paid—Mʳ⁚ Madison Jʳ [LC]
built an addition for his wife and himself

In the fall of 1794 they returned to Philadelphia. Mʳˢ⁚ Madison [LC:
though she] dropping[LC: ed] the sober shades [LC: dress] of "the Friends"
and enough of their restraints to allow her to enter freely into a gayer Society, (which best pleased her husband and suited her his position) retained
for many years the name, and *always* their fundamental principles [MC: of
that religion] that love of truth, abhorrence of vice, and universal benevolence [MC: of character], which had been so deeply implanted by her father
parents.

Most truly happy was she [LC: on] returning to Philadelphia and to the
many loving friends of her girlhood! they gathered round her, rejoicing in
a prosperity which they all shared! then, without reproach of conscience,
it became her duty, as well as a very great source of pleasure to grace
with her beauty the Republican Court of Lady [LC: drawing room of Mʳˢ⁚]
Washington!

Mrs: R. B. Lee her dear friend and [MC: former] bridesmaid, when married to Mr: Todd relates that at this time she was driving with her in a
an close carriage near Philadelphia, when some gentlemen, passing in a
hack, caught a view of her face and repassed her coach so often that the
spirited driver, who suspected admiration for his mistress was the cause,
struck with his whip, whereupon a pistol was instantly fired at him and
passing through the carriage in front of those two ladies, just allowed them
to escape with their lives—the desperate men, drove away rapidly, and Mr:
Madison when he heard of this outrage, did what he could to discover
the perpetrators, but in spite of his efforts could not succeed in tracing
them. [LC]

Mʳˢ⁚ Madison's recollections of Dʳ⁚ Franklin, with whose daughter, Mʳˢ⁚
Bache, she was intimate, were very pleasant. He was fond of the society
of the young, and in return much beloved by them, As he was a sufferer

---

11. Mary Cutts may have meant "redemptioner," which was a person who sold their
services to a ship's captain in exchange for passage to America.

from gout, they delighted to gather round [MC: visit] him and listen to his conversation, so instructive and [LC: so well] adapted to the capacity of his hearers [LC: agreeable]— On one occasion She used to say the only quarrel [LC: rudeness] in which, she ever entered [LC: was thought she was [misbehaved?] was with Dolley [MC: daughter of the celebrated Dᴿ:] Witherspoon, daughter of the instructor of her husband, They had congregated in his room when [LC: met in the room of Dᴿ: Franklin and] the kind old gentleman told [LC: asked] her (Dolley Payne) to hand him a glass of water, the former [LC: her [. . .]] seized and presented it first [LC: before he,] whereupon the latter [LC: she thoughtlessly] struck the officious hand!— Dᴿ: Franklin rebuked her by saying "Dolley, Dolley I am ashamed of thee!"— It was a lesson to her through life! [LC: she never forgot]. Dᴿ: Franklin died the 15ᵗʰ: of April 1790. The King [MC: of France] and Convention went into mourning for him, so did the House of Representatives, the Senate refused, General Washington would not allow the Executive to wear mourning [MC: the outward sign of grief], for he did not know where to draw the line of distinction.

Mʳˢ: Madison and her sisters were intimate with the daughters of Governor [MC: Thomas] McKean, particularly so with Sally, who married the Marquis Carlos Martinez d'Yruho,[*]¹² [LC: then] minister from Spain. He was appointed in 1796. She was gay, witty, dashing and independent as any Court beauty could be! a few of her letters at different intervals have been preserved—to save trouble she seems to have written alternately to the sisters, as some of the [LC: to Mʳˢ: Madison and her sister Anna, afterward, Mʳˢ: Cutts.] and as they were descriptive of [LC: the] Philadelphia Society, we regret [LC: of the time, it is to be regretted that] so few small a number are [LC: still] in existence—the following describing the fashions belongs to this date.

My dear Anna,

Philadelpʰⁱᵃ:, Friday June 10ᵗʰ: 1796

Yours dated the 19ᵗʰ: of May, was handed to me the day before yesterday by Mᴿ: Grove, and really I have never been more astonished, than I was, at the contents of it; you give me a compleate scolding, you say you have written me several letters and have not received a single line from me, but my *good Anna,* you ought to hear first what I have to say in my vindica-

* de'Yrujo

12. Carlos Fernando Martinez Yrujo, Marquis de Casa, married Sarah (Sally) McKean.

tion, before you proceed to judge me without either judge or jury, in the first place; I do positively assure you it [LC: this] is the only letter I have received from you, except the one I writ which you writ [LC: wrote to] me at the time your sister Dolley did, and that, I did not receive until near [LC: nearly] three weeks after the [LC: its] date of it [LC], now, mademoiselle, I have cleared myself and pray you can do the same, for I have written you two, one of them was dated the latter end of April, the other the middle of May, besides one which I wrote your sister Madison, about ten days before I received your hers and yours (which was written on the same sheet) [LC] in which I gave her all the news of Philadelphia from your departure until that period, and which was equally for the inspection of Mary and yourself. Grove look's a great deal better than he did in the winter, he says he has been travelling through the greater part of Virginia, and in consequence feels much better. Your letter for Eliza Matthews, I sent to her yesterday morning by Dr: Butts, who came to town a few days ago, he knows where she lived, and [LC] begged me to let him take it to her as he knows where she has heard a great deal in her favor, and wishes to be introduced to her, and I am certain she got it before yesterday at one o'clock and went from here with it, to her. [LC] You tell me, you hope I will pardon the liberty I [MC: you] take in enclosing it to me. 'Pon [LC: Upon] my life! I will have you to know, mademoiselle, that such a heinous, terrible wicked thing, is unpardonable, and I fear was it to be tried by a Court Martial, that they would certainly shoot you off hand on account of it. Now, my dear Anna, we will be done with Judges, Juries, Courts, both martial and partial, and we will speak a little about Philadelphia, and the fashions, the beaux, Congress and the weather— What w do I not make a fine jumble of them, what would Harper or beau Dawson say were they to know it—ha, ha, ha—mind you laugh here with me!— Philadelphia never was known to be so lively at this season, as at present, for an accurate account of the amusements I refer you to Mary's letter, if she pleases to shew it, but you must make the agreement with each other, she will tell you about Philadelphia, and you must tell her the fashions—you see, I should make an excellent judge, for I should weigh all my cases in a scale, in order to be just, and not condemn the people, as somebody I know did, can you guess who!— I went yesterday to see a doll, which had come from England, dressed to shew us the fashions, and also, I saw [LC: besides] a great quantity of milinary, they wear chemises with the plaits made [. .] the back, high in the neck, so as to wear no handkerchiefs [LC], very long trains, and they festoon them up around the bottom [LC], with loops of bobbin and small covered buttons, the same as the dress, you are not confined to any number of festoons but put them according to your fancy, and one cannot conceive what a beautiful effect it has, there is also a robe which is pleated very far back, open, and ruffled down the sides, without any train, being even with the petticoat. The hats are quite a different shape from what they used to be, they have no slope in the crown, scarce any rim, are turned up at each side, and worn very much on the side of the head, several of them are made of chipped wood, commonly known by the name of cain [LC: cane] hats—the hats at present are all lined, one that has come for M^rs: Bingham, is lined with white and trim[LC: m]ed with broad purple ribbon put round in large puffs, with a bow on the left side, and another fashion is to put the ribbon in stripes up the crown so as to meet in a point on the top of the crown, with a large bow there, and another to the left side, the beau bows have a great many ends to them, the bonnets are all open on the top, thro which the hair is passed, either up or down, as you fancy, but latterly they wear it more down than up, it is quite out of fashion to friz or curl the hair, as it is worn perfectly straight. Earrings are very fashionable. The waists are worn about two inches longer than they used to be, and there is no such thing as long sleeves now, as they are worn half way above the elbow, either drawn or plaited in various ways, according to fancy, they do not wear ruffles at all, and as for elbows, Anna, ours would be alabaster, compared to some of the ladies who follow this fashion, they do pin black velvet or any colored ribbon round the bare arm between the elbow and sleeve. There has [LC: have] come some new fashioned slippers for the ladies, made of various colored kid or morocco, with small silver clasps fixed on them; they are very handsome, and make the foot look remarkably small and neat. The millinery last received is allowed [LC: thought] by every body to be the most handsome and most tasty received for a long time. All our beaux are well, the amiable chevaleir is perfectly recovered and is handsomer than ever, I mentioned to him last evening that I had received a letter from you, and that you desired to be remembered to him, he seemed much pleased at your attention and desired I should give his best love to you when I wrote, so did Fatio, and good M^r: Viar, so you see my dear Anna, that I do keep my promise tho' you do scold me so much. Poor M^r: Mecare looks pale and low spirited. I saw him yesterday and told him I should write you, he appeared perfectly delighted and told me to give his best love to you— **Mind Anna,** [MC: that] you write me a long answer to this, and that very soon, for I will not write you again until you do!

I remain, dearest, your sincere and affectionate friend,
Sally McKean

Miss Anna Payne To M^rs: A. P. Cutts

My dear Anna,

Philadelph^ia September 3^d 1796

I received yours by M^r: Taylor and gave [LC: delivered] the enclosed M^rs:
Crosby to give to Betsey Matthew's. [LC]

My dear girl, you can have no idea [LC: my dear girl] what rare romps
[LC: pleasant times] I have, there is the charming chevalier, the divine
Santgana, the jolly Viar, the witty and agreeable Fatio, the black eyed
rougeish Lord Henry, the soft love making Count de [   ], the giggling, fool-
ish C . . . r the slovenly E—r [LC] and sometimes the modest good Meclare
who are at our house every day. We have fine riding frolics and musical
parties—however, I will refer you to my letter to your sister Madison, as I
am confounded tired of writing this being the third long letter I have written today. M^r: and M^rs: Jaudenes[13] set sail about the middle of July, with
the two dear little children, in good health and remarkably fine spirits—.
I am to receive a large packet of papers from them as soon as they arrive
in Spain, telling me all the news and also a very elegant Spanish Guitar,
on which I intend to learn, Signor Don Carlos has given me a few lessons
on that instrument. I have one at present lent to me by Don Santayana—
and we have a famous Italian singer, who came with the minister, he can
play on every instrument, I will not except one—he is the drollest [ ] [LC:
creature] you ever saw— He sings divinely and is generally the leader of our
fine concerts oh, my dear Anna, I am serenaded every night with divine
music, I must say so for it is more than common music.

I long with the greatest impatience for the month of October, to have the
pleasure of embracing my dear Anna.— for heaven's sake make as much
haste to town as you can for we are going to have one of the most charming winters imaginable— Santa anna [LC: na] and Fatio send their compliments to you and so also does good M^r: Viar and Meclare told me to be sure
and give his best and most sincere love to you, he looks quite handsome
and is smarter than ever.

God bless you my dearest and believe me to be your sincere friend and
admirer.

Sally McKean.

The following letter was addressed [LC: about this time] by M^r: Madison
to M^r: James Maury—a Virginia gentleman who had formerly been a companion and friend at school— M^r: Maury was [LC: and who was] appointed

13. Mr. and Mrs. Jose de Jaudenes y Nebot, a Spanish diplomat and his wife.

Consul at Liverpool by General Jackson Washington, and retained it under every succeeding administration until recalled by General Jackson [LC: a post which he held for more than twenty years].

Dear Sir,

Philadelphia Jan^{y:} 18^{th:} 1797.

M^{r:} Mason and myself lately received your packets of London papers, by the Alexander Hamilton, which were very acceptable as they brought us the earliest accounts of some of the important articles contained in them. I send in return several packets by Captain Joseph Prince, who is to sail from New York and to whom I cannot conveniently transmit any thing of a more bulky nature. Captain Prince is a brother in law of M^{r:} Ber[LC: c]kley, clerk of the House of Representatives and formerly known to you in Virginia. He will be very sensible to any kindness it may lie in your power to shew his friend; and they will have a proper claim on his acknowledgments also.

This country is extremely agitated by pecuniary distresses, and the mercantile ones which begin to thicken on it. The unfortunate Treaty intended to appease our [LC: one] nation is bringing us into trouble with several. You will see that the House of Representatives is engaged on the question of a direct tax. The result is a problem not yet to be solved. It is expected the executive will comm[unicate] in a few days a full state of the controversy with France.

After a warm contest for the succession to General Washington, t[he] vacancy will be filled by M^{r:} Adams. He has seventy one votes and M^{r:} Jefferson sixty eight. The division would be [. . .] nicer, but for the failure of one of the returns from a County of this State, in time to be counted and other casualties in other States had a share in favoring M^{r:} Adams. M^{r:} Jefferson it is now well known will serve in the secondary place attached to him.

This being the last Session of Congress of which I shall be a member, I must at the same time that I return you—thanks for all your past favors, request that your future ones be addressed to Orange. Virginia—and that they may not be sent on the calculation that I shall get them free of postage.

With great esteem, I am dear Sir, / Your most obedient humble servant

J. Madison J^{r:}

In 1799 M^{rs:} Madison, accompanied by her husband, made her last visit to her Uncle and Aunt Winston. They lived near her old home in Hanover

County, Virginia, Col Isaac Winston was a man of cultivation and sound judgment, and one whom M^{r:} Madison regarded with the highest respect, he was also, one of the few [LC: those], to whose opinion M^{r:} M—— [LC: M^{r:} Madison] would sometimes yield his own, we find, by letters interspersed at [LC: through] different periods of his career, that advice from this quiet country gentleman was given at different periods for many years. M^{rs:} Madison was particularly attached to his daughter, [LC: afterwards the wife of D^{r:} Beckwith] who was much with her after the marriage of her sister, Anna. Miss Winston was witty and full of repartee, adding much to the charm of M^{rs:} M——'s circle. M^{r:} Madison was parted from his [MC: wife] at this time but a few days—only long enough for him to engage round in Richmond.[*]

When members of the "society of friends" neglect their attendance at meeting or disobey the regulations of the Society it is the duty of the elders to warn them of their danger and bring them back, by persuasion, to their fold. If such warning is not heeded, then they are read out of meeting— Such we presume, was the case with Anna Payne, who was at Montpelier, under the guidance of M^{rs:} Madison when the following notice [LC: letter] was received [LC: from two ladies of that religious Society, from which Miss Payne had not formally separated herself.]— Very young, with an exquisite ear for music, she sang and played on any instrument that to which she had access, without cultivation but with remarkable accuracy. This taste naturally caused a fondness for dancing, [MC: and] these were the sins which she had not the courage to renounce.

"3rd m^g 8^{th:} 1799.

"As friends concerned for thy welfare and for the support of our Christian testimonies, we make use of this opportunity to remind thee of the conference we had when last together, on occasion of the deviation of thy conduct and appearance from the self-denying profession, we, as a religious society believe ourselves call'd to hold forth to the world, and as we have not heard from thee since on the subject in much affliction we request thou would acquaint us with thy sentiment thereon in order to enable us to come to some conclusion in the case that if there is a conformity in thy behavior and appearance to the principles we profess a certificate may be sent to place thee as a member of the monthly meeting within the company of which thee resides, the name of which thee will please to inform us of

* she married D^{r:} Beckwith and resided in Alabama.

it; but if no such conformity has taken place, we are of opinion it will be best the case should be taken to the monthly meeting of which thou art a member, to be there resulted agreeable to our discipline. As we believe thy friend who hands this will be careful to forward an answer we request thee will be so kind as to forward furnish him with one, if thee does not, nor we do not hear from thee soon after receiving this (as thou art at such a distance from us that friends cannot conveniently visit thee on the occasion) we think it likely a testimony will be issued against thy conduct. Although we have written thus plainly, we can assure thee, it is with affectionate desires, that thou may be favored to see the necessity of denying self, and be enabled to take up thy cross daily and follow Christ our holy leader in all his requirings, that so in the end thou mayst receive the Crown of Life, which the Apostle saith 'the Lord has promised to them that love him.'

Hannah Yorkes and Sarah Tomkins["]

Richmond Monday night

My dearest,

December 2^d 1799

Neither the chart of your uncle, or the memory of your brother could save me from two errors on our way down, we made out, notwithstanding to reach Town before sunset. I found at Mr Watson's a room prepared for me, and an empty one immediately over it, but they are both in a style much inferior to what I had hoped. You must consequently lower your expectations on this subject as much as possible before you join me, which I shall look for about the time you suggested. I have found it more convenient to let Sam remain until tomorrow morning, than to start him today. He will be able to execute the journey in one day with ease, with an empty carriage. I have procured for your Uncle, a paper. which is for tomorrow morning, in which there is an account of the success of the Republicans in Holland—against the British and Russians, particularly the latter. He will see also, the first fruits of the session in the change of the Speaker and clerk. Colonel Smith had eighty and odd votes, against fifty odd, and Mr Wirt ninety odd against forty odd— The former Chaplain and Sergent at Arms were reelected.

Present me affectionately to all around you.— always and truly yours

J. Madison J^r [LC]

General Washington died in December of 1799—the following summer, Mr Jefferson, accompanied by M^r and Mrs Madison and her sister, made a visit of condolence to Mrs Washington at Mt Vernon, here Mrs Madison formed an acquaintance with Miss Henly,[14] a favorite neice and ward of M^rs: Washington's, who afterwards married Tobias Lear, private Secretary of Mr Madison General Washington.— this casual acquaintance ripened into lasting affection. M^rs: Lear has been many years a resident of Washington, her health always delicate, she rarely visits, but her house has always been the resort of her many friends, especially the young, who love, within her quiet walls to receive advice and sympathy! When this tribute to the memory of her early friend was suggested, she heartily seconded the suggestion and gave what information she could, and letters [LC: and allowed the use of such letters as she possessed]. Her having been so long a cherished inmate of General Washington's family would alone make her an object of deep interest, This lady often mentions little peculiarities of [LC: and many are the incidents she can recall in regard to] that illustrious pair. An interesting fact we [LC: remember to have] heard her state, that, once dining alone with General and M^rs: Washington, he remarked it was the first time such an event had occurred for forty years.

In the winter of 1800, M^rs: Madison's youngest sister, Mary, was married to General J. G. Jackson,[15] a prominent member of Congress from Harrison County, Virginia, He was many years in Congress, and M^rs: Madison had the great happiness of seeing her every winter in Washington as long as she lived. which was until the year 180— when she was carried off in [LC: this was not for a long period as she sank under] a rapid decline. M^r: Jackson died in 1825, while serving as Judge of the United States Court in the Western District of Virginia.

{{*End of first bound document*}}
{{*Second bound document begins*}}

In 1809, M^r: Jefferson's eight years of chief magistry [MC: Presidency] expired and M^r: Madison was chosen by the people as his successor— We will not say that it was an event which caused much happiness to either M^r: or M^rs: Madison, they saw difficulties and dangers ahead, which had been warded off by the last administration, difficulties which must be arranged, peaceably, or by war. The attack on the Frigate Chesapeake[16] had for some

14. Tobias Lear married Frances "Fanny" Dandridge, niece of George Washington, his third wife.

15. John George Jackson (1777–1825), who married Mary Payne, and later, Mary Meigs.

16. The USS *Chesapeake* was a heavy frigate of the U.S. Navy. On 22 June 1807, it was fired upon by HMS *Leopard* of the Royal Navy for refusing to comply with a search for deserters. The *Chesapeake-Leopard* Affair became one of the "affairs of honor" that led to the War of 1812.

years caused much ill feeling between England and America. In the year
1809 Mʳ Erskine,[17] who wished to conciliate the two countries, made fair
and liberal proposals to the government, which were cordially accepted,
and the prospect of this happy adjustment gave unfeigned satisfaction to
the American People. But as soon as Mʳ Erskine despatches reached London, they were disclaimed he was accused of having exceeded his instructions and recalled. He was succeeded by Mʳ Jackson,[18] who was haughty,
proud and unconcilliatory, and made himself so obnoxious to the Cabinet
and counsellors that Mʳ Madison was compelled to decline diplomatic
intercourse with him.— This step was approved by a majority of Congress,
and he also was soon recalled by his Government. Mʳ Foster[19] was immediately sent in his stead—his pleasant and agreeable manners formed a
contrast to those of his predecessor—he identified himself with society and
was, in consequence, a favorite with Mʳˢ Madison and her coterie, several unceremonious notes from him to her shew how well he sustained his
social position, while he, answered in his political diplomacy adjusted the
long pending and harassing difficulties which impeded the English Government from making heretofore making reparation for the Frigate Chesapeake. This long delayed justice was accepted by the president a short time
before the declaration of War.

To the citizens of Washington (though they have no vote) the election of
a new President is of peculiar interest to them, as by change of Administration their social position is so much disarranged. Long cherished affections
and friendships broken up—to say nothing of their political preferences.
What wonder then, that an event which placed Mʳˢ Madison in the "White
House" should give such general satisfaction and pleasure! She had endeared herself to all classes; the poorest beggar could come to her with
confidence, and confide his or her cares and wants, sure of an attentive
and sympathizing audience if possible, she would send them on their way
rejoicing—if not, she gave them comfort and advice, causing them to feel
they had in her—a friend. To the powerful and arrogant, she would accord
all their vanity exacted.— She would say, it was not her place to treat them
otherwise. One of her peculiarities was, never to contradict any one— and
that was one of the earliest lessons she inculcated in the young people by
whom she was [MC: always] surrounded.— Receiving so many congratula-

17. David Montagu Erskine (1776–1855) was a British diplomat and politician.
18. Francis James Jackson (1770–1814) was a British diplomat.
19. Sir Augustus John Foster (1780–1848) was a British diplomat and politician.

tions she could not but reciprocate the pleasure it gave her friends to have her in this exalted position, she saw nothing but flowers in her path, from the thorns she turned aside. Her countenance, beaming with inward happiness made friends wherever it glanced! It delighted her to do good: petitions from afar and near were showered upon her; she was never annoyed, by them, and always answered them favorably, if possible; as her influence over her husband was unbounded and seldom exerted in vain. Many, whom the world little knows, are indebted to Mʳˢ Madison for independence and position in society—she never said so, for she never betrayed a confidence, but grateful letters have proved [MC: it and] recorded thoughts that outlive and facts, which outlive the spoken word! Mʳ Madison's administration consisted of George Clinton [MC: of New York] vice president afterwards Elbridge Gerry of Massachusetts—The Secretaries of State the were first Robert Smith of Maryland then James Monroe of Virginia; those of War— William Eustis of Massachusetts four years, John Armstrong of New York, little [mr] James Monroe January 19ᵗʰ 1813. James Monroe of Virginia September 26ᵗʰ 1814. William H. Crawford of Georgia March 2ᵈ 1815 Secretaries of the Navy—Paul Hamilton of S. Carolina March 7ᵗʰ 1809. William Jones of Pennsylvania January 12ᵗʰ 1813; Benjamin W. Crowninshield of Massachusetts December 19ᵗʰ 1814.

Post master generals—Gideon Granger continued in office. R. J Meigs of Ohio, March 2ᵈ 17ᵗʰ 1814.

When it became necessary to change a member of the cabinet or any other office holder—Mʳ Madison never said in place of in sending the name of his successor to the senate for confirmation, merely mentioned the name to fill the appointment, but never said "in place of so and so, dismissed." So great was his refinement of feeling, he never wounded the most sensitive, if it could be avoided by silence on his part. Governor Coles tells us that visiting Mʳ John Adams at Quincy, the old [MC: venerable] statesman asked him "how often Mʳ Madison lost his temper—" Mʳ Coles, who was his private secretary, instantly answered "never Sir, I have been with him day and night and never saw him even impatient." So great was his equinimity of disposition!

The following just remarks are from the pen of his friend Mʳ C. Ingersol.[20] "Undertaking the Presidency at a time of the utmost difficulty, he

20. Charles Jared Ingersoll (1782–1862) was an American lawyer and Democratic member of the U.S. House of Representatives from Pennsylvania. Ingersoll later toasted James Madison as the "Father of the Constitution."

continued in it, by re-election, during the established period of eight years, and when he retired, left the country in the highest degree glorious, prosperous and content. It cannot be, but that future ages will look back to his administration as one [MC: a time] of great trial and great renown. The Constitution which has succeeded in Peace triumphed in War. M^r: Madison was always the same, victory never elated, defeat never depressed him beyond measure, always calm, consistent and conscientious, there was confidence that he would do right come what might. Exposed to that deluge of abuse which the leading men of free countries, with a licentious press, cannot avoid, he was perfectly serene and unmoved by any vindictive emotion; true to friends, patient with adversaries, resolute and forbearing even with public enemies. All the emergencies of war never once betrayed him into infringements of the Constitution."

M^r: Madison invited M^r: Edward Coles of Albemarle to fill the responsible office of private secretary, which office his brother Col. Isaac Coles had held with M^r: Jefferson. This invitation was very unexpected and found M^r: Coles on the eve of Departure to the Western Country, but his friends advised him to defer this journey for the present and accept the appointment, which he did. Early in life he was imbued with the belief that the possession of slave property was essentially wrong—from that moment all the energies of his enthusiastic nature were bent on the manumission of his own, So soon as the death of his father put him in possession of his proportion, he took them with him to Ohio, afterwards to Illinois, and then gave them their freedom, still employing them as hirelings. Soon he became prominent in that new State and was elected [MC: its] Governor for several years. Successful in after life, he attributes his good fortune to this early effort, which his friends thought would be attended by ruin. He was private Secretary for six years to M^r: Madison, during the most interesting period of the Presidency— Intimate with M^r: Jefferson and M^r: Monroe, few minds are more stored with historical events and pleasant memories, on which he delights to dwell than his own! He is now a resident of Philadelphia, in which city he followed the example of M^r: Madison by marrying a lovely girl, belonging to the Society of Friends.

M^rs: Madison was a foe to dullness, wherever She went she promoted gaity and happiness, she returned all visits that were made her by ladies, and it gave her pleasure to do so. Her "dove parties" composed of the ladies of the Cabinet and foreign ministers, when their lords were engaged in formal Diplomatic dinners, were exceedingly popular, her private receptions, her lotteries, in which every guest had a cadeau, are still remembered. To say nothing of her drawing rooms where all parties appeared, knowing that they should all share her kind welcome and benignant smile, she felt that is was her duty to pour oil on the waters of discord, and draw malcontents into the fold of her husband, and successful she was for few would [MC: oppose] the partner of such a wife! With the hospitality of a Virginian her house was always filled with guests— A few of them, conspicuous for their wit and beauty we may mention as having enlivened her house for more than one winter, Miss Maria Mayo, afterwards, Mrs: General Scott, Miss Susan Wheeler, afterwards, Mrs: Commodore Decatur, and Miss Tudor, afterwards Mrs: Commodore Stuart, there reigned as belles, and *there*, it is said became engaged to their respective heroes. The three Miss Catons, to whom England also gave the award of beauty, and the lovely and fascinating Madame: Buonaparte,[21] though she was then harassed by [MC: the selfishness of] Napoleon Buonaparte, the beautiful Misses Murrays, sisters of Mrs: John Mason, who was the chosen friend of Mrs: Madison—Mrs: Ellenor Custis, granddaughter of Mrs: General Washington[22] and hosts of others equally celebrated, often lent their charms to adorn her drawing room— We must not omit to mention Miss Coles,[23] the sister of Mr: Edward Coles, accomplished and agreeable, she married the Honorable Andrew Stevenson, and was there, her having aided Mrs: Madison in the entertaining of her guests, was not among the least of her recommendations to the delightful society, which she enjoyed at the Court of St: James, where her husband filled so creditably the high post of Minister, under the appointment of General Jackson.

In 1809— her sister Lucy, of whom we have previously spoken had the misfortune to loose her husband, George S. Washington resisted as long as possible the belief into [MC: in] the inroads of this fell desease, finally, went, when too late to South Carolina and there died.

[MC: Mrs: Madison's] sister Mrs: George S. Washington [MC: was then a widow.]— Her husband had resisted as long as possible the inroads of Consumption, finally, when too late to regain his health went to South Carolina, and died in 1808, soon after his arrival— Mrs: Washington was still young, very pretty, animated, full of repartee and impulse; forming a contrast in [MC: figure] as well as dignity to Mrs: Madison. she also enlivened

21. Elizabeth Patterson Bonaparte (1785–1879), known as "Betsy," was the daughter of a Baltimore, Maryland, merchant and was the first wife of Jérôme Bonaparte and sister-in-law of Emperor Napoleon I of France.
22. Eliza Parke Custis (1776–1832) married Thomas Law (1759–1834) in 1804.
23. Sarah (Sally) Coles Stevenson (1789–1848) married Andrew Stevenson, Speaker of the House of Representatives (1827–34) and U.S. minister to Great Britain (1836–41).

his home department of M⁼ M until the spring of 1812. when she married Judge Thomas Todd of the Supreme Court—and made her future residence in Kentucky. Judge Todd died in 1826

When M͞ʳ Madison came in from his cabinet to dinner, generally fatigued and exhausted with the grave affairs of state at that harassing period, he would say, the hearty laugh which she caused him was as refreshing as a long walk. Sprightly conversation acted as a charm on M͞ʳ Madison, who was naturally serious and thoughtful; and that was a sufficient incentive to M͞ʳˢ Madison always to have a cheerful and happy household. M͞ʳˢ Cutts usually passed her winters in Washington. M͞ʳˢ Madison always fond of children, petted and spoiled those of her sisters as well as her own son.

M͞ʳ Joel Barlow[24] was a great admirer of M͞ʳˢ Madison's and on all occasions spoke of her as "the Queen," He brought to her drawing room M͞ʳ G. W. Irving and M͞ʳ [MC: Robert] Fulton[25] presenting them as his sons— M͞ʳˢ Madison curtsied and promptly said "they were sons of whom he might well be proud." M͞ʳ Barlow responded "yes, surely, I have had the pick of the world." M͞ʳ Joel Barlow was a distinguished poet, philosopher and politician, he was born in the village of Reading, Connecticut, about the year 1755. He was one of ten children, but his education was not neglected. He wrote "the Columbiad" ["]Prospect of peace" and much more. He married Miss Baldwin, daughter of the Honorable Judge Abraham Baldwin, of New Haven, afterwards of Georgia which State he represented for many years in the Senate of the United States. In 1792 he chose France for his residence—at this time he formed an intimacy with M͞ʳ Fulton the accomplished mathamatition, who lodged in the same hotel with him, and afterwards, M͞ʳ Barlow, when he went to his own house invited him to live with him, which invitation was accepted. and M͞ʳ Fulton remained seven years his guest. In 1805 he returned to America and purchased the beautiful residence of Kalorama where he resided, devoting himself to his favorite pursuit of Literature. In 1811 he was sent by M͞ʳ Madison as Minister Plenipotentiary to France, to negociate a treaty of commerce with Napoleon, after making every possible effort he failed— In 1812, he was invited by the Duke de Bassano to a personal conference with the Emperor at Wilna, in Poland. He started immediately but did not reach his destination, owing to

24. Joel Barlow (1754–1812) was an American poet, diplomat, and politician.

25. George Washington Irving (1783–1859) was an American author, essayist, biographer, and historian of the early nineteenth century. He was best known for his short stories "The Legend of Sleepy Hollow" and "Rip Van Winkle." Robert Fulton (1765–1815) was an American engineer and inventor, widely credited with developing the first commercially successful steamboat.

the inclemancy of the weather, he was attacked by inflamation of the lungs and died the 22^{d} of December 1812—at Larnavica, in Poland. Mrs Barlow returned, to Washington, accompanied by her sister Miss Baldwin, who aft and died in 1822 She had no [MC: children so she willed] Kalorama, the most beautiful gentleman's seat in the neighborhood of Washington to [LC: to her Cousin Mrs Baldwin from whom it was purchased by] her sister, who had married Co^{l} G. Bomford of the Army—where she resided until so very recently, that her hospitality, her benevolence, and the happy anticipations [MC: of pleasure] which were entertained by young and old, from a visit to Kalorama are too well engraven on our hearts and memories to require repetition.

Many gentlemen as well as ladies added interest to society, who were [MC: marked] by peculiar excentricities [MC: of talent] or perhaps it were better to say "their organ of individuality was more decidedly developed", among them we may mention Mr Thomas Law,[26] (the youngest brother of Lord Ellenborough) he was very absent minded; He had married the gay Ellanor Custis, with whom he seems to have had little sympathy, as they were seperated by mutual consent Mrs Law resuming her maiden name. We are told that some years afterward he met her at an evening party on Capitol Hill, in the same house where he had seen her for the first time. Mrs Madison, and many others who had been there on a similar occasion were also present, he looked at the guests, the pictures, the furniture, and [MC: he forgot] the lapse of time, and the old associations brought back old feelings, he walked up to his wife and spoke to her after a silence of five or six years— She in astonishment exclaimed "You do not know to whom you are speaking." He darted off, and said to a friend, "Yes! I was deceived, the delusion is perfect."

Two foreign gentlemen requested through him an interview with the President, the interview was granted—at the appointed hour, Mr Law appeared with his friends, but had totally forgotten their names, rank and the object of their visit, which he was to explain—so he merely said "they were from Brazil."

It was he who went to the Post Office to enquire for letters; the clerk said "for who Sir." Mr Law answered "do not you know, do not you know"—the officer politely said "he had been there but a few days." after some difficulty he remembered his name and said *Law*, the young man looked through the

26. Thomas Law (1756–1834) was a British-born Washington speculator. He spent his early years in India, where he amassed a considerable fortune. In 1796, he married Eliza Parke Custis Law, Martha Washington's granddaughter.

list and asked the first name— M[r:] Law again troubled, asked the name of the city Postmaster. "Thomas; Thomas Munroe—" "that is mine! Thomas Law." A friend The gentleman (Gov[r:] Coles) from whom we had the narration, asked him "if this was really so." M[r:] Law smiled and said "he must plead guilty![""]

Moore[27] the lyric poet, visited America during M[r:] Madison's administration and gave rise to many amusing incidents, owing to his stature and extremely youthful appearance. Talleyrand was several years in the United States—also Chateaubriand, Volney, General Moreau, Joseph and Jerome Buonaparte—[MC: and] D[r:] Priestly the celebrated philosopher and polemical divine—he died in Philadelphia.[28]

When Melly Melly,[29] the first Turkish Ambassador arrived in Washington M[rs:] [MC: Madison] gave him a party composed of the beauty and fashion of the Metropolis, after he had bid good night, (for then it was not considered polite to take French leave) a noise was heard in one of the anterooms. In passing out, he had caught a glimpse of a large fat black negress, who made her appearance from the kitchen with coffee. Melly Melly suddenly threw his arms round her and said [MC: exclaimed that] she was the only handsome woman in America. M[rs:] Madison often spoke of a youthful band, calling themselves "M[rs:] Madison's guard" they came from a neighbouring town to be inspected by her, she was highly pleased, invited them in and feasted them. When the hour of departure arrived, they were troubled, but said nothing—she saw signs of evident uneasiness in their open countenances—and said "What is it my friends?" The commander a youth

27. Thomas Moore (1779–1852) was an Irish poet, singer, songwriter, and entertainer, now best remembered for writing the lyrics of "The Minstrel Boy" and "The Last Rose of Summer."

28. Charles Maurice de Talleyrand-Périgord (1754–1838) was a French diplomat; François-René, vicomte de Chateaubriand (1768–1848), was a French writer, politician, diplomat, and historian; Constantin François de Chasseboeuf, comte de Volney (1757–1820), was a French philosopher, historian, and politician; Jean Victor Marie Moreau (1763–1813) was a French general who helped Napoleon Bonaparte to power, but later became a rival and was banished to the United States; Joseph-Napoléon Bonaparte (1768–1844) was the elder brother of Napoleon I of France, who made him King of Naples and Sicily (1806–8), and later King of Spain and the Indies as Joseph I of Spain (1808–13); Joseph Priestley (1733–1804) was an eighteenth-century English theologian, Dissenting clergyman, natural philosopher, educator, and political theorist.

29. Sidi Soliman Melli Melli was the first Tunisian ambassador to the United States.

of twelve stepped forward and confessed, "they had no money to return with." She instantly sent for her purse and emptied it with so much pleasure into his hand that she won the hearts of those happy boys! more by what she said, than by what she gave, for they would accept no more than a sufficiency to take them over the river.

M^rs. Madison's servants were singularly attached to her, of these, two, were well known in the annals of Washington— John Siousa, a French man who came to this country as a seaman on board the French Frigate Didon, which was accompanied by the Cybele, another frigate, in the year 1804, their officers were commissioned to take back Jerome Buonaparte, whose marriage with the beautiful Miss Patterson, had offended his brother Napoleon. He was appointed door keeper at the President's House. On M^rs. Madison's return to Washington in 1837—this honest man renewed his services without any expectation of remuneration, and was devoted to her interests. He is still living—very aged, too aged for service. He was offered a pension by the Bank of Metropolis, where he had been a faithful messenger, ever since the Branch Bank of the United States in Washington had been discontinued, in which Institution he had occupied the same position since the burning of the President's House in 1814. The old soldier would not receive the offered pension, He is known as "French John."

Another, although of a different color, was Joe Bolen, a splendid specimen of the negro, his sole pride was in his master and mistress, with every honor they received, holding his own head the higher! With his own wages he soon freed himself, and when M^r. Madison retired from public life, he laid aside his whip and said he would never again use it, and wept like a child on being parted from his handsome greys. M^r. Madison's equipage was always driven four in hand as were those of most of the gentry at that time. Poor old Joe, spent his money freely and was obliged the latter years of his life to sell oysters for a living!— Paul, a handsome mulatto boy, and favorite page of M^rs. Madison's, sighed for freedom, and having sufficient money ran away to New York, but when his funds were exhausted he sighed remembered his home of ease, and wrote imploring his master to receive him again, which he did, and beleiving in his repentance, his journey to New York was never mentioned! This boy when he became a man, was a very efficient one, and remained with M^rs. Madison until a few years previous to her death, when again enamoured with freedom, she allowed him to purchase it for a very small Sum.

So harmonious was her disposition, she never argued a point, if friends or relations indulged in satire or wit, in her presence, which might wound the feelings of others, she would quickly leave them; and when the peculiar and welcome sound of her returning high h returning sound of her high heeled shoes gave token of her approach all ill feeling would be forgotten or suppressed and the topic changed, so well known was her dislike to contention; for she always said "I would rather fight with my hands than my tongue." Particularly neat in her household and other arrangements, cleanliness and fresh air were for many years her only physicians. Rising early her domestic duties were attended to before breakfast, then she would come near the sleeping apartments of her guests, to awaken them with her bird like carol, at the sound of her loved voice they would spring up with the exclamation "Why did you not waken me before!" Children always followed her, at Montpelier the little negroes would gather in her train, from the different houses of "her people" when she took her morning rounds, she never repelled them, but when she returned to her own dwelling, she would think of some service they might perform, and send them trooping on their way, in summer it was to gather her the beautiful wild flowers which adorned the vallies and meadows, in winter to pick up chips [. .] some errand of mercy to some a superanuated grand dame, of their own color. Returning breathless from these errants of love, if she had suitable gifts, they were given, if not, the kind smile and thanks of their mistress was enough! It Every thing seemed as if they could not do otherwise then love her; even the favorite cattle on the lawn, whom she had carressed and stroked with her hand, would give her a sound of recognition and walk after her, so she was always sure of company. I We have often been amused in Washington, when she was passed eighty, to see her on the pavement, before the inmates of her house were awake, attended by a little black boy of three summers, on one side, and an old cat the other, moving slowly and surely as she did herself. Taking her arm in ours, we would ask if she was a witch with such attendants. She would answer playfully "they seem to desire exercise, and I do not object to their companionship."

her gentle rebukes were always effective, when children which o ought to be clean and had no excuse for soiled dresses or aprons, came into her drawing room, without these proprieties having been attended to, she would say "come sweet one" and lead her to her store room, and there with her great shears, (the only scissors she ever used) cut them out a garment to replace the soiled one, pin it together and put it on the wondering child— who instantly ran to the mother or nurse—who required no second hint— These garments varied, from the unbleached cotton for the use of servants

to the pin dotted india muslin, for which she had a great fondness—when
the rebuke was intended to be [MC: very] slight, she would send one of
her own "Court" dresses to be cut on a smaller scale, which of course was
never done [MC: but carefully put away until the child could appreciate the
gift.]— An admirer of M^rs: Madison's says, when he first saw her, she was
a child, he was elegantly dressed, but he stood wrapt in admiration of the
French Artificials in her head dress, in immitation of fruit, his mother told
him he was impolite, but M^rs: M— asked so kindly what was the cause of
his it, that attracted his attention, that he answered promptly "the beautiful grapes and cherries!" M^rs: Madison instantly put her hand to her head,
disengaged them and made him happy by their possession!

After every effort in an honorable point of view failed to secure peace,
and the aggressions of the enemy on our coast and navy were too frequent
and too daring to be borne any longer, M^r: Madison sent a message to congress [MC: which was still in session] ably written and conclusive, so War
was declared the 18th: of June 1812. M^r: Jefferson writing from Monticello to
M^r: Thomas C. Flournoy under date of October 1st: 1812, says "servile inert-
ness is not what is to save our country, the conduct of a war, requires the
vigor and enterprise of younger heads. All such undertakings, therefore are
out of the question with me, and I say so with the greater satisfaction, when
I contemplate the person to whom the executive powers were handed over.
You probably may not know M^r: Madison perfectly personally, or at least
intimately as I do— I have known him from 1779, when he first came into
the public councils, and from three and thirty years trials I can say conscientiously that I do not know a man in the world of purer integrity, genuine
republicanism more dispassionate, disinterested and devoted to genuine
republicanism than himself, nor could I in the whole scope of America or
[MC: and] Europe point out an abler head. He may be illy seconded by
others, betrayed by the Hulls and Arnolds[30] of our country, for such there
are in every country, and with sorrow and suffering we know it. But what
man can do will be done by M^r: Madison. I hope, therefore, there will be
no difference between among republicans as to his reelection, and we shall
know his value when we have to give him up, and to look at large for his
successor."

30. This likely refers to William Hull, who served in the War of 1812. His surrender of the Northwest Army on 16 August 1812 was considered treasonous. "Arnold" is
probably a reference to the famed traitor Benedict Arnold.

The declaration of war had been so long delayed that, when it finally passed the Senate, few were prepared. In all measures of similar importance, there are two if not more decided parties, so this wise movement was not exempt from its opposers. These were principally from the North Eastern States, who though they had suffered most from aggression, still feared the brunt of the war would fall upon them. Some were in its favor, but still thought more extensive preparations should have been made before the final mandate was given, others said it was unnecessary, that treaties and other pacific measures would have sufficed. While Great Britain fancied she might continue her aggressions against so peaceful a nation without chastisement. The most harrassing and unceasing cause of complaint was the constant attacks upon our sea coast, the impressment of sailors, while nominally searching for deserters. Our gallant navy and all seafaring men were burning with impatience for an opportunity to avenge their wrongs! So that class of our countrymen received the declaration of war with unfeigned joy!

"Britannia rules the waves" had for unnumbered years been the motto of our mother country, and her prowess on the waters was undisputed! Very little attention had been paid to an increase of our navy since the Revolution. General Washington and the succeeding presidents had proposed its enlargement but with so little zeal that the project had never been carried into effect. "In the years of 1811 and 1812 it consisted of but ten sloops frigates, five of which were laid up in ordinary, ten sloops and smaller vessels, and 165 gun boats, only sixty of which were in commission, yet the brave band who manned them made the year 1812 one if not *the* most glorious, in the annals of American history! "On the 21st: of June, within one hour after the official proclamation was received the squadron set sail in pursuit of a British convoy, which had left Jamaica on the 20th: of the proceeding month." Ramsey.

The names of the first frigates [MC: Squadron] were the President, 44 guns, commanded by Commodore Rodgers, the United States by 44 guns, Commodore Decatur the Congress 36, captain Smith, the Hornet 18, and the Argus 16 guns, The first conquests were made by Commodore Porter who commanded the Essex of thirty two guns—he captured a transport of two hundred soldiers on the third of July, the thirteenth he ran down the British sloop "Alert" and after an action of eight minutes he conquered her, So confident was her officer of success that he made the first attack.

But the victory which seems to have made the greatest impression was that of commodore Isaac Hull,[31] who commanded the Frigate Constitution of forty four guns. Its announcement came at a time immediately after news of the inglorious defeat of General Hull, who was commander in chief of the Army in the North Western frontier, had cast gloom and consternation wherever it was known, so the rebound of gratitude to the brave officers was commensurate with the small hope they had of success against an enemy in [MC: so powerful an] enemy in her strong hold, the ocean.

The desire for conflict with the Frigate Guerriere was more powerful than that felt towards the conquest of other vessels, because her officers had ridiculed, what they called our puny Navy, insulted our flag and boasted of their superior seamanship, besides sending constant challenges to from their commander to ours. offic After much manœvering and skilful management, which our nautical knowledge is too limited to describe, the enemy's vessel was brought sufficiently near to be dismantled and [MC: almost] destroyed. After a conflict of thirty minutes, she surrendered, but the fire from the Constitution had rendered her useless, so she was set on fire and soon blown up. This victory occurred on the 19th: of August 1812— The loss was small on either side, but the wounded were more unequal [MC: being only] seven Americans and sixty three of the enemy[MC: 's] men. Commodore Hull's arrival in Boston on the 23d: of August, created a great sensation, many of the officers were promoted and Congress voted them fifty thousand dollars to pay [MC: as recompense] for the loss of the Guerriere.

The news gave real satisfaction in the Metropolis, a magnificent ball was given to the victorious officers. Lieutenant Hamilton, son of Mr Paul Hamilton, Secretary of the Navy, was entrusted with the flag of the conquered frigate—he arrived the night of the ball and was met in the Hall by Mr Coles, the private Secretary of the President, who suggested that there could be no more appropriate opportunity of presenting it than the present occasion— Most of the guests were assembled among them [MC: were] his parents and sisters. Mrs Madison and the Ladies of the

This ball was [MC: said to be] given to the Navy generally, and to Commodore Stuart in especial in return for one he had recently given on board his Frigate, at the Navy Yard to the citizens of the District. In the midst

31. Isaac Hull was the commodore of the USS *Constitution* and forced the surrender of the British frigate HMS *Guerriere* on 19 August 1812. He later commanded the U.S. Pacific Squadron (1824–27).

of their enjoyment it was rumored that Lieutenant Hamilton, (son of the Secretary of the Navy, Hon: Paul Hamilton) had arrived and was in the Hall beneath, with He was bearer of the flag of the Macedonian and of Despatches from Commodore Decatur. A scene of confusion instantly occurred, the gentlemen rushed down to hear and to see. Governor Coles (Mr Madison's private secretary) proposed that they [MC: should] bring it up to the ball room, which suggestion was taken, as there seemed no better occasion to present it than the present. The gentlemen and ladies of the Cabinet were all present, [MC: amongst them] his parents and sisters, cabinet as well as many of the most distinguished belles— The Secretary Mr Hamilton and his son when entering the room, gave him his arm, and walked to the platform where Mrs Madison and the Ladies were standing. [MC: He was] followed by Commodore Hull, Commodore Stuart, Captains Morris and Tingey each bearing an end of the flag, when they approached Mrs Madison. Commodor Stuart let his end fall, either by accident or design (the motive has been much questioned, but we can only state the fact)—one of the Ladies said instantly, "trample on it, trample on it!" M^{rs} M— drew back instantly, [MC: and said, "Oh! Not so!"] while the lady advanced and put her foot upon it!

Many interesting anecdotes of those days might be related, but as the figurants are still living we fear to be too personal.

The naval victories we have mentioned were but the begining, they followed in quick succession—the Squadron under command of Commodore [MC: Rodgers] captured a packet with two hundred [MC: thousand] dollars in specie. The Argus was equally successful capturing merchantment, and so obtaining an equal sum. The United States under Commodore Hull brought in the Macidonian of forty nine guns and three hundred men— as usual the loss of the Americans was very small. The United States was very little injured but she had to return to bring the conquered Frigate. Commodore Decatur received the same gratifying reception as did Commodore Hull and his officers. This victory was followed by that of a Sloop of War, the Wasp, commanded by Captain Jacob Jones, though in a disabled condition she succeeded in boarding the Frolic of twenty two guns. In this encounter Lieut Biddle distinguished himself. It was a hard fought warfare, resulting in great loss to the crew and officers of the Frolic they having but three officers and a few seamen left. The officers were deprived of their hard earned prize, for perceiving a schoon sail, they soon found it to be a British Frigate of 74 guns—and to avoid pursuit from so superior a force they reluctantly [MC: abandoned her]—however, Congress gave them twenty five thousand dollars for her [MC: *page torn*]

The Constitution was fated for even greater renown. When her command was resigned by Commodore Hull—Commodore Bambridge succeeded him and the twenty ninth of December he encountered the British Frigate Java of forty nine guns and carrying 400 men. she was soon taken into possession, but finding she had been so much injured by the fires of the Constitution, she was burnt, and the officers and men taken on board of our own vessel, where they were treated with courtesy and consideration, this humane and gentlemanly behavior was acknowledged by the English. We have not mentioned half the officers who gained lasting glory, apt we know, that we have already encroached on the privileges of other and abler biographists—we are acquainted [MC: with] two accomplished and distinguished scholars, already engaged [MC: in] writing the life of Mr Madison [MC: (others are in the field)] consequent of this particular war; and as Mrs Madison's mission was one of peace, we will confine ourselves to her, until the invasion of her house by the British "*Warriors.*" Peaceful as she was, we cannot deny the deep interest she took in the nations welfare and her husbands honor—some few letters to her sisters will shew her interes thoughts were disturbed by pending danger.

In 1813—Mr Madison entered into his second term of Presidency, he had 129 votes and De Witt Clinton, 89. Elbridge Gerry was Vice President having 131 votes Jared Ingersoll of Pennsylvania having but 68 votes.

During the War, Mrs Madison's course was marked by her efforts to destroy rancerous feeling—then so bitter between Federalists and Republicans. The Ladies as usual participated strongly in it, one, whose name is well known and who has just gone to a better world, we hope, drove to Mr Madison's door stood in her chariot and loosened her beautiful hair which was celebrated for its length, and said she would gladly part from it to hang Mr Madison! Mrs Madison found it difficult to forgive this insult to her husband, but she did, not however before the Lady changed her politics.

A week before the British entered the city of Washington, Mr Monroe, the Secretary of State, mounted his horse and rode to Benedict, a small village on the Patuxent, and there witnessed the landing of the forces of the enemy; he, knowing how badly prepared was the seat of government for defence, instantly sent a vidette to Mr G. Graham and Mr S. Pleasanton, clerks in the State department, authorizing them to save the public papers and records by taking [MC: and to take] the best care [MC: of them] in their power. These gentlemen sent for [MC: coarse] linen, and had large bags made, which they filled with the valuable records of the Revolutionary war, the, then, unpublished journals of Congress, the Correspondence of General Washington, his commission, resigned at the close of the War, &c &c. M^r: Pleasanton obtained carts for the conveyance of these bags to a grist mill two miles above George Town, on the Virginia Side of the Potomac.

While engaged with these papers, in the passage way between the two departments (State and War) General Armstrong, who was passing, paused and told them, they were taking unnecessary precaution. He did "not beleive the British intended to fulfil their threat of coming to Washington." M^r: Pleasanton replied "in every emergency it is well to be prepared, and we *all* believe they will come."

Fearful that in case of invasion, the mill would be wantonly destroyed, M^r: Pleasanton—hired cards carts and waggons in the neighbourhood and conveyed them himself [MC: his important trust] to Leesburg. Va—35 miles from Wa. and placed them in an empty house, under charge of the Rev^d: M^r: Littlejohn— Much fatigued from his journey he slept soundly, the next morning he was told that the flames ascending from the seat [MC: burning] of the governmental buildings—were distinctly seen during the night.

The English, just previous to the burning of Washington, used many strategies to obtain the papers of M^r: Madison—spies were inducted into the President's house disguised as women, suspected by their efforts to enter M^r: Madison's private office—anonymous letters were received threatening his life by the dagger or poison, and friendly ones of warning, which enabled him to counteract schemes aimed at his life. These were for the greater number disregarded, until the last moments, when the English officer in command sent word to M^rs: Madison, that unless she left, the house would be burned over her head! "News came that the English had landed forty miles below the city, their destination was unknown. Several roads lead across the country to the city, and several to Baltimore, when it was ascertained that Washington was their destination object, the Commanders of our Army, for unfortunately the command was divided, at least authority over General Winder was claimed by the Secretary of War, could not agree on the route to be chosen, nor the measures to be adopted to oppose the British forces, who were advancing in the country. In this dilemma the President went to Bladensburg accompanied by several members of the Cabinet, when they unexpectedly found the two armies engaged."

So unexpected was their onslaught in the President's house, that M^rs:

Madison expected dinner company that day [MC: this dinner, which was never served, was dug out in partial preservation by the workman when the House was rebuilt], the following is from M^{rs}. Jones wife of the Secretary of the Navy.

My dear Madam,

Washington, August 24th. 1814

In the present state of alarm and bustle of preparation for the worst that may happen, I imagine it will be mutually convenient, to dispense with the enjoyment of your hospitality today—and therefore pray you to admit this as an excuse for M^r. Jones, Lucy and myself.

M^r. Jones is deeply engaged in dispatching the Marines and attending to other public duties. Lucy and myself are busy packing up ready for flight: but in the event of necessity we know not where to go, nor have we any means yet prepared for the conveyance of our effects. I sincerely hope the necessity may be averted, but there appears to be serious cause of apprehension. Our carriage horse is sick, and our coachman has left us, or I should have called last evening to know what M^{rs}. Cutts had determined upon. I feel great solicitude on her account.

Yours very truly and affectionately.

E. Jones.

When M^{rs}. Madison was convinced that the British officer only waited her departure to begin his work of destruction, M^r. Madison was still in Bladensburg, and she in momentary expectation of his return. Her first thought was to save the public papers, and the Declaration of Independance, the second, to preserve the portrait of General Washington* said

---

* [MC: note] John Siousa's testimony about the removal of the portrait of General Washington, seems to have had great weight with M^r. Charles J. Ingersoll, at the time and for more than a quarter of a century afterwards. it was said M^{rs}. Madison was said to have cut the picture from the frame, aye, and believed also! More recently, as time's shadows lengthen, several have thought to deprive her of the credit due her. M^r. C. J. Ingersoll who has endeavored to ascertain the truth says "such as near as can be ascertained, is the truth of its rescue, which has been involved in Newspaper polemics to part of the honor"

The picture was certainly placed in a hack by M^r. Jacob Barker and M^r. De Peyster of New York. How was it possible to admit a portrait the size of life into such a conveyance? except by taking it from the inner wooden frame? and is it possible that with the cry of "the British are coming" sounded every moment by kind friends and terrified servants, that time would be taken to draw the many *tacks* necessary to confine the

to be by G. Stuart, (now hanging in the President's house) in this she was assisted by her friends Mʳ˙ R. G. De Peyster of New York and Mʳ˙ Jacob Barker,[32] who not knowing what else to do with it, took it in a hack and gave it in charge of a poor woman living a few miles from George Town, where it remained six weeks. Her own personal property was forgotten though in after years she often spoke with regret of her piano, book cases and other handsome furniture, and presentation gifts to herself, which busts and cases of medals which were consumed by the devouring element! We must in justice to the officer " ([MC: who] obeyed orders [MC: Admiral Cockburn)] acknowledge that he expressed a desire to save every thing that belonged to Mʳˢ˙ Madison, but in the hurry and fright, no one could come forward to name her possessions. We were recently told by a lady from New York, with whom he was acquainted, that he had said so great was his admiration for Mrs [MC: M.s] character, that if he had known her property he would himself have brought it out! as it was he took a beautiful pair of vase from the mantel, thinking they must have been hers, and placed them in safe keeping! Mʳˢ˙ Madison appreciated his courtesy. On leaving her drawing room for the last time, her eye caught a sight of the gilt eagles, which ornamented the cornices, those American trophies must not be left, So she instantly recalled her friends and had them taken down and conveyed away in safety with the other national articles. Mʳ˙ Madison arrived soon after she left, a few gentlemen were with him, among them were Mʳ˙ Richard Forrest and Mʳ˙ Richard Cutts, the latter said that Mʳ˙ Madison took books and told him to put them in his carriage, and wine he placed at the door ready to be conveyed to the exhausted Soldiers, but there was no way to transport them. So the British had the benefit of those costly wines [MC: and rare volumes].— As Mʳ˙ Cutts was proceeding up Pennsylvania Avenue his horses were unharnessed [MC: and taken by the invaders] and he was left to find his own way to Montgomery, where was his wife, on foot, as the best way he could.

We have heard Mʳˢ˙ Madison say that she seemed to have lived a lifetime while waiting at the President's house for the return of her husband, she cared not where she went, but Her fear that he would be taken pris-

---

canvas to the board, no, the carving knife which Mʳ˙ Ingersoll says "she held in her hand" must have been in this moment of necessity, as asserted and undenied at the time, if there should be any doubters the following letter from Mʳˢ˙ Madison written not long before her death will forever settle a question to which she attached so little importance.

32. Robert G. L. De Peyster (1795–1873) was a New York merchant; Jacob Barker (1779–1871) was an American financier and lawyer.

oner amounted to agony!— Her sister, Mᵣˢ Cutts had gone early in the day, where, though she was to join her, she scarce knew— When the final order came from Mʳ Madison that she was to delay no longer, she dared not linger but was driven to George Town, where she was joined Mʳˢ Jones and other lady friends, even then, she had not courage to proceed without Mʳ Madison so returned, and met, him and accompanied him to the Virginia shore, and saw him cross to the Virginia shore. He was accompanied by Mʳ Rush, Mʳ Monroe Mʳ John Mason and Mʳ Carroll. Her friends lingered in George Town until until she joined them, under the escort of Mʳ J. Graham and nine volunteer companies. It was three o'clock before she left the President's house, so by the time the party left George Town, the shadows of evening were falling fast. They drove about two miles and a half beyond the heights and stopped at the residence of Mʳˢ Love. The lady was ill but made every preparation the house could afford for her unexpected guests. Mʳˢ Madison sat at the window all night and watched the lurid flames ascending on high! John Siousa was the first [MC: last] to leave the house. When all had departed he took a favorite Macaw (which will be duly noticed) and the key locking the front door, took also the key to the residence of the Russian Minister, Mʳ Daskoff[33] whose house was protected by the flag [MC: of] his country. Mʳ Madison passed the night at Mʳ Cooke Fitzhugh's in Fairfax County. A panic filled the defenseless city, so soon as they saw the flames rise from the Presidential abode. It was rumored that all were to be destroyed by the fire or sword, those who could fled in every direction, while some few raised the Tory flag with hostile hearts and real English feeling! The object of the enemy was to obtain possession of the President and important papers. Disappointed in these expectations, after the degrading pastime of a few bonfires of private [MC: residences belonging to] unoffending residents and the principal public buildings, they left the city just before dark the 24ᵗʰ of August 1814. Alexandria suffered much more from these invaders, who gained neither laurels nor commendation from their own country.

Many houses were offered to the houseless President, on the return of himself and Mʳˢ Madison, the day after [MC: and] while the ruins were still smoking! He chose that of Mʳ John Tayloe of Mount Airy,[34] commonly known as "the Octagon" and there remained a year, until the corner

33. Andrei I. Dashkov (1776–1831) was the Russian minister in Washington from 1811 to 1817.

34. John Tayloe III (1771–1828) was a wealthy Federalist landowner who built the famed Octagon House.

house of the seven buildings was put in order for him. The "White House" was not rebuilt until too late for his occupancy, it was refurnished for M^{r:} Monroe. [*]

Washington Feby 11th 1848

Dear Sir,

I did not receive your favor, containing the newspapers and therefore in my impatience to assure you of my gratitude for the interest you take in my defence in the little narrative of the picture rescued. You will see by the enclosed what was said at the time. The impression that M^{r:} Carroll saved Stuart's portrait of Washington is erroneous. The paper which was to have accompanied your letter has not reached me, but I have heard that his family believed that he rescued it. On the contrary M^{r:} Carroll left me to join M^{r:} Madison, when I directed our servants in what manner to remove it from the wall, remaining with them until it was done. I saw M^{r:} Barker and yourself (the two gentlemen alluded to) passing and accepted your offer to aid me in any way, by inviting you to help me preserve this portrait—which you kindly carried between you to the humble but safe roof which sheltered it awhile. I acted thus because of my respect for General Washington—not that I felt a desire to gain laurels, but if there be a merit in remaining an hour in danger of life or liberty, to save the likeness of any thing, the merit in this case belongs to me.

Accept my respects and best wishes,   D.P.M.

To R. G. L. Depeyster
Westport
Connecticut

Tuesday Augt. 23rd. 1814.

Dear Sister:

My husband left me yesterday morning to join Gen. Winder. He enquired anxiously whether I had courage or firmness to remain in the President's

---

* On the return of M^{r:} and M^{rs:} Madison to Washington they went to the house occupied by M^{r:} Cutts in F Street (now the abode of the family of [MC: M^r] J. Q. Adams) that day it was very difficult to procure provisions, as so few of the citizens had returned—and to add to their discomfort there was the most tremendous storm that was ever remembered to have occured in the neighbourhood, the city was at one moment illuminated by brilliant flashes of lightening, at another darkened by heaving black clouds of rain. A great deal of dammage was done [MC: for] many years afterwards the noble trees, which were uprooted from the earth and lay prostrate like, mighty giants, were pointed out as testimonials of the power of the Storm King!

House until his return on the morrow or succeeding day, and on my assurance that I had no fear but for him, and the success of our Army, he left me, beseeching me take care of myself, and of the cabinet papers, public and private. I have since received two despatches from him, written with a pencil; the last is alarming, because he desires I should be ready at a moment's warning to enter my carriage and leave the city; that the enemy seemed stronger than had been reported, and that it might happen that they would reach the city, with intention to destroy it.

I am accordingly ready; I have pressed as many cabinet papers into trunks as to fill one carriage; our private property must be sacrificed, as it is impossible to procure wagons for its transportation. I am determined not to go myself until I see M^r: Madison safe, and then he can accompany me, as I hear of much hostility towards him;x x x x x x x x x x

disaffection stalks around us.x x x x My friends and acquaintances are all gone—even Col. C— with his hundred men, who were stationed as a guard in this enclosure.X X French John (a faithful domestic) with his usual activity and resolution, offers to spike the cannon at the gate, and to lay a train of powder which would blow up the British should they enter the house. To the last proposition I positively object, without being able however, to make him understand why all advantages in war may not be taken.

Wednesday morning 12 o'clock. Since sunrise I have been turning my spy glass in every direction, and watching with unwearied anxiety hoping to discern the approach of my dear husband and his friends, but, alas, I can descry only groups of military wandering in all directions, as if there was a lack of arms, or of spirit to fight for their own firesides!

Three o'clock. Will you believe it, my Sister? We have had a battle or skirmish near Bladensburg, and I am still here within sound of the cannon! M^r: Madison comes not. May God protect! Two messengers, covered with dust, come to bid me fly; but I wait for him. x x x x x x x x x x x x x x At this late hour a wagon has been procured, I have had it filled with the plate and most valuable portable articles belonging to the house. Whether it will reach its destination, the Bank of Maryland, or fall into the hands of British soldiery, events must determine.

Our kind friend M^r: Carroll has come to hasten my departure, and is in a very bad humor with me because I insist on waiting until the large picture of Gen. Washington is secured, and it requires to be unscrewed from the wall. This process was found too tedious for these perilous moments; I have ordered the frame to be broken and the canvass taken out; it is done, and the precious portrait placed in the hands of two gentlemen of New York, for safe keeping. And now, dear Sister, I must leave this house, or the retreating army will make me a prisoner in it, by filling up the road I am directed to take. When I shall again write you, or where I shall be tomorrow, I cannot tell!

The forgoing extract has been already in print, it was written selected by a talented [LC] lady [LC: of talent] who wrote a sketch of M^rs: M for the Portrait gallery—a letter to a neice in answer to the request [MC: for incidents] says "give my kind love to M^rs: Smith and tell her it would give me pleasure to do what she recommends, and that I hope it will not be long before I make the effort, tho' I cannot promise much, as I cannot give her any thing of importance *in my own eyes*— I have other letters beside the one the extract was taken from—which continue the little history of War times and my especial difficulties: but egotism is so repugnant to my feelings nature, that I shrink from recording my own feelings, acts or doings— You may tell this to M^rs: S—whom I consider a kind friend and amiable lady"

The kind "Friends" never lost their love for M^rs: Madison, whenever they came to Washington, she received them affectionately and cultivated the acquaintance of the few residing in the District—we believe there are but fe numbers are much reduced, though those bearing the names of her favorites still exist. Janneys Littles, and Wetherells and Shoemakers &c— Friend Little's name was always mentioned with peculiar tenderness, by M^rs: Madison and her sisters, any thing she advised always received attention, of course, this advice only extended to their moral and bodily health. We find a note summoning their attendance [MC: and requesting their signatures] as witnesses to her daughter's marriage in 1810— When the "elders" came to Washington, they were On invited to expound their religious views in Congress on the Sabath in the Capitol, and an attentive [MC: audience] was always secured.

In 1814—when the war was partially over, M^r: and M^rs: Madison went to Montpelier for a month or two to recruit and rest after the turmoil and excitement they had so lately undergone— Then it was she received a visit from her faithful friends Rebecca Hubbs and Sarah Scull—whom she entertained with the respect and kindness due to their moral worth. By the following letter they seem to [MC: have] been satisfied with their mission in its essential parts, with an assurance by their own judgement that she could not be corrupted by the adulation she received, could not corrupt her pure and pacific disposition.

Rebecca Hubbs
7th Month 13th 1814

Dear Friend

Thinking it may be acceptable I put pen to paper to write thee a few lines In part to inform thee of the manner in which we got along and my safe return home. The kind reception we met with when at thy dwelling has caused my mind to be much with thee and Thine. Since we parted from you Particularly. So Dear Dorothy for Several Days after when at a Clear Flowing Brook with the Help of thy Kindness we poor pilgrim's were Refreshed on the way which Seemed to Satisfy as a set meal at a full Spread Table and though we were Strangers in a Strange Land yet at times was Enabled to rejoice that the lord had [. . .]unted us worthy to suffer shame for his name sake. we was favoured to get along [. . .] well and arrived at Baltimore the Day Preceding the yearly meeting where I received a Letter from Home and w[. . .] Informed that my dear babe [. . .] very Ill and by accounts Could not expect her to recover Oh my Dear Friend I found it hard for a woman to forget her sucking Child Yet sometimes it is Possible. The next Day after this news my beloved Companion Sarah Scull was Taken sick. This Centured my mind in deep Humility before the Lord and Thankfull for my own Health Desirous that every trying Dispensation may be prosperous In their errand to me I endeavoured to resign my will to the divine will and committed my Dear Little babe my Life and my all to the Lords Disposal then Parting with my Companion in Sickness at Baltimore after [. . .]ting a few meetings set out for home where through the protection of Divine Mercy I arrived safe found my Husband and Children in good Health and my dear babe recovered of her Sickness for which I was Thankfull and though nothing Having nothing to Boast of but Weakness and infirmities yet Desire Humbly to bow before the God and father of all our Sure mercy and in awfull reverence acknowledge that in the Lord Jehovah is everlasting Strength.

And now my dear friend having visited Thy Dwelling much bowed Down in mind under a Sense of my own weakness having none but the Lord to appeal to

To Justify me with [. . .] to relieve my mind of its exercise and be found in Obedience To the most high whose Dreadfull Judgment Should be more Terrible to us and more Justly to be feared than the face of Clay on the Assults of mortals.

Dear friend mayest thee be enabled to Obey the voice of Christ which Speaks in the secret of the Heart So as to be at Peace with god come what will. Thou Hast a precious Talent Committed to thy trust by the King of Kings and my souls desire for thee is that thou may more and more come out of all that Cumbers to seal the virtue of Truth to Operate in and redeem thy Souls from all the difficulties that [. . .] or may attend thee My wishes for thee and thine is That you may be supported under every exercise of mind and witness the living Presence of Jesus Christ whose life and power in the Inward part as they are fi[. . .] is more than all the words that can be spoken of which thou hast at times been Sensible but we cannot help expect to get to Heaven or [. . .] religion without witnessing Conflict with that which was again [. . .] Vanity, Pleasures, Ambition and avarice at times [. . .] at the celestial [. . .] But permit me as one Knowing the terrors of the Lord To entreat thee with my own Soul to not risk our eternal felicity for all the fading things in this World but rather prize the crown Immortal that fadeth not away. Assuredly I think Dear Dorothy I shall ever remember with gratitude of Heart thee and thy beloved Companion your Kind and Christian Entertainment of us little ones God will not be wanting to reward your Love with Dessirous to be had In remembrance by thee Dear Dorothy in Love I Conclude and remain thy Souls well wisher

L. Rebekah Hubbs

To Dorothy Madison

My Love to thy Dear Antient Mother-in-law If Living who I believe is not far from the Kingdom of Heaven. From

Rebekah Hubbs

NB Please excuse my bad writing Near Woodstown Salem County N. Jersey Sarah Scull Joins in that Love which neither Time nor Distance Can erase

LETTER FROM THOMAS B. JOHNSON, POST MASTER AT NEW ORLEANS, TO MRS. MADISON

New Orleans 19th January 1815

Madam,

I had confidently hoped from the events of the last fourteen days, to have announced to you in this letter, the departure from our shores of the implacable foe, who, trusting to our supposed disunion and disaffection, has had the temerity to assail us at our very thresholds, but, although he still maintains a precarious foothold on our soil, be assured Madam he speedily must abandon it, covered with disgrace.

Madam, the American Army in Louisiana has gained immortal glory. It has made a defence against the most valiant and fortunate troops of

Europe, excited to desperation by resistance and staking its all of reputation on the die, unsurpassed in the annals of military warfare, its leader, achieving in one hour the object of a whole campaign, the preservation of the State from conquest and the overthrow of its invaders.

The eighth of January will form an epoch in the callends of the republic. It was on the morning of that day the British, led by Mr. Edward Packenham, attempted to storm our lines and to force a way to the city, at the point of the bayonet. Advancing in full confidence with this intent, and encouraged to it by their Commander, his watchword booty and beauty, They were suffered to approach within twenty yards of our batteries unmolested; at which moment a fire from our guns and our musquetry opened on them, with such irresistable effect, they gave way at all points flying in the utmost confusion, leaving the ground strewn with their dead and dying. You may conceive, Madame, what a spectacle of carnage must have met the eye after the battle, when you learn that in killed, wounded and missing, the loss of the enemy exceeded two thousand; eight hundred being left dead, their Commander in chief killed. Generals Gibbs and Keene severely wounded, and the flower of their Army the 4th and the 21st almost exterminated.

On the other side of the river we were momentarily dispossessed of a battery by the enemy (the guns of which, however, we had time to spike) in consequence of a part of our troops being seized with a panic, in spite of the better countenance maintained by their comrades to the last and the exhortations of their Officers, not to dishonor themselves. But it was attended with a further disaster, Colonel Thornton retreating almost immediately badly wounded.

twelve o'clock. Intelligence has this moment been received from General Jackson that the British have evacuated the country. The rear of their army compleated the retreat to their shipping last night, leaving behind them, many of their men, desperately wounded, besides several peices of cannon. The city is in a ferment of delight. The country is saved, the enemy vanquished and hardly a widow or an orphan whose tears damp the general joy. All is exultation and jubalee. What do we not owe a protecting Providence for this manifestation of his favor?

Permit me to offer you my congratulations on this auspicious termination of our trials and dangers and to assure you of the respect &c

The next most important step in Mr. Madison's administration was the final signing of peace the treaty of Peace. At first difficulties were presented, thrown in the way by England. She would not accept the mediation of Russia. Messrs. J. Q. Adams, Albert Gallatin and James A. Bayard were to meet at Gottenberg.— It was afterwards decided the meeting was to be [MC: held] at Ghent, they were there joined by Messʳˢ: Clay and Jonathan Russell. Mʳˢ: Madison's son was attached to this Embassy—he had only recently left a most excellent catholic institution, under charge of the Bishop of Maryland, and reluctant as she was to part from this idol of her affections, the present opportunity for foreign travel, seemed too favorable to be neglected. Especially as most of the gentlemen were individual friends, whom, she hoped would guard her son from evil. At this period he was represented to be perfectly free from all pernicious habits—from the time of his absence until his return her solicitude was extreme.

The evening before the arrival of the news, that the Treaty had been signed, some friends who were passing the evening with him [MC: Mʳ: Madison] said, he was very desponding and scarcely spoke (he was then living at the Octagon) the next day a rumor came, that a letter had been received in Boston, favorable to his wishes—and a few hours afterwards the diplomatic budget arrived. Though a shade glow of contentment gradually overspread his countenance and the shade of disquietude passed away, as he perused the satisfactory documents, still no word of rejoicing was spoken. His cabinet was summoned and then the glad tidings were announced. It was signed the eighteenth of February 1815

The annexed letters were written by Mʳˢ: Albert Gallatin, those addressed to her by Mʳˢ: Madison were promised us, but were not found.

New York July 2ⁿᵈ 1814

I understand my dear friend that you did not receive any letters from Payne by the last arrivals. I will communicate to you with pleasure what Mʳ: Gallatin says of him. He says, Todd & Millegan left St. Petersburg before them and took the Sweden route, found Gottenberg and the coast frozen and after a long detention came by the way of Copenhagen & joined them at Amsterdam the day before they left it. that Payne had gone on a visit to Paris, and was to return to Mʳ: G. in three weeks, he set off the 7ᵗʰ of May from London. He will have a very pleasant jaunt no doubt. Dallas expected to follow him. Millegan was gone on a Message to Gottenburgh. I can not write you a long letter as I am afraid of being too late for the mail, and I wish you to get the information as soon as possible, for I know you must be anxious. Remember me to Mʳˢ: Cutts and believe me your very sincere friend,

H. Gallatin

End of Cutts Memoir I

Cutts Memoir II

Transcribed by LEE LANGSTON-HARRISON,
CATHERINE ALLGOR, *and* JAMES T. CONNOLLY

In the year 1801 M^r. Jefferson was elected President and M^r. Madison appointed Secretary of State. Albert Gallatin of Pennsylvania succeeded S. Dexter who remained for a year [MC: as Secretary of the Treasury], Henry Dearborn of Massachusetts, Secretary of War, Benjamin Stoddard continued in office. Robert Smith of Maryland succeeded him in 1802— and as Secretary of the Navy—Joseph Habersham, was continued in office but succeeded in 1802 as Se Postmaster General by Gideon Granger of Connecticut.

Washington had undergone but very little improvement since M^rs. John Adams's description of it in her memoirs, the houses were few and far between, in many places the roads not opened, the beautiful square in front of the President's house not distinguishable from the open common, many original trees still growing in the midst of this new city,— In bad weather the roads [MC: were] almost impassable, but there was an excellent and respectable society, belonging to the three District cities, Alexandria, George Town and Washington, independent of those accomplished ladies and gentlemen who were high in Governmental office, and added their charm to the resident society among the old land holders the names of the Tayloes, the Brents, the Carrolls, [MC: Digges Youngs Finsouks] and many others are still prominent. M^r. John Tayloe of M^t. Airy built in 1799 the largest house in the city. General Washington watched the progress of its erection with much interest. John [MC: M^r] Tayloe was the wealthiest man in Virginia, the owner of a thousand negroes—he lived in very handsome style, as became his wealth, nor was there any attempt at Competition. necessity compelled all to keep their carriages, owing to the extended [. . .] Annapolis, the seat of Government, was celebrated for its balls, the elegance and aristocracy of its society. This gentleman [MC: Mr Tayloe] was also celebrated [MC: famous] for his splendid racehorses— Races were then in high favor and attended thrice a year by the most fashionable and even fastidious ladies as well as gentlemen.

Coming to Washington in the spring of 1801, M^rs: Madison was quite young, happy, hopeful and very beautiful!— she still wore her accustomed Quaker cap—her neck covered with a thin kerchief, otherwise, her dress was expensive and fashionable—fond of society she mingled freely with all and soon became without an effort the favorite "of society". A great deal of social intercourse was maintained, even including attendance at the great balls at Annapolis—but parties began at seven and broke up at ten & it was considered quite dissipated to stay later [MC: than] eleven. The representatives [MC: diplomatists] from foreign courts also figured conspicuously in this large circle. England's representatives were Lord and Lady Bagot, Lord and Lady Erskine and Mr Foster. M^r and Lady [MC: M^rs:] Deschamp from Russia. M^r and M^rs: Pichon from France. Melley Melley from Turkey, &c[35]

In the winter of 1801, M^rs: Madison's youngest sister was married to Genl: J. G. Jackson, prominent member of Congress from Harrison County Virginia, he was many years in Congress and to M^rs: Madison's happiness bringing this sister near her every winter. He died in 1825, while serving as Judge of the United States Court in the Western District of Virginia.

M^rs: Madison, aided by her sister, usually presided at M^r: Jefferson's whenever he gave entertainments. His two daughters were married and enjoying their domestic life in Virginia. Of these, M^rs: Randolph,[36] the eldest, who was particularly fitted to do the honors of the highest station, paid her father only two visits in Washington—during the time of his administration. This lady had been introduced into society in Paris, at a very early age. She was but twelve when her father took her with him, when he was appointed minister, and had been placed under charge of Madame de Fentis—until her education was compleated. Her presentation was during the reign of Louis the sixteenth, just before the French Revolution, but her education in France had taken nothing from the natural frankness and

35. Sir Charles Bagot (1781–1843) was an English diplomat who was married to Mary Charlotte Anne Wellesley-Pole Bagot (ca. 1786–1845); Frances Cadwalader Erskine (1781–1843) was the wife of the British minister; Louis-Andre Pichon (1771–1850) was a French diplomat married to Alexandrine-Emilie Brongniart Pichon.

36. Martha Washington Jefferson Randolph (1772–1836) was the daughter of Thomas Jefferson, the third president of the United States, and his wife, Martha Wayles Skelton Jefferson.

simplicity of her manners, so between M$^{rs.}$ Madison and herself there was a congeniality in the kindheartedness and benevolence of their dispositions. They remained intimate friends until the death of M$^{rs.}$ Randolph in 1836. His second daughter, who married M$^{r.}$ Eppes,[37] was exceedingly beautiful in person, but very diffident and retiring in manner, she died young, while M$^{r.}$ Jefferson was President. The sisterly intercourse existing between M$^{rs.}$ M— and M$^{rs.}$ R— sometimes gave rise to amusing mistakes. One day M$^{rs.}$ Randolph had engaged to call and make some visits with M$^{rs.}$ Madison, but when she came M$^{rs.}$ M— was not well enough too much indisposed to accompany her. M$^{rs.}$ Randolph found it much colder then she had anticipated. "Take my pelisse, and hat, to correspond," said M$^{rs.}$ Madison, and in her carriage M$^{rs.}$ R— drove off to the very persons of all others, whom she wished to avoid, owing to the mistake of the servant, and was generally announced as M$^{rs.}$ Madison, producing much pleasant feelings where friends were mutual. A lady (M$^{rs.}$ M^{c}I.) to whom a visit in her case was improperly received her as M$^{rs.}$ Madison, when the mistake was discovered she extricated herself from the dilemma by saying that she did not know of her being in town. M$^{r.}$ Jefferson was devoted to his daughter and wished to have her always at Monticello, where she and her daughter her as M$^{rs.}$ Madison, when the mistake was discovered, she extricated herself from the dilemma by saying that she did not know of her being in town.

M$^{r.}$ Jefferson was devoted to his daughter and wished to have her with him always at Monticello where she and her daughters lived until his death. M$^{r.}$ Jefferson had made a will some years previous, but as his end approached he found himself embarrassed and his daughter portionless. This evidently disturbed his thoughts—so the author of the Declaration of Independence remembered the good he had done to his country and left his daughter as a parting legacy to her "My daughter to my country" were among his dying words. Two States North Carolina and Louisiana acknowledged the gift by each presenting her with ten thousand dollars. Her son in law, M$^{r.}$ N. P. Trist[38] was presented by M$^{r.}$ Adams with a clerkship an office in Washington—which induced M$^{rs.}$ Randolph to choose it for her abode—and there she resided with her daughters, beloved and admired by all who knew them. M$^{r.}$ Jefferson placed the following lines in the hands of his daughter just before dying.

37. Mary Jefferson Eppes (1778–1804), born Mary Jefferson, was the younger of Thomas Jefferson's two daughters who survived infancy.

38. Nicholas Philip Trist (1800–1874) was an American diplomat and personal secretary to Jefferson, friend to Presidents Jefferson, Madison, and Monroe.

"Life's visions are vanished, its dreams are no more
Dear friends of my bosom why bathed in tears?
I go to my father's, I welcome the shore
Which crowns all my hopes or which buries my cares
Then farewell, my dear, my loved daughter adieu!
The last pang of life is in parting from you
Two seraphs await me, long shrouded in death
I will bear them your love on my last parting breath!"

The following inscription was copied by Governor E. Coles from the tombstone erected to the memory of his wife, by Thomas Jefferson

"To the memory of Martha Jefferson
daughter of John Wales
born Oct. 19th: 1748 o. s.
Intermarried with Thomas Jefferson
January 1st: 1772.
torn from him by death
Sepr 6th: 1782
this monument of his love is inscribed."

We subjoin one or two familiar notes from the president to shew how much he depended upon the lady of his Secretary of State.

"Th. Jefferson begs that either Mrs: Madison or Miss Payne will be so good as to dine with him today, to take care of his female friends expected."
May 27th: 1801.

"Thos Jefferson was much disappointed at breakfast this morning, not having until then known of the departure of Mr: and Mrs: Madison and Miss Payne—he hopes they will come and dine today with the Miss Butlers, who were assured they would meet them here, and summer with Mrs: Gallatin and Mrs: Madison —affectionate salutations."
June 4th: 1801.

"Thomas Jefferson presents his respectful thanks to Mrs: Madison for the trouble she has been so kind as to take on his behalf. Nothing more is wanting, unless (having forgotten little Virginia) a sash or something of that kind could be picked up any where for her. The amount and the person from whom the earrings and pin were bought, Thomas Jefferson will also ask of M^rs: Madison. He presents his affectionate salutations.["]

July 10th: 1805.

Cannons of etiquette to be observed by the Executive.
by President Jefferson.

first. Foreign ministers arriving at the seat of government pay the first visit to the ministers of the nation, which is returned; and so likewise on subsquent occasions of reassembly after a recess.

second. The families of foreign ministers receive the first visit from those of the National ministers, as from all other residents and as all strangers foreign or domestic do from all residents of the place.

third. After the first visit the character of stranger ceases.

fourth. Among the members of the Diplomatic Corps, the Executive government and its own principles of personal and national equality, considers every minister as the representative of his nation, and equal to every other without distinction of grade.

fifth. No titles being admitted here, those of foreigners give no precedence.

sixth. Our ministers to foreign nations are as private citizens while here.

seventh. At any public ceremony—to which the Government invites the presence of foreign ministers and their families, no precedence or privilege will be given them other than the provision of a convenient seat or station with any other stranger invited, and with the families of the national ministers.

eighth. At dinners in public or private, and on all other occasions of social intercourse, a perfect equality exists, between the persons composing the company, whether foreign or domestic, titled or untitled, in or out of office.

ninth. To give force to the principle or equality or pèle mêle, and prevent the growth of precedence out of courtesy, the members of the Executive, at their own houses, will adhere to the antient usage of their ancestors, gentlemen in mass giving [. . .] precedence to the ladies in mass.

tenth. The President of the United States receives visits but does not return them.

eleventh. The family of the President receives the first visit and returns it.

twelfth. The President's family in public or private.

thirteenth. The President, when in any state, receives the first visit of that Governor and returns it

fourteenth. The Governor of a state, does in his State, receive the 1ˢᵗ⋅ visit
of the from Foreign Ministers.

The Legislative and Judiciary branches, being coordinate with the Executive, this list does not assume to lay down rules for them, but expressly
declars declares the proceeding not to affect them in any wise.

Mʳˢ⋅ Madison was always conciliatory and [MC: always] willing to waive
her rights when their being waived involved no principle of vital importance. Etiquette she delighted to throw aside at all times, she liked no form
which separated her from her friends— the following relation from herself
is one example, (it was elicited on the occasion of the first large diplomatic
dinner given by President Polk). One of the foreign ministers was dis-
pleased at what he considered a breach of etiquette in his and his cabinet
handing the wives of their own ministers instead of those of the diplomatic
corps, as formerly had been done—not as a right, but as a courtesy— Mʳˢ⋅
Madison said that in 1804, Mʳˢ⋅ Merry,[39] wife of the English minister, a
lady who came to the country impressed with ideas of her own superiority, publicly asserted that she intended to teach the Americans etiquette,
and how to behave themselves— This was repeated in the presence of Mʳ⋅
Jefferson, who instantly said, "I will put her in Coventry"—and secured
Mʳˢ⋅ Madison's promise to dine with him the day after, at a State dinner—
she went—he advanced to hand her in, she stepped back and said, "take
Mʳˢ⋅ Merry," he answered "not so" and persevered in handing the Lady of
the Secretary of State. The next day Mʳ⋅ Madison gave a dinner, when the
same etiquette was observed—Mʳˢ⋅ Merry who was very sensitive at what
she deemed an insult, ran and seized her husband's arm and was handed
by him; she considered herself illy treated, complaints were made to thier
Government and Mʳ⋅ Merry was recalled. He was a country gentleman,
and she it was said, had been a bar maid in her father's inn where Mʳ⋅ Merry
first saw her and was charmed with her beauty and they were married, but
it was not a very fortunate union, and she was separated from him, and
ended her career in Paris, where she attracted much attention.

Her Mʳˢ⋅ Madison's presence of mind rarely forsook her—she never
allowed herself to be carried away by fear, tho' her nature was one of
extreme timidity— When the Indian Chiefs came to Washington it was the
fashion to entertain them; One evening after they had been entertained

39. Elizabeth Death Leathes Merry (d. 1824) was the wife of the British minister
Anthony Merry.

by Mʳˢ˙ Madison, she retired late to her chamber and while she was disarranging her cap at the mirror, she saw reflected in it from behind the door the face of a wild Indian!— She paused a moment to avoid suspicion, did not catch his eye—then walked quietly into the next room, rung the bell, returned to her position at the mirror until the bell was answered by a tall negro man, who soon shewed this son of the forest that he had made a mistake in ascending instead of descending from the drawing room—

At this time the death of Alexander Hamilton, by the ambitious Burr created great distress in political and private circles. So intimately connected was he with Mʳ˙ Jefferson and Mʳ˙ Madison—[. .] [MC: that they] felt his loss as noble natures alone can!— Mʳˢ˙ Madison in several letters written at the time mentions it with horror! Cultivated, intelligent refined and accomplished as was Aaron Burr, from that moment his star evil star was in the ascendancy! disappointed in the Presidency [MC: and] a few years afterwards in his attempts to take possession of the beautiful Island of Blennerhassett, he was tried and acquitted in Richmond by the subtlety of the law, which he knew could not reach him, else, he would not for his own accord have surrendered himself to justice—not acquitted in the eyes of the world, very little is known of him afterwards, and that little unworthy of historical note.

Baron Humboldt[40] also visited Washington [MC: in] the summer of 1804 with a suite of very charming gentlemen. His *fame* has been more fully established since then, but he could not please more now, with his laurels gathered, than he did then, while they were being culled.— We have recently been gratified by hearing the pleasure with which this learned man recounted his reminiscences of Washington and especially of Mʳˢ˙ Madison— He was much pleased with our republican simplicity, the ease of social intercourse and with the estimation placed on [MC: our] ladies. Mʳ˙ Jefferson invited him to a review of the militia, he was struck at their want of proper organization, having comparing them with the veteran soldier of his own country, and the splendid troops of France, and [MC: even] the President's plain blue coat worn while reviewing them [MC: all were matters of surprise.] He could not forbear asking why he did not wear a uniform. Mʳ˙ Jefferson answered "to shew the superiority of the civil to the military power."

40. Friedrich Wilhelm Heinrich Alexander Freiherr von Humboldt (1769–1859) was a German naturalist and explorer.

Thomas Jefferson requests the favor of the honorable M^r C[. . .] to dine with him the day after tomorrow at half after three or at whatever hour the Senate may adjourn rise.

The favor of an answer is asked

Wednesday Jany 27th: 1802.

When Meley Meley the first (and we believe the only) Turkish Ambassador arrived in Washington, M^rs: Madison gave him a party composed of the beauty and fashion of the Metropolis, after he had bade good night (for then it was not considered polite to take French leave) a noise was heard proceeding from one of the smaller rooms. It was his habit to walk round and [yon?] wherever he could obtain admittance, so, he caught a glimpse of a large fat negress, who made her appearance from the kitchen with coffee. Mely Mely suddenly threw his arms around her, saying, "she was the handsomest women he had seen in America, that she resembled one of his wives, for whom he had given an incredible price—and who was a trad for a camp one camel"!— This was made known to the guests by his interpreter and his singular taste caused much merriment.

He was a fine looking man, his costume as handsome as gold, silk embroidery and Cashmere could make it.— Very stately in deportment— [MC: at parties,] always surrounded by the ladies, who conversed with him freely, one, was curious to know of what beautiful fabric his turban was composed—never having seen muslin so fine!— He took it from his head and presented it for nearer inspection—it was plaster of Paris.

In [MC: February] 1803 Captains Lewis and Clark were sent by M^r: Jefferson to explore the Missouri River, [MC: and discover the best communication with the Pacific Ocean] in this expedition a great deal of interest was taken by the cabinet and especially the ladies. They were much entertained, and ere their departure on this perilous journey, souvenirs were sent them, and they were fitted up with Camp equipage and every thing thought to be suitable for them. M^rs: Madison, with her usual sympathy was very much distressed for she believed they never could return from that land of savages—however they did "return" after an absence of four years, full of hair breadth escapes and marvellous adventures—and as many specimens as they could bring from so far off, in the wilderness! these specimens were divided among their friends, and M^rs: Madison had part of thier silver cooking utensils, valuable from association and the long journe and successful journey performed. M^rs: Madison often spoke of them, [MC: late in life] but, never could realize how much more adventurous her countrymen had since been!

Mr: Jefferson rewarded These brave [MC: pioneers] were afterwards rewarded, one (Captain Lewis) by being appointed Governor of Louisiana, the other, (Captain Clarke) receiving the appointment of Governor of Louisiana General of the Militia and agent of the United States for Military affairs Indian Affairs, in that department.

Poor Captain Lewis met with a melancholy end to his successful career, all his life he had been subject to attacks of hypochondria— On September 15 1809—while travelling in the Chickasaw nation, symptoms of this derangement were strongly developed, and during the temporary absence of the woman with whom he lodged, he took advantage of being left alone in the house, to destroy his own life!

M^r: Jefferson writes to his friend D^r: Barton[41] of Phil^a:, 27 February 1803 and speaking of this interesting expedition says, "It was impossible [MC: to find a] [. . .] who to a complete science in Botany, Natural History, Mineralogy and astronomy, joined the firmness of constitution and character, prudence, habits adapted to the woods, and familiarity with the Indian manners and character, requisite for this undertaking. All the latter qualifications Lewis has. Although no regular botanist and cetera, he possesses a remarkable store of accurate information on all the subjects of the three kingdoms, and will therefore readily single out, whatever presents itself new to him in either, and he has qualified himself for taking the Longitude and Latitude necessary to fix the geography of the line he passes through. In order to draw his attention at once to the objects most desirable, I must ask the favor of you to prepare for him a note of those in the lines of botany, zoology, or of Indian history, which you think most worthy of observation."

In January 1803, M^r: Monroe was sent on a special mission to England, two years afterwards on an especial mission to Madrid

It was in this year that Gilbert Stuart, our celebrated painter, came to Washington, where his renown was fully appreciated—as well as his extraordinary genius. He was born in 1754—of Scotch parentage, received his first lessons in painting from a gentleman of that country, named, Cosmo Alexander; he was professionally a painter but was supposed to have come to the country for political purposes. M^r: Stuart's powers of memory and

41. Benjamin Smith Barton (1766–1815) was an American botanist, naturalist, and physician.

[MC: observation] were so strong that he could paint pictures from recollection at the early age of twelve. He was also devoted to music, and very remarkable for his colloquial abilities, he contrived to arrest the attention of his sitters by a variety of anecdotes, with which his wonderful memory was amply stored, and he had the [MC: tact] to discover their favorite topics and always conversed on those, interesting them so much that they would forget themselves and appear in their natural character. A friend of M^rs: Cutts writes to her from Washington, May 7th: 1804. "I can tell you nothing new. Stuart is all the rage, he is almost worked to death, and every body afraid that they will be the last to be finished.["] He says "the ladies come and say, "Dear M^r: Stuart, I am afraid you will be very much tired, you really must rest when *my* picture is done." M^rs: Robert Smith is sitting now, so is M^r: Madison." This executive painter was considered very partial in his paintings, always favoring those whom he liked best— Most of the prominent residents of Washington had their portraits taken by him, so there still remain many in the city of Washington.

In 1804, M^rs: Madison's sister Anna was married, how great [MC: was] her grief in parting from her, the following letters will convey some idea. Requiring something to love, her affection was concentrated on this neice sister whom she had reared and who was as her own child. Richard Cutts, whom she married, "was a member of Congress from the District of Maine, then constituting a part of the Commonwealth of Massachusetts—he was descended from one of the earliest founders of New England, and inherited that inextinguishable love of liberty freedom, the envied yet venerated but peculiar characteristic of the English pilgrims, He received his early education at Harvard University, at which institution he was graduated in 1790, in the 20th: year of his age. Following the bent of his inclinations, having studied law, Mr: Cutts engaged extensively in the pursuit of navigation and commerce, though at the same time deeply involved in the vicissitudes and ardently devoted to the duties of political life. At an early period of his career, after the close of his studies at the University, he visited Europe, and added to his stock of knowledge acquired at the seat of science the stores of experimental instructions acquirable early in the school of observation and inquisitive travel.

On his return from Europe, after serving two successive years as member of the General Court of Massachusetts, he was at the age of 29, in 1800 elected by the people of his district (but two opposing votes) a member of the House of Representatives of the United States. He took his seat on the 7th: of December of 1801—commencing with the administration of M^r:

Jefferson and through six successive Congresses, constantly sustained by the continued consistency of his constituents, he gave a firm, efficient and undeviating support to that administration and to that of his successor M^r: Madison, until the close of his first term, 3^d: March 1818, having patriotically sustained by his votes, non-importation, non-intercourse, the embargo and finally war, as measures called for by the honor and interests of the nation, although ruinous to his private fortune, since the greater part of his property consisted of ships, the loss of which if [MC: captured or] destroyed, might, as thus it did, reduce him to poverty." We have quoted thus far from a sketch made of him by the Honb^l J. Q. Adams. Col Thomas Cutts, [MC: his father] was the wealthiest man in Maine, he used to say he [MC: could] journey for a week and always sleep in his own house—his residence was on Cutts Island, a beautiful place in the Saco river, the Saco falls were just opposite, and could be heard for two miles distant—their descent is very rapid and the scenery altogether wild and romantic, the Indians had even then hardly left this favorite resort of theirs—a place on in the rocks under the falls is still pointed out as the residence or hiding place of a Sagamore of Saco—and a beautiful girl, whom he had enticed away from her friends to live with him. Col. T. Cutts inherited his property from his father Richard Cutts of Portsmouth, N. H. who was descended from one of three brothers, among the earliest settlers in New Hampshire, one of themselves [MC: (John Cutts)] was first colonial President of New Hampshire—of his sister lady Ursula Cutts, many wild legends are told, one we [. .] she was murdered by the Indians as well as her whole household.* Indeed, Portsmouth was at one time celebrated for its wealth, the magnificence of its entertainments, and its hospitality, Particularly before the Revolution. The wealth and grandeur of the Pepperell family has become legendary— General William Pepperell's [MC: grand] son, commanded at Louisburg, soon after his success against the French, he went to England, King George 2^d: asked, "in what way he could reward him for his services." The General answered, "Only by keeping a sufficient number naval force on the banks of Newfoundland to protect

Many years after the death of Colonel Thomas Cutts, some enterprising travellers were struck with the tremendous water power of the Saco river near the falls and its suitableness to turn a mill. These gentlemen on their return to Boston, formed a company for its purchase from the heirs. This was soon done, and it is near the site of the "York Manufacturing Company." one of the most flourishing in New England— Of course, much of its romantic scenery is destroyed by the [. . .] brick buildings and the hum of the busy wheels— the several thousand fishermen for whom I find employment there." Struck by the seeming disinterestness of the reply, his majesty caused to be made for, and presented to him, a superb snuff box, now owned by M^{rs:} Ward, having on the cover in bas relief, the very appropriate representation of Diogenes and Alexander. "The city of London presented him with a long table covere of solid silver covered with an extensive service of plate. He was made a [MC: Baronet] in 1746. He had but two children— the son, and pride of his heart died at the age of twenty five. Gaiety was then banished from the mansion. The old hero commenced preparations for his own disolution. His daughter Elizabeth married Hon^{ble:} Nathaniel Sparhawk of a counsellor and Judge. Soon after the decease of his son, Sir William made his will, entailing his property on many generations, and the name of Pepperell, which all the heirs were to assume. Notwithstanding the entailment, this princely domain was confiscated, because in the possession of the last Baronet of the name, "who was a mandamus counsellor, and of his brother, also refugee loyalists of 1776." The remnants of the mansions of this family still remains, though tenanted by several families of fishermen who did not like the inroad of strangers, whose curiosity takes them to the place— Like *all* old houses in New England, money is said to be built up in its walls—and somnambulists have often pointed out the parts of the arches where is was concealed, but we have not heard whether any was ever found, as the *masonry* is "generally too substantial to be broken." [MC: So we have been told, when curiosity prompted us to enquire how much was discovered.]

Of a later date, still, built before the Revolution is the mansion of General Knox, at Thomaston, Maine—he was the greatest favorite among General Washington's generals—and retired to this beautiful retreat at the age of 45, after the Revolution. It bore the same name as M^{r:} Madison's residence, and was equally famed for the its [MC: the] extended hospitality of its inmates— M^{rs:} Knox^{42} was the daughter of Secretary Flucker of Massachusetts, and it was her mother who was engaged to the son of Sir William Pepperell, great preparations were made for the wedding—a house was built and furnished by Sir William. the gay party were assembled, they were standing before the clergyman when suddenly the lady turned from the groom, walked up stairs saying she would not marry him—all were

42. Lucy Flucker Knox (1756–1824) was the daughter of Thomas Flucker, the royal provincial secretary, and the wife of General Henry Knox.

in consternation and a few days afterward the disappointed bridegroom dropped dead in the street and the bridal preparations were turned into funeral preparations. M^rs. Cutts writes to M^rs. Madison [MC: sister writes to her] in 1804 "We have not yet made our visit to General Knox—M^r. C— has received two very pressing letters from him to hasten us, but it is more than an hundred miles and I have an antipathy to make such an addition to my journey, notwithstanding my desire to see the country and most of all their Princely establishment, which is the wonder of the Eastern World!" M^rs. Knox outlived her husband eighteen years and remained at this beautiful retreat until her death.

We have made a digression in favor of "old houses," still, we have not said half we wished, for we have a strange fancy for those time worn relics of the past, and would delight to repeat the many legends told of their antiquated tenants, whose pride, aristocracy and eccentricity have crumbled into dust! and these traditions we believe, as they are and why should we not, as they are handed down from generation to generation by those who did not change their fealty—[. .] [MC: and so much of our biblical and historical lore is transmitted to us in the same way] [*Two lines of cancelled text, illegible*]

The marriage of M^rs. Madison's sister to so prominent a member of Congress was a scene of great gaïty—it was an [.] irresistible opportunity for M^rs. Madison to give pleasure to every body, so every body was invited to the Secretary of State's—some of the attendants are still living—many presents were sent as tokens of affection and [sentiment?]—these consisted principally of embroideries, from sleeves to pincushions, poetry and paintings, all the workmanship of her friends—we mention them merely to shew the difference between the present magnificent gifts—and the simple ones, fifty years ago. M^rs. Dashcoff sent the usual Russian bridal present— two wine coolers, one filled with salt, [MC: the essence of life] the other bread—the staff of life— There was then, but one Church in Washington of which Parson McCormick (who performed the ceremony) was rector—this church was at the Navy Yard, and attended by the President, Cabinet, foreign ministers (who were not Catholics) and citizens for the convenience of Washingtonians, he often preached in the hall of the Senate on [Friday?] [. . .]. When other churches sprang into life, M^r. McCormick was a clerk in the State Department, and had charge of the gifts sent by foreign potentates [MC: to the President of the United States [*long line of text, illegible*]] and not allowed to be accepted by individuals [MC: who held any appointment under our government]—among them, was the snuff box presented by the Emperor Alexander to Honble: L. Harris[43]— Mr: McCormick would say, "admire the diamonds outside—before you look in, the two there, are so much handsomer, they throw the others in the shade—" then, after all possible delay, until curiosity was at its height, he would suddenly raise the lid, and instead of diamonds the polished surface would reflect the eager *eyes* of the admirer of diamonds those precious stones. After being ourselves disappointed we enjoyed with him, the pleasure of seeing others disappointed [MC: likewise defeated in their expectations].

This was the first separation of M^rs: Madison from her sister, so began their correspondence, some of these letters we publish, as they give greater insight into her character, than those written more formally, and after she has learned to be cautious in expressions as becomes the wife of a statesman.

In 1805 M^rs: Madison injured her knee, and was for a time under charge of D^r: Elsy, then a prominent physician [MC: in Washington]—but from want of care on her part, it threatened to be a very serious accident. M^r: Madison became alarmed and insisted in placing her under the strict rules and regimen of D^r: Physic at Philadelphia—the progress of her recovery she notes in the following letters addressed to M^r: Madison and her sister.

To M^rs: R. Cutts

Washington, June 4th 1805 Philadelphia

My dearest Anna,

I now write your from my bed, to which I have been confined for ten days with a sad knee, it became a painful tumor—and two doctors were called in, their applications of caustic burning by chemical action, give me hope of getting well—but heaven knows when!

Now my dear, I must tell you of M^rs: M's airs. I told you we had been unusually intimate, she had met the French here and had been very sociable with Madame, but the other evening she came in high good humor to pass some hours with her patient as she styled me, when Merran came in and mentioned that the General and his family were walking near the house— M^rs: M. instantly took the alarm and said they were waiting for her to depart in order to come in, seized her shawl, and in spite of all I could say, marched off with great dignity, and more passion, you know when she pleases she can get angry with persons as well as circumstances.

43. Levett Harris (1780?–1839) was a diplomat from Philadelphia and U.S. consul at St. Petersburg in 1803.

Yesterday we had brother George Thornton and Laurence Washington to spend the day. Mamma and Madison dined at Young's. I was confined to bed. John presided below and then sound of Virginia hilarity echoed through the house! George coughs incessantly, looks thin, is hoarse, but has no idea of dying. Since I wrote you, two days past, I have heard sad things of Tourreau,* that he whipped his wife and abuses her before all the servants—do not breathe it in your country as it will make you then all so odious—as he desires to be! I pity her sincerely as she is an amiable and sensible woman. I have a letter from Mount Vernon inviting me there, but alas it seems I shall walk no more!

Ever yours, D.

If my beloved sister, had received my last from Washington, she will be unhappy to find that I was obliged to take this journey in so dangerous a season, but it proved a very dangerous [LC: pleasant] one, as I was easier riding than in any other position, my health and spirits revived every day that I.

To M^rs. R. Cutts

Washington July 8th, 1805

Still my dear Anna, must your sister write you from bed—my knee will keep me in Washington longer I fear than will be conducive to our health or

---

* Genl. Tourreau was minister from France under the reign of [. .] Egalité—and his career is said to be such as would characterize that epock, tho' an aid to Napoleon his origin was very obscure— While in power, he was very cruel in the extreme—in the rapid change of popular favor, he was condemned to be executed, it was the custom the evening before to put marks on the doors of those to be guillotined the next day, his wife, then a servant girl employed about the jail, rubbed the mark from his door, and so his life was saved. He rewarded her by marriage. It proved a very unhappy alliance. He treated her so badly that she threatened to return to Paris, and laid her plans accordingly, unknown to him, as she thought, but he, tho' he appeared blind, watched her with the eyes of a lynx. he and ardently wished her departure, while she, poor woman, fancied it was the greatest punishment she could inflict on her rebellious Lord. Col Isaac Coles (private Secretary to Mr Jefferson) who was going to France in the same vessel was requested by Genl Toureau to take charge of her and see that she was treated with respect. He also gave him money for her [MC: expenses] but this was to be kept secret from her until they sailed. When told, this she was much excited and would have returned had she dared!

General Tourreau was a remarkable man in his appearance, tall, dignified, a profusion of snow white hair, heavy black eyebrows and whiskers—bowed often and profusely.

interest. We have nothing new to tell you the town is tolerably vacant and dull. The President goes in one week and we were all to go about the same time, but for the reason given. I feel now very impatient to be in Orange, as I have some confidence in the change of air—poor M. N. went off last week [LC: at Staunton] on her way from the springs, this place is healthy yet, but terribly warm and dry! I had a friendly note from the President yesterday begging me to get* Virginia's wedding garments, with trinkets and dresses for all the family. I shall ride to the stores but cannot get out to shop for them—very little variety in George Town—but I must do my best for them. I am to be at the weddings if I can the last of the month, but I have scarcely a wish and no expectation of going. I should rejoice to be with you, dear Anna, tho' I could not have the pleasure of playing the nurse to you now, as I never get down but to ride or dine with company.

I spent the morning of the 4th at the President's, sat quite still and amused myself with the mob. Why did you not tell me you staid with M$^{rs:}$ Latrobe? She was two or three days with me. M$^{r:}$ and M$^{rs:}$ Merry are at Baltimore going on as they did here fighting and exposing themselves.

Farewell your own sister D.

Philadelphia 29th July 1805

If my beloved sister, has received my last from Washington, she will be unhappy to find that I was obliged to take this journey in such a dangerous season, but it proved a very dangerous [LC: pleasant] one, as I was easier riding than in any other position, my health and spirits revived every day that I rode. We breakfasted at Grey's ferry this morning and I now write from my bed—but oh how dismal are all things to my view, in this place without you, and I in this sad condition. But D$^{r.}$ Physic has seen my knee and says he will cure it in a month, this ought to comfort me, but Anna, if I was not afraid of death, I could give way to most immoderate grief. I feel as if my heart was bursting—no mother, no sister but fool that I am! here is my beloved husband sitting anxiously by me, who is my unremitting nurse—but you know how delicate he is! I tremble for him! One night on our way he was taken very ill, with his old complaint, I thought all was over with me, I could not fly and aid him as I did formerly—but heaven in its mercy restored him next morning—and he would not pause until he heard my fate from D$^{r.}$ Physic.

---

* Virginia Randolph, who married M$^{r:}$ Archibald Cary.

Philadelphia, 1805 31st July

My dear Sister:

We are in excellent lodgings in Sanson S$^{t.}$ and I feel quite like another being!—My knee is better, D$^{r.}$ Physic has splinted it—not a step can I take but this process is to cure it we hope, and the Doctor thinks it gives me no pain, but from the fixed position. I have had the world to see me. M$^{r.}$ and M$^{rs.}$ Lenox, Miss Kean, M$^{r.}$ and M$^{rs.}$ Hase, Sally, Marquis and M$^{rs.}$ M, M$^{rs.}$ Rush, Stuart and every body of every description to see Madison—we have invitations to the house of one dozen of the gentry, but withstand all to be at ease here. Madison is well and sends his love to you both, as I do. I dare not write half I wish as I am laying in bed and dare not, cannot get up. We have heard from Mamma, she is now easy about me, she will go on to Uncle's where we shall follow when I am well—will write you in a day or two all about everything.

Your devoted sister, D.

Philadelphia, August 2nd 1805

You ask who is kindest to me here and I can tell you that among a numerous sett the Pemberton's bear off the palm. I can never forget Betsey!—who has been as you would have been to me—my poor knee is no better, so difficult and tedious is it to heal— Yet D$^{r.}$ Physic* says it it will and must soon be well—he has applied caustic three times since I wrote you, which is a sad thing to feel, but it does every thing that the knife would do—it removes all impediments to a cure, but increases the work of healing. I

---

* D$^{r.}$ Physic had been was an inmate of M$^{r.}$ J. Todd's family when M$^{rs.}$ Madison first married, and she had the greatest confidence in his skill, as well as friendship [MC: towards him] founded on thorough knowledge of his sterling qualities. So had M$^{r.}$ Madison, inspired by his skill in curing her knee, for the cure treatment of similar cases he was celebrated "His management of deseased joints, by perfect rest, [. . .] and diet, is a happy substitute for the errors generated under the use of the term scroffula or white swelling, and ending either by amputation or death!—sometimes both"—see life of D$^{r.}$ Physic.

He was a very reserved and absent minded man, as well as one of great probity— It is said that when he was engaged to be married he went one evening to see the lady of his choice, she sent him word she could not see him as she was too much indisposed, not caring to return to his books, he wandered about and finally went into the theatre, a place which he rarely attended—there to his utmost surprise, was the object of his affections, he was so disgusted at her falsehood that he never spoke to her again. He afterward married Miss Emlin of Phil$^{a.}$— He died in 1837. He was a man of deep feelings and the death of a patient often laid him up from excess of sensibility.

have not yet seen where I am and the longer I stay the less I care for the vanities, but shall enjoy them much too well at last I suspect.

N. M. L and S. L. made me a visit last night, they remonstrated with me on seeing so much company, and said it was reported that half the city of Philadelphia had called upon me. This lecture made me recollect the time when our Society used to control me entirely and debar me from so many advantages and pleasures, altho' so [LC: utterly] out of their power, I really felt my ancient terror of them revive to a disagreeable degree—this crowd, more like the attendance in a new play, has really become tiresome—yet I cannot help it, nor can all my vanity make it more than tolerable &c. Your own forever, DPM.

To M^rs: Madison

Washington August 7th 1809

My dearest,

We reached the end of our journey yesterday at one o clock; without interruption of any sort on the road. M^r: Coles had been here sometime. One, if not two of the expected dispatch vessels of England had just arrived, and M^r: Gilston after a short passage from France, entered Washington about the moment I did. You may guess therefore the volumes of papers before us. I am but just dipping into them, and have seen no one as yet except M^r: Smith for a few minutes last evening. What number of days I may be detained there it is impossible to say. The period you may be sure will be shortened as much as possible. Every thing around and within reminds me that you are absent, and makes me anxious to quit the solitude. In my next I hope I shall be able to say when I shall have this gratification, perhaps also to say something of the intelligence brought me just brought [me!] I send the paper of this morning which had something on the subject. I hope the communications of Gilston will be found more favorable than is stated. Those from England can scarcely be favorable, when such men hold the reins as we have latterly had to do with. M^r: and M^rs: Erskine are here. His successor had not sailed on the 20th of June.

God bless you and be assured of my constant affection

J Madison

The beautiful and valuable Counterpane, which does so much credit to the skill and ingenuity of Miss Wildes, has just now been received. I beg she will accept my sincere thanks for the singular favor. It is greatly augmented by the expressions of kindness from my unknown friend. I hope she will believe that I cannot forget her, and that she will add to my obligation by accepting from me some token of my regard.

DP Madison

January 20th 1810

M^{r:} Serurier[44] was minister from France the last few years of M^{r:} Madison's administration, and resided part of the time at Kalorama[45]— While minister, he married (we believe in New York) a lovely girl, in her sixteenth year, her parents, M^{r:} and M^{rs:} William Pagot were refugees from the Island of S^{t:} Domingo—they escaped when she was a child of 7 years—exceedingly beautiful, she saved the life of her parents at that epoch. The vessel in which they left [MC: the Island] was searched by the negroes, and they were discovered, and would have been murdered, had it not been for this courageous child, who rushed forward and threw herself at the feet of the inhuman savages, and with clasped hands, implored them to spare the life of her parents— The negroes, astonished at so much loveliness and courage, listened, and said they "could not kill the parents of such a child!" M^{rs:} Serurier had made friends in Washington, so she did not [. .] who were prepared to welcome this lovely and fascinating stranger—it is said at that time she was a perfect dream of beauty, full of enthusiasm and gratitude for [MC: the] kindness shewn her by M^{rs:} Madison, she repaid her by the most childlike love—M^{rs:} Madison which M^{rs:} Madison received and returned in full— Twenty years afterwards, when she [MC: M^{rs:} M.] had returned to her country home, and M^{r:} Serurier was again Minister to the United States—M^{rs:} Madison wrote and invited her to come immediately with her husband and family to Montpelier—which invitation was of course accepted, and a few weeks of happy intercourse soon passed—and they parted, their affection only the more firmly cemented by this reunion, which was their last.

My dear friend,

On this day eight years ago I wrote you from the retirement of Sully—to congratulate you on the joyful event that placed you in the highest station our country can bestow. I then enjoyed the proudest feelings—that my

44. Louis-Barbé-Charles Sérurier (ca. 1775–1860) was the French minister to the United States from 1811 to 1816.

45. The Washington home of Joel Barlow.

friend, the friend of my youth, who never had forsaken me, should be thus distinguished and so peculiarly fitted to fill it.

How much greater cause have I to congratulate you, at this period for having so filled it as to render yourself more enviable this day, than your successor, as it is more difficult to deserve the gratitude and thanks of the community than their congratulations—you have deservedly received all this of all.

Being deprived, by the sickness of my child from joining the multitude today in paying my respects to where they are due, I feel the sweetest consolation in devoting myself entirely to you.

My heart clings to you, my beloved friend and has done so for the last fortnight, with a selfishness that produces the keenest feelings of regret and tho' my domestic habits, more than inclinations, have prevented my taking advantage of your kind invitations to be more with you yet I felt a security and pleasure in being with so near you, and a confidence in your affection, that constituted my chief pride as a citizen I assure you. But the period has at length arrived when we must again part. You will retire from the tumults and fatigue of public life to your favorite retreat in Orange, and will carry with you principles and manners not to be put off with the robe of state; having been drawn from maternal breasts, and nurtured from the example of those dear pious parents, to whom you ever resigned yourself with such filial obedience and devotion as to bring their blessings on your head.

Talents such as yours were never intended to be with remain inactive— on retiring from public life, you will form a more fortunate arrangement of your time, be able to display them in the more noble and interesting walks of life—you will cherish them, my dear friend, in a more native soil, they will constitute the chief felicity of your dear venerated husband, and descend in full perfection to your son. I remember at this moment in my last conversation with my venerable Uncle Parrish, your father's friend, he said of you, "She will hold out to the end, she was a dutiful daughter and never turned her back on an old friend, and was charitable to the poor."

Thus the blessing of this good old man went with you, better even, we are taught to believe, than the sounding trumpet of fame!

Will you do me the favor, my dear friend, for it is near my heart that you, should, to take advantage of some leisure moment, to say something for me to your highly respected husband. In the fullness of my gratitude I can express nothing, but shall ever hold in sacred remembrance the highly valued friendship and confidence he has shewn my husband.

I rejoice to hear that you do not leave the city very soon. I may hope to enjoy your society, tho' I presume your engagements are many I shall reserve myself to meet you on a future occasion.

I must ask your pardon for thrusting such an epistle at you, but it releeves my my heart and will not, I trust wound yours—it demands no other acknowledgment at present than a cordial reception. It grows dark, and you shall have this tonight.   Believe me truly yours,

Eliza Lee

From Judge Johnson of the Supreme Court

Washington Sunday 1817

I am this moment on the eve of leaving Washington, and shall leave it without a parting interview with one whom I must be indulged in the liberty of comprising among the most respected and most cherished of my friends.

But you, Madam, cannot mistake the feelings which dictate to me this mode of making you an humble tender of a most affectionate Adieu.

You are now about to enter upon the enjoyment of the most enviable state which can fall to the lot of mankind. To carry with you to your retirement the blessings of all who ever knew you. Think not, madam, that I address to you the language of flattery. It is what no one, but yourself would hesitate at conceding. And be assured that all who have ever enjoyed the honor of your acquaintance, will long remember, that polite condescension which never failed to encourage the diffident, that suavity of manner which tempted the morose or thoughtful to be cheerful, or that benevolence of aspect which suffered no one to turn from you without an emotion of gratitude.

Permit, Madam, one who has shared his due proportion of your attentions, to make you a tender sincere tender of the most heartfelt gratitude and respect and to wish that you may long enjoy every blessing that heaven dispenses to the meritorious.

Do me the favor to tender to Mr Madison also, a most respectful Adieu and a cordial and sincerely friendly one to your Son.

Very respectfully,

William Johnson, Jr.

[*Four lines with missing words due to a tear in the right side*]

When the eight years of chief magistracy had expired and the helm of *the United States* was no longer under the guidance of M^r: Madison—the citizens of the [*page torn*] cities seemed as if they could not sufficiently [*page torn*] his beloved wife; balls public and private [*page torn*] given; one in George Town out shone all others, the walls were covered with transparencies, [MC: Paintings and verses] executed on white velvet and most richly framed These were sent to Montpelier and ever afterwards hung in a favorite room of M^r: Madison's, constant and happy reminders of by gone days.— Poetry, prose and gifts were also showered upon them.

At that time Montpelier contained 2500 acres. The range of mountains with which it is surrounded, are called the the Blue Ridge, belonging to the Apalachian. They extend as far as the eye can reach, forming successions of landscapes varied at every turn, from the wildest to the most cultivated, immense waving fields of grain, tobacco &c. [MC: in sight] the mountains cultivated, tho' so many miles distant, shewing distinctly the residences—which were often explored with the Telescope, which was part of the portico furniture, and used to spy the road where carriages and large parties were seen almost daily winding their way from afar to this harbor of hospitality, to stay as long as they could, sometimes for days, sometimes for months—none ever left without regret! Situated on the route to the far famed Virginia Springs, strangers, enquiring for the novelties of the neighborhood, were told at Orange Court House [MC: that] they were only five miles from Ex president Madison's. The punctilious Northerner, often hesitated about the propriety of "intruding," but the cordial welcome they would receive and the inducements offered for the prolonging their visit, assured them of the pleasure it gave the inmates of that household to gratify the wishes of others— We have visited many of the finest residences in our country and been most hospitably entertained, still the heart lingers on its first acquaintance with the beautiful and good at Montpelier— we have been asked to describe it. After doing so, [MC: we] have looked around at the elaborately carved oak work; the highly polished and tapestried walls, high ceilings and luxurious appertenances of the present elegant homes in our country, then, suddenly struck with their greater beauty have wondered wherein was the difference! May we not think that the *inmates* shed the peculiar charm over the whole?— An able pen, describing Montpelier says "there were few houses in Virginia that gave a larger welcome, or made it more agreeable, than that over which Queen Dolley—the most gracious and beloved of all our female soverigns reigned; and, wielding as

Montpelier, engraving from *Homes of American Statesmen* (New York: Alfred W. Upham, 1860), p. 181.

skillfully the domestic, as she had done worthily and popularly the public sceptre, every thing that came beneath her immediate and personal sway, the care and the entertainment of visitors, the government of the menials, the whole policy of the interior—was admirably managed, with an equal grace and efficacy."

July 5th 1820

I have just received yours, my dear sister, and rejoice that you are all well and that your friends are about you

Yesterday we had twenty persons ninety persons to dine with us at one table—fixed on the lawn, under a thick arbour. The dinner was profuse and handsome—and the company very orderly. Many of your old acquaintances—among them the two Barbours— We had no ladies except mother Madison M$^{rs:}$ Macon and Nelly Willis the day was cool and all pleasant—half a dozen only staid all night, and are now about to depart.— Co^l. Monroe's letter this morning announces the French Minister, we expect him this evening or perhaps sooner, tho' he may not come until tomorrow, but I am less worried here with a hundred visitors than with twenty five in Washington this summer especially— I wish you had just such a country home as this—as I truly believe it is the happiest and most independent life, and would be [*page torn*] for your children.

Your devoted sister
D.P. Madison

It was necessary again to enlarge the beautiful mansion at Montpelier, embedded in its mountains!— M^r: Madison senior died soon after M^r: Jefferson's election to the presidency, and as his eldest son [MC: Ambrose] was dead, James, succeeded to the homestead and adjacent broad acres. His mother still lived and retaining the use of all the original part of the house, (until her death) kept up the ancient style, and the use of the servants, who had grown old in her service, One, "Old Sawney" (the very picture of Time with his scythe) waited upon his mistress at 90; to be sure he went to sleep [MC: in] handing a glass of water, almost his only duty.

He had his house and ground, where he raised his favorite vegetables, cabbages and sweet potatoes—as well as chickens and eggs to be sold to "Miss Dolley" as M$^{rs:}$ Madison was called by the old lady's servants.

General de La Fayette[46] when he visited Montpelier in 1825, said one of the most interesting sights he had witnessed in America was when he visited the log cabin of Granny Milly, 104 years of age, whose daughter and granddaughter, the youngest nearly 70 were and [MC: were] all too old [MC: at rest retired] from their labors, were [MC: and] living happily [MC: together]; their patch of ground cultivated for them; their food and raiment supplied by "Mass Jimmy and Miss Dolley." Their residence in "the Walnut Grove" was a pleasant walk and an object of interest to M$^{rs:}$ Madison's [MC: young] relatives, who would save part of their luxurious breakfast and to take, themselves to those good old people, and return with the gift of a potato or fresh egg— and Sometimes, an old chest, would be rummaged

46. Marie-Joseph Paul Yves Roch Gilbert du Motier, Marquis de La Fayette (1757–1834), often known simply as Lafayette, was a French aristocrat and military officer. He was a general in the American Revolutionary War

to shew them the only treasure of Granny Milly, which was an old worn French copy of Telemachus[47]—which had been given her as a keepsake by the wife of the gardener Bezée. None but an eye witness can know of the peace and ease of these sable sons of toil! to retire with health and not a care for the morrow and surrounded by their progeny, on those planta- tions which remain in the same family over a century! Death of the master *occasionally* but only occasionally, changes the scene for the young!—but rare, indeed, is the instance of a Virginian, purchasing the estate, objecting to the incumbrance of superannuated slaves, who love their homes, from which, in many cases they have never been five miles— No, they stay with their indulgences, happy and free, until death leaves the log cabin [MC: vacant] free for other occupants!

Mrs "The old lady" as she was usually called, returned the primitive hours of her childhood as well as furniture

No, they stay with their indulgences, happy, because contented, until death leaves the log cabin free for other occupants!

That region of Virginia is particularly healthful and seemed to be very beneficial to the native Africans, of whom, there were several over one hun- dred [MC: years of age] on the plantation.

M^rs: Madison Senior—or "the old lady" as she was usually called kept up the primitive hours for meals to which she had been accustomed, and her time for receiving visits from the guests of her son was after her dinner and before his.

M^r: Madison honored and loved his mother; his house was the resort of the distinguished men of the time; foreigners, tourists, artists and writers failed not to visit himself and Mr Jefferson and they esteemed it a privi- lege to be taken at two o'clock, her audience hour, from the pictured hall and mirrored walls, to the old time wainscoted and closseted rooms of this most excellent woman!— she was proud of her son who had never given her a moments anxiety, save for his health, during a long life.

She was a lady of excellent education—strong mind and good judg- ment, active and well to her last moments; she took an interest in [. . .] modern events, as well as people the many friends whom by whom she was surrounded; the love and admiration she bestowed on her daughter in law, who studied her comfort, was ever apparent. She lived to be ninety

47. A figure in Greek mythology, he was the son of Odysseus and Penelope, and a central character in Homer's *Odyssey*.

eight; her usual seat was on a couch in the centre of a large room, a table in front, on which was her bible, prayer book and knitting; these divided her time—the gloves and stockings, with the name knit in [MC: (by her)] were precious gifts to her grandchildren— Our earliest recollection is seeing Madame de Neuville[48] (wife of the French Minister) sitting near this [MC: old Lady] talking of the French Revolution and darning a Camel's hair shawl, in which we could see no beauty—but which, she said, was very handsome.

The Montpelier Mansion had a very large and wide portico supported by pillars in front of the house, and here, Mr Madison always exercised in stormy weather, walking his allotted number of miles, In the centre of the gravel walk to the gate, was a, [MC: large] tin cup, which had been there for years; after every rain it was brought to him to measure the quantity which had fallen. On the right hand a short walk from the house was a beautiful temple, surmounted by a structure of Liberty; it was built over the icehouse which made it very cool; close to it was an immense mulberry tree, this building was intended, but never used, for his study; rows of well grown silver pine led to it from the house, a loud echo also lent its charm to the place. On the left were clumps of rare trees of which the weeping willow and the silver poplar predominated; these concealed the out buildings so necessary to such an establishment. Behind the house was another portico, not so large as the one in front; from this you stepped down on an extensive lawn, bounded by ha ha. Beyond, prominent among others, were two tulip trees, so much alike that Mr Madison called them his "twins"; they are still standing in fields rendered useless by a present of the seed of the Tiger lilly; they were sent [MC: from France] by Genl. de la Fayette, with other esteemed flowers, and spread so rapidly that Mr Madison found it impossible to uproot them—among the "other esteemed flowers" was the common thistle which, grows too luxuriously by our road sides, it was marked, very rare, and raised with care until it proved so unpopular a flower!

Mr Madison was fond of Horticulture, and had many fine specimen on the lawn, among them, the pride of China, which its odoriferous and beautiful lilac blossoms, the Osage Orange, and all the forest trees at its boundary.

At some distance from the house was the garden laid off in the shape of

48. Anne-Marguérite-Henriette Rouillé de Marigny Hyde de Neuville (1729–1849) was the wife of Jean Guillaume Hyde de Neuville, French minister to the United States.

a horse shoe by an experienced French gardener, who lived many years on the place; his name was Beazee; he and his wife came to Virginia at the time of the French Revolution and left Mr Madison's shortly before his death to return to "La belle France." They were great favorites with the negroes, some of whom they taught to speak french— Madame contrived a hat to shade Mrs Madison's eyes; it was hideous, but she liked it and when she took her morning rambles always called for her "Beazee bonnet."

The choicest fruits, especially pears, were raised in abundance, figs bore their two crops every summer, which Mr Madison liked to gather himself; arbors of grapes, over which he exercised the same authority. It was a paradise of roses and other flowers, to say nothing of the strawberries, and vegetables; every rare plant and fruit was sent to him by his admiring friends, who knew his taste, and [MC: they were] carefully studied and reared by his black the gardener and his black aids. The "old lady" had her separate garden and gardener, and allowed no innovation on the primitive style.

The pillars of this South portico were twined with ever blooming roses and white Jessamine, which reached up to the terraces, and were sweet welcomers to the stranger, whose early morning impulse was to open their chamber doors glass doors and walk out for the pure mountain breeze and Italian Scenery! Mrs Madison brought the sweet briar also near; these were the only flowers, allowed to approach the house, except green house plants; among them we must notice a superb Cape Jessamine; each bud as it appeared bore the name of those she loved most, and each morning she would examine them nay, more frequently, she would examine them, and it was almost distressing, should a favored one die without maturing! her husband, son and sisters were always first named, then came her guests and favorite friends.

She had one pet brought with her from Washington, a large Macaw—it was a splendid bird and seemed happy and proud when it spread its wings and screamed out its French phrases, which it had been taught by John Sioussa— It was very fond of M^r and Mrs Madison, but the terror of visitors. "Polly is coming!" was the mode of frightening the children of the household as some of those now grown little ones [MC: now grown] can tell! Her career She was very old, [MC: and] her career was recently brought to an end by a night hawk, which pounced upon her, when, one night by the carelessness of servants, she was not brought to her perch in the hall.

The cattle were all of the finest breed, Mr Madison raised the Angola Sheep, so famous for their wool—the pet Durhams were allowed to come near the house—also, his favorite horse, "Liberty" which had grown old in his service, was petted, fed and stalled alone; he well deserved his name; not a gate which he could not open—nor, any outrage which cattle could commit was not, by the negroes, ascribed to "Liberty" Mᵣ Madison, in his humorous way, often repeated these amusing and generally false tales of his disused horse, but never curtailed his freedom.

The drawing rooms was covered with Persian carpet, the walls entirely covered with mirrors and pictures [MC: among the latter were] many by Stuart, Washington, Jefferson, Adams, [*Erasure*] himself and Mrs Madison [MC: by that renowned artist] the Declaration of Independence, and some of its signers, *were* conspicuous. Statuary, beautifully chisseled occupied the mantel. Mᵣ Madison's favorite seat, was in a campeachy chair, the sofas were covered with crimson damask—three glass doors, opening in the centre on the back portico, displayed the entwined pillars and lovely lawn

The halls and passages waxed and highly polished; one, connecting the "old lady's" apartments with the elegant ones of her son, was hung entirely with oil paintings, generally from the ancient masters; choice engravings every where else—the walls of the large dining room were also covered with pictures, all of interest, having some history attached to each; a large Napoleon in his ermine robes, Louis the fourteenth, Confucious, the Chinese Philosopher, an African king, an occasional portrait of some favorite servant by a good artist—a painting in water colors of Mᵣ Jefferson by his enthusiastic admirer and *lover* Kosiousco, views of Constantinople and Sᵗ Petersburg, framed medalions, testimonials of respect and admiration from crowned heads and simple citizens, a large, long and wide well polished mahogany table, with [MC: and] the sideboard borne down with silver, the accumulation of three families, are well remembered.

Adjoining the dining room was Mᵣ Madison's sitting room, it was furnished with chairs and bedstead* of iron, high posts and heavy canopy of crimson damask—bought by Mᵣ Monroe, when special agent (or Mᵣ G. Morris) from the dismantled palace of the Thuleries—also many pieces of china which belonged to the ill fated Marie Antoinette; here, were hung the trophies from the George Town ball beside mirrors and pictures; an arm chair and desk completed the furniture of the room. The last few years of his life, his fingers were so affected by rhumatism that here he dined at his small table, near the door [MC: in this room] (having his dinner cut for

---

* This is now in possession of his nephew Mᵣ J. Hancock Lee of Orange Cy. Va

him) placed near sufficiently near the door of the dining room for him to converse with his guests.

The statuary filled [MC: a room, which] that went by the name of "clock room" out of respect to an old fashioned English Clock which for years had regulated the establishment and still actively performs its duty in his nephews house, relieved [MC: by its removal] from the task of ticking, year in and year out, to the marble ears of Jefferson, Washington, Jefferson, Adams, Paul Jones, the Emperor Alexander and his Empress. La Fayette, Baldwin, Barlow, Gallatin, Clay &c besides Guido's Hours, Cupids, and Psyches—and what M^{rs:} Madison valued most, a profile of M^{r:} Madison in marble, one of the most successful efforts of Carracci, who lost his life in prison because he designed the [MC: machine] Infernal.

We must not dwell too long on these familiar scenes, but mount the carved staircase in "the old lady's" part of the household, and enter the library; plain cases, not only round the room, but in the middle with just sufficient room to pass between, these cases were well filled with books, pamphlets, papers, all, every thing of interest to our country before and since the Revolution, this is no exaggeration; we much recollect the wealth and literary taste of father and son; in addition was the celebrated library of Lord Dunmore, purchased by the elder Madison—what became of this valuable collection?— M^{r:} Madison willed to his wife 300 volumes, to be by her selected, then to the University of Virginia (of which he was Proctor) the residue, of which it had not editions—since M^{rs:} Madison's death the University claim the remainder, saying that their editions are more modern consequently, not the same; the creditors of her son also claim them, so they, much dwindled away, were recently removed to a room in the Court House at Orange Cy. Va, still disputed property.

M^{r:} Madison altho' no sectarian, was a religious man, as may be seen throughout his career in life. He attended the Epi

M^{r:} Madison, tho' no Sectarian had that religion of the Bible and of the heart, so visible throughout his career in life. When possible, he attended the Episcopal Church; The nearest to his residence, was at Orange C. Va. five miles distant, and the county roads of Virginia need no description!

Camp meetings were always well attended by the first families, where they went with their families servants for days and sometimes as long as they lasted. The young always anticipated especial pleasure, nor did the elders enjoy the social intercourse less, with neighbors some of whom they had not seen since the last "meeting"

M^rs: Madison soon fell in to the Country customs. Barbacues were then at their height of popularity. To see the sumptuous board spread under the forest oaks, the growth of centuries, animals roasted whole, everything that a luxurious country could produce, wines, and the well filled punch bowl, to say nothing of the invigorating mountain air, was enough to fill the heart of an anchorite with joy! A friend and neighbor of M^r: Madison's, who has passed eighty *summers,* not winters, is still hale and hearty, and keeps up the old custom of having the bowl passed from lip to lip by his guests before the announcement of dinner! At these feasts the woods were alive with guests carriages, horses, servants and children—for all went— often more than a hundred guests. All happy at the prospect of a meeting, which was one a [MC: scene] of pleasure and hilarity. The laugh with hearty good will, the jest, after the crops, "farmer's topics" and politics had been discussed. If not too late, these meetings were terminated by a dance, as there were generally some violins taken by their merry owners, and good musicians were these "Uncle Tom's" and "Uncle Sam's." The Negroes, like the birds of their woods, have their sweet wild notes, filled with melody— but their songs and dances need no encomium! The guests regulated their departure by the number of miles they were from home, allowing themselves just sufficient time to jog back before dark, and the slaves animated by the sight of the enjoyment of their masters and mistresses, of whose feast they have partaken, when their duties are over, assemble in the largest cabin, call in house servants and field hands, tune up the violin and make the plantation resound, until morning, with their gaiety and mirth. These customs have not yet left Virginia entirely left Virginia. [*Two lines of cancelled text, illegible*]

A Virginia Custom, perhaps not peculiar to that State, was to build up in the wall wine to ripen with age. M^r: Madison Senior did not forget this and his son after the death of his mother reaped the benefit of his forethought; he also, had wine his wine put away in the pediment of the portico, this until his death on his retirement from public life until his death was favored above all new importations, and will doubtless be remembered by many [MC: for whom] he brought it forth and always called it his "Batchelor Wine." He also had his "Washington Wine," [MC: imported] with the General's. Medeira was his favorite produce of the grape, his sense of taste was very keen. Governor Coles, tells us that one evening, returning from the theatre [MC: in Washington] with a party, the careless driver caused the carriage to upset, they walked home with M^r: Hamilton Secretary of

War, he prevailed upon them to go in, and produced wine, which Mr Madison said recognized, saying, "this must be from the brand brought to Norfolk of a certain vintage," he knew its flavor, as he had some of the same importation. Mr Hamilton who was very polite and courteous, thought he was mistaken as he had bought it in Baltimore— Mr Madison took another glass and said, "No, I am not mistaken, this was the same importation as mine" Mr Hamilton smiled and gave up the point, afterwards as a matter of curiosity he wrote to his merchant in Baltimore and found that he had purchased in Baltimore Norfolk, and Mr Madison was right.

As the plantation was large, the neighbors were not very numerous, Governor Barbour of Barboursville, Judge P.P. Barbour of Frascatti, the M^r and Mrs Howard, Mrs Dr Willis, his neice and the daughter of Ambrose Madison his two sisters Mrs Macon and Mrs Conway [MC: also] Mr W. C. Rives 15 miles distant and even Mr Jefferson—whose distance was thirty miles, was considered a neighbour, though the roads bad enough now, were then [   ] almost impassable; for this they seemed to care little. With their coach and four, skilful driver and outriders, to hold it up should there [MC: be any danger of it falling] they would journey from five to thirty miles to dinner, beginning the day before, if necessary.

Mr Madison dearly loved and was proud of his wife, the ornament of his house—she was his solace and comfort, he could not bear her to leave his presence, and she gratified him by being absent only when duty required. No matter how agreeably employed he was her first thought, and instinct seemed to tell her when she was wanted—if engaged in conversation, she would quickly rise and say "I must go to Madison." On his return from riding round the plantation she would meet him at the door with refreshment in her own hands.

Mr G. W. Featherstonhaugh who was an [MC: accomplished] English gentleman who wrote a geological survey of our Western Country—made many visits to Montpelier, charmed with its inmates. This letter, was in 1832 when he wrote in the album of her neice the following lines, which we believe were never published.

Mr G. W. Featherstonhaugh[49] a friend of Mr Madison's and an accomplished English gentleman made him several visits; during his last he

49. George William Featherstonhaugh (1780–1866) was a British geologist and geographer who initiated the Albany and Schenectady Railroad and was a surveyor of the Louisiana Purchase for the U.S. Government.

wrote the following lines which he gave to M^rs: Madison's neice—we believe they were never published. M^r: Featherstonhaugh, is a [MC: as well as a] distinguished Geologist!

MONTPELIER[50]

"Here! at this gate, the swelling Sylvan range,
The stately mansion, with its pictured halls,
I'll bid adieu. Perhaps this is the last
Of all this excellence, that life may lend me time
Me time to look upon. Here let me stand
And look, and say, even from my inmost heart,
Peace be within these walls! the peace of heaven,
May it forever reign within your breasts,
Ye gentle inmates of that honored roof.
Never two purer hearts, amid the lands
And varying climes I've known, have I observed.
Thrice blessed and honored they, whom even age
Adorns, with brighter excellence; in whom
Fidelity, mutual respect, and love,
And mutual tenderness unite. Behold
That noble dame—see her gracious bearing—
The cordial welcome to her numerous friends
Observe her Zeal; her hospitable cares.
But mark the keen solicitude, the thought,
Constant ever to him, there, where he lies,
Alive in an immortal Spirit, though
The lofty cares of more than fourscore years,
His sinews have unstrung, each day she lives
But for to watch over his precious life.
Soft is the Pillow from her careful hand.
Never was man more blessed in such a wife,
Never was wife more honored in her mate.
Hail Madison! among the living sons
Peerless, of fair Virginia's golden soil

50. Montpelier Research Database, #23424, Montpelier Foundation. The transcription team thanks Michael Quinn, Director, and Lynne Dakin Hastings, Vice President for Museum Programs, both of James Madison's Montpelier, for permission to use this transcription.

Of all its generous children first art thou,
Save for the memory of him, whose name
Shines above all men's names: in whom the love
of Country and of Virtue far surpassed,
The love of life. He, whose glorious days, men
Where Christendom extends, by one consent,
Have hailed the type of human Excellence:
A glass for men to look in, when they need
To curb the wild ambition, that weak minds,
Leads oft astray, and makes historic names,
The curse and Shame of human annals, when,
They might be Gems like that of Washington.
His great example was not lost on thee,
Whose life has passed in loyalty to truth.
The tree of Liberty, planted by him,
Well hast thou nurtured! Now, its spreading boughs
Give shade to all: and thou shalt be revered
Whilst time shall last, forever shall our sons,
Raise in this land the honored names,
Of Washington and Madison—the types
Of human wisdom—patriot probity,
Blest be thy future days, long mays't thou live,
To love thy friends; to know how much thou art loved,
Long may the wisdom of [MC: all] ages past,
Oft from thy gentle lips and hallowed heart,
Be poured into the listening ears of men,
As mine have drank it in:—and when thy sun,
Declines at length into the golden West,
To rise refulgent to a brighter day,
May the immortal mind Still turn to God
Bearing thee onward in thy Course to heaven."

> September 1832.
>
> G. W. Featherstonhaugh.

When M$^{rs:}$ Madison left Washington in [MC: April] 1817—her sister M$^{rs:}$ Cutts had become a resident of that city; a daily correspondence was kept up by the two sisters. After the death of the latter in 1832 her letters were reclaimed by M$^{rs:}$ Madison requested her neices to return letters which were strictly confidential between these united relatives her wishes were complied with, a few letters addressed to them (whom she called her adopted children) will shew her private character, in very few cases can we give whole letters, as they also were confidential and most of the persons mentioned still living, but there is a good advice prevailing the whole, which emanating so truly from one who so eminently possessed the secret of "success in life," which deserves to be remembered.

Friday 16th. September
Feby 2d:.

My sweet Mary, [LC: Doubtful]
My dear Dolley,
I hasten to answer your kind letter in or

The poetry on the company of Mrs: Adams was excellent and I am glad to find you have a good taste, but above all I rejoice to hear through my correspondants, that you were a good nurse and devoted to your dear sick mother— Yes, I love you and Mary a thousand times more, if possible, than I ever did, since I hear you are dutiful daughters— Continue to write me about her when you can spare the time from her side (which I do not wish you ever to leave). Give my love to dear Thomas and tell him to write, when Mary and you are engaged. Kiss my sweet Dick for me, but Mary first on my account. I feel very grateful to all those ladies who are so kind to your mother and could love the blackest *Indian* who was kind to her! indeed I feel as if I could bribe the whole world to make her well!

Adieu my own sweet girls   D.P.M.

Take care of all my letters to your mother until she is able to read them, hide them from every eye under lock and key

Montpelier 16th September [LC: 1831?]
My sweet Mary

I hasten to answer your kind letter, in order that I may the better obtain your forgiveness in the case of having mislaid your letter to Louisa! I can neither find nor trace it, after much search and I think it has been put into the fire by Miss Becky whose hurry to kindle a little fire for her master, made her collect every thing like paper on or about my table this rainy morning. It was a short letter and I hope you will recollect enough of it to write over and add more, for your amiable correspondant, to whom give my assurance of love. I am grieved that your Mamma is unwell, but trust it proceeds from fatigue, do persuade her to go to Mrs: Bomford, and not to worry herself with household or any business. I hope the bustle and alarm of *Insurrections* are over in the city—tho' I hope all will be on guard ever after this. I am quiet, knowing little about it and that I cannot help myself if, I am in danger. I beleive there is none at present.

Tell M^r: Trist I send *him* a few letters leaves [MC: from the Cape Jasmine] if not the whole flower of his dear lady who is now blooming, when all her contemporaries have changed color and are passing along! emblematic of her good heart and disposition, whose fragrance will last until the end! You will find enclosed a leaf from each of the flowers name—as follows, Monsieur and Madame Serurier and two sons, M^rs: Cutts and M^rs: Madison—the bride and groom Lear, M^rs: Lear, Dolley and yourself with M^rs: Trist's.

Your uncle Madison still wears the bead ring you placed on his finger, I see him look at it every now and then— My eyes are very weak, still I am writing you a deal of nonsense. I have notes that tomorrow will bring with it, to me, a large party from Richmond and the lower country, Mayos &c Payne is on the wing to his mine with three gentlemen in his train.

Adieu! ever yours, D. P. Madison

From M^rs: Madison to D.P.M. Cutts.
My dear Dolley,

December

I have been for the last three or four days the most disconsolate person you can imagine—with a violent tooth ache else, I should have returned the book and a thousand thanks for your agreeable letter and handsome gloves, which fit me to a charm.

I will keep the book, unless you prevent [LC: forbid] me, until I read the second volume; yet to come and send them both by Walter—who is summoned to Philadelphia on the 1st Monday in January and who will leave us in time for Washington in time to attend the Court Martial. The little anecdote you tell about the Roux's has, I confess, added to my curiosity. In my last I informed you that Walter and Payne had been detained abroad by bad weather, but now they are safe and sound with us—we have played chess, read and talked together all this time without even the appearance of ennui. Thank my dear Marey for her kind note, I rejoice in her recovery, for which I know she is indebted in a great measure to the judicious nursing of a good mother.

I expect Madame Serurier has been very kind in her sickness as she seemed to love her while here. I hope you will soon be at the parties and will give me a detail of what is going upward, amidst the various characters in Washington. I have long been confined by the side of my sick husband and never see or hear interesting subjects except him, and should therefore be a dull correspondent. Your Uncle is better now than he was a few days ago and I trust will continue to mend; his hands and fingers are still so swelled and sore as to be nearly useless, but I lend him mine. The music box is now playing near me, it seems adapted to solitude rather than a city where variety reigns. Our mountains are white with snow, the winter's wind is loud and chilling—I hope you will take more than usual care of yourselves this winter, I wish I could cover you with furs, but, if I dared to indulge in wishes! Good night love

Yours ever DP.M.

To DPM Cutts

Montpelier 10th March 1830

I am now seated pen in hand to write you, my sweet girl, tho' in my very bad humor for the success I desire, in producing an amusing letter—such should mine be, in answer to your short, tho' kind one.

Imagine if you can, a greater trial of patience than seeing the destruction of a radiant patch of green peas, by frost! It came last night on the skirts of a storm, and while I was lamenting that our dear midshipman, should ever be exposed in such a wailing winds, my young adventurers were wrecked off their moorings! but away with complaints, other patches will arise, and I will mourn no longer, over a mess of peas or of pottage, but would rather meet you at the next party, where I hope you intend to go—or, if you espy me not, by the side of your favorite, be assured I am unavoidably detained at home, from whence I shall breathe many wishes for your happiness there, and wherever else you go. I had indeed, my "quantum sufficit" of gaiety in Richmond, but what I enjoyed most was the quiet hospitality of the inhabitants, among whom I should like to spend my winters. In Washington I had most [LC: old] acquaintances and if they were now as they used to be in those times, my old partialities would still be felt. But I confess I do not admire the contention of parties, political or civil, tho' in my quiet retreat I am anxious to know all the maneuverings of both, the one and the other, so, be not timid in laying their claims before me, no one shall see statements but myself. I hope you became acquainted with Miss Preston, she is very large of her age, and a most amiable woman, should her father and herself be in town still in the city, present them my best love. I wish that circumstances would have permitted you to have accepted M^{r:}

V. B's invitation, but I cannot doubt that you had good reasons for declining. You know that I saw him and his sons in Richmond. By the bye—do you never get hold of a clever novel, new or old that you could lend me? I bought Couper's last, but did not like it, because the story was too full of horrors.

Adieu! my precious D. think of me as your own friend and Aunt, and write often as you can.

Montpelier Novr 1830

My dear Dolley, [LC: doubtful Mary]

I have been so much engaged in the book you so kindly sent by the last post, that I have scarcely left myself time to thank you for it by this. I will however take an early opportunity to shew my gratitude by a longer letter. If you can send me the Romance of History, I shall be very glad and will make proper dispatch in the perusal. Govr: Barbour is here, he will stay some months away, we have seen the P.P. Barbours here and at their own house lately, Phillippa does not expect to see Washington again soon and regrets it, her father is now a recluse Judge and she a recluse. I find you have no idea yet, of the improvements love can make, or you would not surmise that another, must have courted for John. When he became acquainted with S. Carter his tongue twanged as if sent from a bow! Last winter when I witnessed his attention to her and heard him talk and laugh like a Ganymede, I knew it was Cupid's act by the color! She is a sweet girl and I hope you will see her before here, before long. you and my own dear Mary!

Ever your affectionate Aunt D.P.M.

Montpelier 5th January 1831

My dear Mary,

Yours ending on the 2^d of January came to relieve my oppressed heart with the tidings of your beloved mother's recovery, from that extreme illness under which I knew or feared she was laboring. I had written a week ago, this day, to D and one to you, enclosed to your father, which, I fear you have not received or you would have told me so—and you would have yielded to my pleadings for that single line by every post, which would tell me your mamma is better, and has a prospect of entire health. To secure this, my dear girls, you must keep her room quiet and herself from the slightest agitation or uneasings—that nervousness of which D^r: Sim speaks, must be attended to with all your delicacy of thought and conduct—her sufferings have caused it, now, let no one approach her, who is not sensible of the importance of smiles and comfort to one who had been so near the grave! May heaven sustain and support her long, to bless you both with her protecting love! "the Oxonians" are enclosed; I could not read while my heart was oppressed with fears for you, you will speak of their safety.

All here are well—Adieu, your own Aunt.

To M^rs: R. Cutts

Montpelier August 2^d 1832

Beloved Sister,

M^rs: Mason has just written me to say you are a little better. Your precious daughters whom I shall ever consider and feel are my own children, have often consoled me by their letters, since you were unable to write. Your husband and sons have also written, in all that affectionate feeling towards you which manifested their deep feeling towards sense of your value to them and to me! and altho' my heart is sad within me because I cannot see or assist you, in your long and painful sickness, yet am I thankful to the Almighty for his favors, in bestowing on you such estimable able friends as now surround your pillow!

My dear husband I hope is recovering, tho' slowly being still confined to his bed. He speaks of you every day to me with me, every day with all the partiality and love of a tender brother, and ardently hopes that we may be long spared to each other!

M^rs: Clay did not call to see me with her husband, they understood on the road that General Jackson was at Montpelier, and passed on to Govr: Barbour's. The next day M^r: Clay came for a few hours. The President's visit having been short, they did not meet here. I regretted much not seeing M^rs: Clay, for she would have talked to me of you.

My dear Dolley, Mary, Richard Madison and Richard, as soon as my mind is more calm I will write to each of you. to those amiable friends also, M^rs: B and M^rs: Mason whose goodness can never been forgotten by your own and ever affectionate Aunt DP. Madison

To M^rs: R. Cutts

Yours, beloved sister, came last night, the account of your great and many sufferings fall heavily on my heart! but I will hope the last attack was the crisis of your disorder and that good spirits and a quiet mind will soon restore you to us. I am sure the kindness of your many friends will prove as it ought to do, a charm and cordial against vexations which otherwise might have an influence on your health—Strive to be happy and well, my dear sister, for my sake and for your childrens! What should we do without you! As soon as my eyes are well I will write to dear M^{rs:} Bomford, in the mean time offer her my love and thanks for all her goodness to you. My husband is not as well as he was two [*page torn*] confined to his bed. I will write and tell [*page torn*]— M^{r:} Madison sends you his affectionate [*page torn*] best hopes that you are getting well.

Adieu my dear ever and always
Your sister D.

The sufferings of this beloved one terminated a few short day[MC: s] after the date of the two last letters, and her daughters just as they were entering into womanhood lost a "*good* mother"! those who have not yet met with this greatest of all berievements will ~~forgive~~ skip the coming lines, those who have will sympathize with us in a slight tribute to the memory of "the *good* mother," who would have parted from her heart's best blood for the happiness of her offspring! one who from the height of worldly prosperity and the brightest prospects was reduced, by the continued losses of her husband to a small income, and while he gazed on, his energies paralyzed by what seemed an adverse fate and the decree of Providence—this "good mother" devoted herself to the interests of her children, she brought them up in the fear of the Lord; she implanted her own pure principles in their young hearts, she taught them to listen to "the still small voice within" as she had been taught by her own parents. Her daughters she would never allow to leave her for boarding school, tho' every inducement was offered— she had them taught her own favorite accomplishments, and instilled into their minds a taste for poetry, the clasics and her own love of the beautiful and true! [...]

To M^{r:} C. on the death of his wife.

Montpelier 6^{th:} August 1832

Dear brother—the heart of your miserable sister, mourns with you, with your precious daughters! and your sons with your sons!—Come to us as soon as you can, and bring them with you. I feel deeply interested in all that concerns my sister and her children—I wish to know her will and where you have deposited her remains!—I wish to present myself with gratitude and love to M^{rs:} Bomford, M^{rs:} Mason and to one and all of those excellent friends who have to the end extended their kindness and consolations to my lamented sister!

M^{r:} Madison partakes in our sorrows and in my wish to see you all here.

Shew this to Dolley and Mary, as, I cannot write to them as this moment. I received yours yesterday evening

Yours affectionately, D.P. Madison

M^{rs:} Madison to M^{r:} Clay[51]

Montpelier November 8th 1836

The continued and very severe affection on my eyes, not permitting, but with much difficulty, even the signature of my name, has deferred, dear friend, the acknowledgement due for your very kind and acceptable letter of August 18th. I should sooner have resorted for this purpose to the pen of an amanuensis, but that the failure of my general health combining equal, and sometimes greater suffering, rendered dictation very painful, and hope still flattered me that I might [LC: yet] use my own. So much time having elapsed with but little improvement in my situation, I can submit to no longer delay in offering this explanation of my silence, nor omit the expression of my deep sensibility to that pure and true sympathy which I am conscious I receive from such highly valued friends as M^{rs:} Clay and yourself.

The source of consolation in my bereavement which you suggest, are those which my heart can most truly appreciate. The reflected rays of his virtues still linger around me, and my mind now dwells with calmer feelings on their mellowed tints. He left me, too, a charge, dear and sacred, and deeply impressed with its value to his fame, and its usefulness to his country. The important trust sustained me under the heavy pressure of recent loss, and formed an oasis to the desert created in my feelings. In fulfillment of his wishes, I have therefore, devoted my self to the object of having prepared for the press the productions of his own pen. It will form the surest evidence of his claim to the gratitude of his country and the world. With the aid of my brother, who had prepared copies of the debates in the Revolutionary Congress and in the Convention, under M^{r:} Madison's eye, triplicates have been completed for publication here and abroad. My son went in July, as far as New York, and remained there for the purpose of negotiating with the most eminent publishers and I have had communication with those in other cities, but no offer has been made by any entitled to confidence, which would free me from heavy and incon-

---

51. This letter is "out of order" as regards the narration, but there is no place for it in the manuscript after James Madison's death. Its placement here is yet another scholarly guess.

venient pecuniary advances and the risks of impositions and eventual loss. Under these circumstances I have been advised by a friend to offer the work to the patronage of Congress, asking their aid so far as to relieve the work from the charges upon it, principally for literary and other benevolent purposes, and, after their use by Congress, to give me the stereotype plates. This would at once allow me to throw them into general circulation on a scale that would remunerate me more in accordance with the expectations entertained by the author, and would also allow the price to be so graduated as to ensure their general diffusion.

As this plan was suggested by one favorable to the Administration, he advised also that the channel of his friends, as the majority of those who were to decide on the proposition, should be employed in making it, and pledged their support. This work being a record only of what passed preceding the existence of present parties, cannot associate the name of Mr Madison with either, and therefore its introduction and advocacy by the one, can be no bar to the favor of the other. On your part, I am sure that, in my yielding to it this direction, you will perceive no deviation from the high respect and friendly regard I entertain toward yourself, but approving an adoption of this course as most conducive to success, you will, with your friends, insure it on the merits of the work alone, uninfluenced by adversary feeling toward the source from whence the measure originated.

It was my intention to have gone to Washington, principally with a view to obtain in personal conference the advice of my best friends, but my protracted ill health, and the approach of an inclement season I fear may prevent the journey.

In addition to the three volumes of the Debates (near six hundred pages each) now ready for the press, matter enough for another volume is expected, and nearly four hundred pages copied, of writings and letters on Constitutional subjects, considerable selections have also been made from his early correspondence, which may form a volume on the legislative proceedings of Virginia, and historical letters of the period from 1780 up to the commencement of the new Government. His Congressional and Executive career may furnish two more. His writings already in print, as "Political Observations," a pamphlet in 1795, "Examinations of the British Doctrine," [&]c, it is thought should be embodied with his other works for more permanent preservation.

It is important that these manuscripts should be prepared and committed to the press as early as they can follow the Debates, and the success of the latter will much facilitate the publication of the former, even if

Congress should decline a like patronage to them, a mode which would be much preferred.

The near approach of the time which will call you to your Senatorial duties rendering it uncertain whether this would reach you ere your departure from home, I deem it safest to address it to Washington, whence I hope, on your safe arrival, you will favor me with an acknowledgement of its receipt and any suggestions your friendship may offer.

Accept for Mʳˢ: Clay and yourself my affectionate respects.

Mʳ: Madison's height was five feet, six inches, and he appeared [MC: even?] shorter in contrast with Mʳˢ: Madison—his figure was slight, his face wrinkled and tanned, [MC: to us when he retired to Montpelier] he looked as if he never had been young, so thoughtful was his brow! After leaving Washington he never altered the style of his dress, which was always black cloth, with shorts, knee and shoe buckles, his hair powdered and a small queue behind, the [MC: daily] task of dressing it devolved on Mʳˢ: Madison, she being the only hair [dresser?] to whom she would trust it—A dear lover of fun, and children, whose follies amused him beyond measure, and they, child like, reciprocated this affection with interest. Among the many anecdotes which enlivened his conversation their originalities were often repeated with most zeal. Not unfrequently there was repetition, but his guests, when they watched the play of his countenance, the transition from brilliant mirth through to brilliant mirth found equal interest in that, as in his story. He was long sighted with one eye, and short sighted with the other, in consequence, he never shaved with a glass.

One of his nephews was on a regimen and not allowed to eat meat, his seat being near Mʳ: Madison, when he wished to give him the indulgence, his question was "well, R. if you can prove this meat is [MC: respectable?], you shall have some"— The ready answer was "Lambsquarter Sir!"

Mʳˢ: J. Q. Adams[52] speaking one day of Mʳ: Madison, said that once one occasion she was dining with him [MC: at his house when] he turned and asked her if she "knew the meaning of husband"? she said "no." He told her it meant Houseband, and laughed heartily at the conceit, which he found in Sir Charles Grandison—then, a favorite novel— Few, were as talented accomplished and witty as this Mʳˢ: Adams, a keen sense of the ridiculous tempered by extreme goodness of heart, when would make her pause

52. Louisa Catherine Johnson Adams (1775–1852), wife of John Quincy Adams, was First Lady of the United States from 1825 to 1829.

"Uncle" James Madison, painting by James Wood, 1817. (Virginia
Historical Society [1967.13])

abruptly in uttering a keen sally of wit or brilliant repartee, which might
give pain, but the merry twinkle of her eye was infectious, even were the
cause unknown.

From early childhood, Mr Madison was a profound student, hardly allowing himself sufficient sleep to sustain nature, this early habit, never forsook him. From four to five hours was his allotted time for bodily repose.
He was fond of being read to, and always read in bed, having his light and
book placed on a stand near him.

His diplomatic correspondences were remarkable for their clearness
and precision—in writing; he was choice in his use of words, never originat-
ing when doubtful, referring to some distinguished precedent from among
English authors. Lord Littleton was greatly admired by him, and often his

example [MC: model]. Every word, or expression he used had their true meaning [MC: definition]— Mʳ Jefferson was known to coin words, expressive of his meaning.

He was fond of puns, and often said "He could converse better lying", meaning—while resting on the couch, a repose needed by his feeble frame, and often indulged in when his friends came to sit with him and enjoy his conversation.

An anecdote characteristic of Mʳ Madison's timidity, caused by physical debility, is [MC: was] related of him by a contempo[MC: ra]ry, during the debates upon the adoption of the Federal Constitution. he [MC: He] was desirous of expressing his opinions—but feared becoming too much excited. However he requested a gentleman who was sitting near him to pull him by the coat should he become exhausted! He began his speech, every moment his voice became stronger, and his thoughts [MC: and language] flowed more rapidly—at last sinking into his seat from fatigue he said, "why, why did you not pull me, when you saw me going on as I did" "I would rather have laid my finger on the lightening" was the reply.

The only journey Mʳ Madison ever took from Montpellier, after leaving public life, was to the Convention for revising the Constitution of Virginia, which met in Richmond in 1829— Mʳˢ Madison accompanied him and enjoyed the hospitalities of that city so famed for its warmth of heart and gracious welcome to strangers— she writes to her brother the 15ᵗʰ January 1815

Richmond, January 15ᵗʰ 1830

"My dear brother, this day the Convention finished its session, and we propose to set off for home tomorrow, if the weather should permit. It now rains and blows and looks as if it would do so for two or three days more, yet we hope not and that we may be able to make some small distance tomorrow. This you ought to receive on Monday night, but it will not do to be sanguine, we can only hope for Tuesday."

Mʳ Madison made an annual visit to Monticello the University of Virginia, of which he was a visitor, he always staid at Monticello, the guest of Mʳ Jefferson— Mʳˢ Madison usually accompanied him.

Always a patriot and student, his tastes never forsook him, he was "au courant" with his country's interest and often her advisor—his leisure hours were employed in revising his writings—the notes and Debates in the Congress of the Confederation in 1782, 3, 4. Debates in 1776 on the

Declaration of Independence and also on the Federal Constitution Convention of 1787 &c—now, so invaluable; these it was his wish should be purchased by Congress, this desire was gratified— For many years of Mʳ⠀Madison's life he was a martyr to rheumatism, and for a few before his death could use his hands to write little more than his signature. Mʳ John Payne[53] acted as amanuensis and assisted him greatly in the arrangement of his papers. Mʳ William C: Rives his country neighbor and constant visitor, enjoyed his friendship and confidence and was also of much as also, lent his valuable aid to this distinguished man, whose mental powers, were never dimmed, tho' his body was cramped by desease.

The beauty of Mʳˢ Madison's character then shone forth, her devotion, and singleness of heart—her affection towards him, whom she delighted to honor! every letter she wrote at that time bore the mark of cheerfulness. for five years she never left the plantation to visit, nor his presence for more than an half hour, he was her sole thought! When summoned to his last account, he lingered several days and the physicians would have prolonged his life until the 4ᵗʰ of July—but he would not be unnecessarily stimulated—and died in the full possession of all his noble faculties, the 28ᵗʰ of June 1836 in the 86ᵗʰ year of his age, and [MC: being] the anniversary of the forming of the Constitution by himself! He was distinguished for a serenity of temper and under no circumstances, public or private did he ever speak evil of

An overruling Providence (which says, that a sparrow, the very least and most useless of birds, shall not fall to the ground without His knowlege, and who also says, there is no such thing as chance) watched over the flickering existence of this star, which had so long and so faithfully performed the duties which He had assigned to him during so lengthened a life! and what day could have been more glorious for H him to be translated than the one on which he had rendered such essential service to his Country, the anniversary of the framing of the Constitution! Politicians have said, that but for James Madison, we should have had none. His election to the Convention itself seemed accidental, he suddenly returned to his county on the eve of his election, He and converted two Baptist preachers, by his power of reasoning, the celebrated John Leland was one of them, and this carried him into the Convention.

Had the great work been postponed a few months longer, it would have been too late; the horrors of the French Revolution broke out, and its con-

53. John C. Payne (1782–?) was Dolley Madison's brother.

sequences were felt over the whole world! Two years afterwards an attempt was made to frame a new Constitution, which it required the united efforts of George Washington and James Madison to prevent, in which they succeeded by bravely sustaining the first, and engrafting [MC: upon it] such amendments, as public virtue and necessity required.

M⁗ Madison was distinguished for a serenity of temper and under no circumstances public or private, did he ever speak evil of any one, invariably cheerful, and watchful for the comfort of others, his patience was unbounded— Governor Coles tells us that when President, the deputations and delegates who came to him with advice and instructions were very numerous—to all of which he listened with the utmost attention. on one occasion Gov⁗ Coles remonstrated, M⁗ Madison said, "they have come from New Orleans, Boston or some other distant place, to advise me, surely I may give them my attention for one or two hours."

For an account of his burial we cannot equal the description given by his warm friend, admirer and neighbor Governor James Barbour who was present on the occasion, and afterward wrote his eulogium He says "Ma He was a devoted husband, a kind brother, a warm friend, a good neighbor and indulgent master. Many were at his funeral and must have seen his slaves decently clad attired in attendance, and their orderly deportment; the profound silence was now and then broken by their sobs—they attended the procession to the grave. There are none of us, I fear, who have not drank of the cup of affliction, heavily drugged by the untimely bereavement of a dear child or affectionate companion; such will but too well remember, that so long as the remains continued on earth, the tie that connected us seemed not entirely dissolved; but, while standing on the verge of the grave, and seeing the corpse deposited, and hearing the pious man give utterance to the fearful sentence 'dust to dust' whose fulfilment by some friendly hand flung back its hollow and mournful sound, how it pierced our souls; how we felt that the seperation was now final—that all was gone! At this part of the service it was not only the body servant, who was standing directly by me, that, by his sobs and sighs, showed how severely he felt his bereavement in the loss of a kind and indulgent master, but the hundred slaves gave vent to their lamentations in one violent burst that rent the air, methought it ascended to Heaven, and was heard with joy by the heavenly host, as a redeeming item in that great account, which he, in common with all the sons of Adam, had to meet. And I derived consolation at the moment from a belief, that if, in that great account, slight blemishes here and there, from the inexorable law of our nature, were to be found, this alone would, in the age of mercy, be sufficient to blot out the unfriendly character that bore the record of his infirmity, to be remembered no more.

"Scenes like this give us the true character. Most men in public seek so to act as to escape censure; but it is in the secrecy of private life, where there is no human eye to see, or seeing, no tongue dares to tell, that the heart stripped of all disguise, and indulging its propensities, appears to good or ill in its nakedness. Most happy must he have been over whose remains such testimony is furnished, that, in his public private as in his public life, all was well. What felicity had Madison in his unusually extended age; he had survived all the fathers of the Revolution as well as of the Constitution. To him, as was so happily expressed by the great Western orator to another illustrious patriot, now among the dead, to him was given the high privilege of standing amidst posterity, witnessing their unexampled prosperity, to which he had so largely contributed, and to hear his name daily associated by them with the benefactors of his kind."

Newspapers have copied or promulgated [MC: the error] that no one knew where was his grave. Where should it be but by the side of his father, mother, brothers and sisters and other relatives, in the old family burying ground surrounded by a brick wall, and shaded by his own loved forest trees, forever dead to the pomp of life! Tho' beautiful Montpelier has passed into other hands, this sacred spot has always been revered—should any one attempt to desecrate it, there are his *own relatives* and *neighbours*—with watchful eyes and jealous hearts, willing and able to defend the graves of their ancestors forefathers. Lieut: Genl Scott's only son also lies within the enclosure, having died in childhood at Montpelier.

His will had been made many years previous to his death, shortly before [MC: that event], however, he [MC: revisited it] revised it and added some codicils. His wife, the pride of his [   ] and honor of his [MC: old] age was left sole executrixe—and chief legatee with the exception of legacies to the amount of $21,000. to his nephews, neices, Princeton College [MC: the colonization society], &c &c to be paid out of the sale of "the Debates" &c to Congress, a small parcel of land to Mrs: Dr: Willis, daughter of his brother Ambrose, also a farm to John Payne, who had so ably assisted in copying and arranging the Debates his papers, public and private. Mr Madison requested that no inventory should be made of his estate— The servants were left without reservation to Mrs: Madison—he, expressing a wish that they should not be sold without their consent, except for misbehavior—

which wish, we have reason to believe was respected— Tho' these people numbered one hundred, many of them were superannuated, and more were useless children, which it required a large revenue to cloathe and support— Mr. Madison often complained of the want of money, and was heard to say, a few months before his death, it that he had been compelled at different times to sell portions of his estate to meet his expenses.

When at last this great bereavement, and seperation from Him, with whom she had lived so happily for forty years, came upon her Mrs. Madison, she did not dare give way to grief, but with Spartan courage collected her energies to carry out the views and wishes of her husband as soon as possible. Money was drawn from banks to prevent delay in paying the legacies. Some of Mr. Madison's, and her own nephew and neices were summoned to make a second copy of the Debates &c before their purchase by Congress. Mr. W. C. Rives and Governor Coles also aided with their friendly advice and assistance; hundreds, we might almost say thousands of resolutions and letters from the most near to the most remote portions of the Union poured in, for when the people knell of the death of the fourth President (Him whom they called "the Just") was heard, the people awoke to their loss and with American impulse sat down to offer consolation to his beloved partner! Mes. Gales [MC: and Seaton's][54] short notice was copied in two weeks into 800 of the 1000 newspapers of the country—fortunately for her, Congress [MC: soon] extended the franking privilege to her— Many of her communications required answers, which she, schooled by her husband knowledge, imparted by her husband, knew it was not proper to answer with the pen of an amanuensis— One of her first was addressed to General Jackson, then President of the United States, who sent with a letter from himself the Resolutions of Congress on the death of Mr. Madison.

Montpellier 10th July

"I received, Sir, in due time, from Congress the communication from Congress, made more grateful to me by the kind sympathy which accompanied it.

The high and just estimation of my husband, by my countrymen and friends and their generous participation in their [*page torn*] sorrow, occasioned by our irretrievable loss, expressed through their its supreme au-

---

54. Joseph Gales Jr. and William Winston Seaton were the official printers to Congress and editors of Washington's premier newspaper, the *Daily Intelligencer*.

thorities and otherwise is the only solace of which my heart is susceptible, on the departure of him, who had never lost sight of that consistency, symmetry and beauty of character, in all its parts, which rendered his [LC: own] transcendant as a whole, and worthy of the best aspirations!

I am now preparing to execute the trust his confidence reposed in me— that of placing before Congress and the world, what his pen had prepared for their use, and with the importance of this legacy, I am deeply impressed.

With great respect &c. &c.

DP. Madison."

This constant strain upon her nervous system, at the end of a few months produced its consequences, Her physical strength gave way, the autumn of 1836 and winter of 1837 were replete with sadness and suffering—the pain and agony experienced by overstraining her eyes, confined her a greater part of the time to her confined bed, with the curtains closly drawn—when convalescent, and when [MC: as] Spring came [MC: advanced] she was lifted to her carriage for a short drive, supported by one or other of her neices to walk from room to room, or up and down the portico.

When Summer came her physicians Dᴿ Grimes and Doctor Taylor recommended her journeying for change of air and scene to the White Sulphur Springs— On her return she writes this to Mᴿ Anthony Morris, her life time friend—

Montpelier, September 2nd 1837

Accept a thousand thanks, dear friend, for your two unanswered letters, containing the best advice in the world, and which I have followed as far as I could, on my visit to the White Sulphur Springs, a new world to me, both sublime and terrific, in its character. I passed three or four days at the Warm and two weeks at the White Sulphur, drinking moderately of the waters and bathing my eyes a dozen times a day—The effect was excellent —My health was strengthened to its former standing, and my eyes where white—but on my ride home, of six days they had the fancy to in the dust, they had the fancy to relapse a little, still I cannot refrain from expressing with my own pen (by you interdicted) my grateful sense of your kind friendship on every occasion.

I met with relations and friends throughout "my grand tour" and had every reason to be gratified, but for my own impatient spirit which continually dwelt on my duties at home, yet unfinished. in In truth I felt my five years [LC: weeks] absence from Montpellier as if I had deserted my staff and therefore was not entitled to the happiness every where offered for my participation—and so—I hastened home to work again."

As winter approached, her duties being fulfilled and her brother [MC: and his family, (with the exception of his third daughter, Anna[55] who remained under her charge)] having removed from her vicinity to Kentucky with his family she felt very lonely at Montpelier. From the memory of the past—she dreaded another winter, shut up by the snows from communication with her kind neighbors. Only a few years previous the revolt in the county of Southampton and massacre of the whites had struck terror to the heart of every slave owner,[56] for the first time in her life she was desolate, and feared to remain, she could not use her eyes—what then, her impulse was to come to [. .] Washington, where she had passed so many happy years, in the zenith of her glory—the children of her favorite sister were there—and many of her oldest and best friends—these reasons decided her to pass her winters at the seat of Government, where she owned a house in the most desirable part of the city— So the second [. . .] [MC: year] of her bereavement she left Montpelier.

Her return to Washington was hailed by all—those who had formerly known her and those who desired to know this First "Lady of the Land—" Her house was filled morning and evening with the most distinguished of all parties—each claiming her as their champion—while she with her gracious smile and kind warm heart, made friends with all, and with infinite tact, took no decided part except by giving preference to her friends of the longest standing—

It had been twenty years since she had, yet, she came, as she went the favorite of society the city left the city, the favorite of Society, yet she came, without influence or power, and the citizens welcomed her return and gladly gave her the position she had left. The 4[th:] of July, the 1[st:] of January [MC: and every other gala day] her house was crowded by all parties, persons of distinction who cared not for the Presidential honors of the present day, and who went no where else, visited at M[rs:] Madison. Every "turn out" of soldiery came to salute her at the door.— she would go to her steps, and in return for their huzzas of delight [MC: cheers of gratification], wave

55. Anna C. Payne (1819–1852) was John C. Payne's daughter and became Dolley Madison's companion.

56. On 21 August 1831, Nat Turner, a slave preacher on a Southampton County plantation, led a slave uprising that killed fifty-one white persons. Turner and his followers were later captured and executed.

her kerchief; friends from the high and the low brought their children and grandchildren sure of the individual interest she took in them; to a looker on these sights were very pleasing and amusing touching— Her patience was inexhaustible.

Her friend, M$^{rs:}$ Lear, remonstrated with her on allowing her time to be so much engrossed, by the crowd which thronged her house—she gently laid her hand on her heart and said "I know the cause of these visits, they are for *His* sake, not mine"—flattery had no effect upon her, she easily detected it, but her kind heart never allowed her to shew it, a few have said she was worldly—not so, she had infinite tact, and always saw the good and not the evil, which exists in all, Her memory was excellent— she was noted for never forgetting a name or face, and she was very much guided by the sound of the voice, those who knew her *best* loved her most— In looking over piles of letters we find her strongest friendships have extended from early childhood to old age, for no degree of prosperity, or the attentions of the world caused her to forget those whom she had professed to love esteem, her manner was so lovely, so indescribably fascinating! we have seen care worn men come in out of curiosity, after a few words, they would kiss her hand and shed tears of gratification [MC: and depart soothed and consoled]—perfect abnegation of self seemed her motto. She could not bear to see anyone in want—generous to a fault, whatever she had was shared by those she loved, more than shared, for this generosity was often shamefully abused—*how,* it is not our place to mention.

Mrs Madison's life was not exempt from trials, her son J. P. Todd, whom she loved so devotedly—and who returned her affection with the same ardor was the shame and constant [MC: frequently a] drawback on [MC: to] her happiness. Educated in Baltimore at a Catholic Institution, when he left he was all that a mother's heart could desire. he went to Europe, as attaché to at the age of twenty one, with Mess$^{rs:}$ Adams, Bayard, Clay and Gallatin when they were sent by M$^{r:}$ Madison to sign the treaty of peace at Ghent. It was then M$^{r:}$ Adams said of him, "It is surprising! he has sufficient talent to succeed in any thing he undertakes." Alas! this young attaché, whose position at that time gave him distinction for foreigners designated him "Prince" and treated him as such; his mother's indulgence and the early possession of his fortune [MC: engendered habits which] conduced to his ruin! M$^{r:}$ Madison who had husbanded his property, put him then in possession—he spent it lavishly with a refined taste, he purchased many gems of art and paintings which for nearly half a century adorned Montpelier. On his return to America his mother continued her indulgences; he had no profession, was a favorite in society and with foreign tastes—he had lost the power of applying himself to any pursuit—became a bonvivant, never married—outlived his mother nearly two years, and died, from the effects of typhoid fever taken in Boston.

M$^{rs:}$ Madison thorouhly enjoyed her residence in Washington, where her indulgent friends on account of her age and former station, asked no return of their visits, tho' she did not always avail herself of this kindness privilege, which, to our knowledge, was disputed but once. A lady, the widow of an exemperor was in lodgings at Washington for a short time, and had an ardent desire to see [MC: her], but said it was beneath her dignity according to etiquette to call first upon an expresidentess—when this was told to M$^{rs:}$ Madison she said, "she shall not be disappointed I will go and see her—" The lady was at home and her heart won by this acknowldgment of her rank and the suavity of her visitor.

When necessary to decline a favor granting a favor, she did so with so much tact, that she never gave offence. On one occasion she gave her friend, M$^{rs:}$ P— a cup & saucer, tokens of her regard. She was much pleased and on her return shewed her souvenir to several ladies in the hotel—one, with whom M$^{rs:}$ Madison, was slightly acquainted came the next day, and expressed a desire for one also [LC: a similar one]— M$^{rs:}$ M— could not be so general in her gifts—so answered, with a smile and curtsey, "cannot you persuade your friend to give it you hers?"

Entering again into society, M$^{rs:}$ Madison endeavored to draw a line of distinction to avoid the fatigue attendant on accepting the many civilities offered her; she wished to confine herself to the numerous weddings, she was always solicited to attend, for "brides must have their way" she would say—and also, occasional dinners, tho' her desire to give pleasure often led her, when much solicited, to overstep the bounds of these self imposed regulations, so necessary for her health. Every day brought to her view some ancient friends, with familiar reminiscences—whom, it seemed impossible, in life's history, ever to meet again. Among them was Lord Ashburton[57] whom she had known in her girlhood at Philadelphia, before he married the beautiful Miss Bingham. He was for two years, her nearest neighbor in Washington, and at the twilight hour, when she was most apt to be alone, he would come over, and enjoy youthful reminiscences with her, and those [. .] the unbend from the noncommittal diplomatic formal conversation

57. Alexander Baring, 1st Baron Ashburton (1774–1848), was a British politician and financier.

so characteristic of his conversation [MC: intercourse] with strangers, until other company came in, when he would bid "good evening." Mrs Alexander Hamilton,[58] also whom she had meet fifty years before at Lady Washington's drawing rooms, and who "was quite a matron when she was a bride," for M^rs: Madison did not like to be classed with those who were older than herself—still, we find the old association of their honored husbands drawing them more closely together, and the desire to be in each others society, [MC: proposed] by the following note in M^rs: Madison's hand writing.

"Will my dear M^rs: Hamilton, console me for a tedious reign of influenza by passing the evening of tomorrow socially with me; accompanied by her charming daughter M^rs: Holly? The moonlight and genial weather will favor my hopes of seeing them.

Affectionately, DP Madison
Jany 16th: 1845

The names of those two distinguished ladies were often associated together as patronesses to public balls given on Washington's birth night and other patriotic occasions. M^rs: Hamilton was a most excellent woman, she charitable and benevolent, she caused herself to be beloved by those who came within her influence, her life was prolonged for 96 years, a few, previous to her death, she took long walks from the Capitol to the President's House, and though not robust in appearance, it is said, she enjoyed uninterrupted health.

She was very industrious, fond of knitting, and the small specimens of her workmanship, which she gave to public charity were eagerly sought and brought good prices from those who prized souvenirs of the [. .] illustrious Hamilton. Her daughter, M^rs: Hamilton Holly, who resided with her, still remains in Washington grieving for the loss of a parent so many years her companion and charge— Altho' to the delightful home of her brother, M^r: James Hamilton, on the North River she had been most affectionately invited.

M^r: J. Q. Adams and family, whom she loved, were also winter residents of Washington, as well as her kinsman William C. Preston, Mr Clay, whom

58. Elizabeth Schuyler Hamilton (1757–1854) was the second daughter of Philip Schuyler, a Revolutionary War general, and Catherine Van Rensselaer Schuyler, one of the richest and most political families in New York State. She was a sister of Angelica Schuyler Church and the wife of Alexander Hamilton. She was born in Albany, New York.

her husband wished to be commander in chief during the War of 1812—M^r: Calhoun, M^r: Webster and all that noble band of patriots, since summoned to give account of their stewardships.

In 1844 1848 Mrs [MC: Madison] was on board the ill fated steamer Princeton when the Peacemaker (the name of the canon whose explosion proved so fatal) exp caused such fatal [MC: great] destruction of life! It happened at an hour when dinner was just over, and most of the ladies lingered below to hear the gay repartee and merry songs of the youthful guests. She was seated near M^rs: Upshur, M^rs: Gilmer and M^rs: Kennon, tho' these ladies knew not the worst, fear almost made them frantic in the panic. M^rs: Madison did not loose her presence of mind, but did her best to soothe them and keep the fatal news from them until better able to bear up, under their heart rendering affliction— [MC: on this occasion] She had accompanied President Tyler and family cabinet, without any of her own family— It was a peculiarly sultry afternoon, hot and dusty—when the booming of the canon was heard in Washington—[MC: most exagerated rumors were afloat still] nothing could be known for an hour, the city was in intense excitement—*all* had friends, many relatives, [MC: yet] nothing could be done, when moments seemed like hours. M^rs: Madison returned. Her drawing room was filled with relatives and friends, all intensely anxious. She came in quietly, with her usual grace, spoke scarce a word— smiled benignly—but those who knew her, perceived her faltering voice, and inability to stand without support— she was soon left with her family—but of the horrible scene, she dared not trust herself to speak, nor did she ever hear it reverted to without a shudder!

In 1844 Congress passed a resolution to invite her with whatever friends she pleased to accompany her, to a seat on the floor of the House of Representatives, to shew her appreciation of this high compliment, never paid to any other lady, she went once or twice first on the occasion of the presentation by M^r: J. Q. Adams, of the Camp Chest of General Washington.

At this time began her pecuniary embarrassment—living without any account of expenditure, for all who came partook of hospitality as in former days, she was now, as she said, more than seventy five, and it was too late to change old habits— The superior judgment of M^r: Madison had always and his financial talents had always been a check upon her liberality. For the last few years she had become embarrassed, crops had failed, the overseer had to be heavily paid, negroes food and clothing purchased and plantation expenses—no income from any other source. The Virginia household

of servants in Washington to be supported, her neice (Anna Payne) igno-
rant as herself in financial matters and equally liberal in disposition, was
of no assistance— Her son, as we before mentioned, was fond of his pleasures and dotingly so of his involved mother, involved, while he did what he
could to assist her, by raiding money at a large interest from brokers, this
was present relief but only involved her the more increased her difficulties.

Two years previously (1842) she went to New York—with her nephew
(R. D. Cutts) and had [MC: to have] an interview with M^{r:} J. J. Astor,[59] who
always spoke of M^{r:} Madison as the founder of his fortunes and was profuse
in offers of friendship to M^{rs:} Madison—to him she mortgaged her house in
Washington, many have said the loan was a gift—not so, it was repaid to
the son of M^{r:} Astor, after the death of M^{rs:} M— by her executor.

On her way to New York she revisited Philadelphia, after an absence of
forty odd many years—and found many changes—still it made her glad
to again see the happy faces which advanced to meet her. During her stay
in this [MC: the] Quaker City, she was the guest of her relation Governor
E. Coles.

Washington Jan^{y:} 22^{d.} 44

If you love me, my dear son, write [MC: to] me—tell me when you will
come to offer the papers to Congress and to do something with the 4^{th:}
volume—we are without funds and those we owe are impatient— the time
has arrived now when if lost or neglected will never return to us!— M^{r:}
Rives with whom *only* I have conversed, assured me that if he could do any
thing in it—we should chuse—but he had made himself so unpopular—that
no *open* efforts of his would do any good to my interest and therefore some
influential member of the lower house should be chosen and employed.—
Oh, my son! I am too unhappy not to have you with me, and not to have
even your opinion and directions, what to do myself or what individual to
engage and at what time!— Do not let this often repeated request offend
you or hurt you my son— but reflect on the misery of your mother, when
she sees that nothing but a happy and early result of this duty will give her
bread or continue to her what is better a respectable standing before the
world—but I will say little more—as it is not good for me to write.

You have no doubt seen in the papers a Resolution of Congress invit-

59. John Jacob Astor (1763–1848) was a German American businessman who was
the first multimillionaire in the United States.

ing me to a seat—and my answer— It is nothing in my eyes or my heart, nor would compliments even higher, unless you and myself were on safe ground with our creditors.

Astor's interest is due the 19th: of February—can you obtain it for me? Miss Legaré's best respects to you

ever your affectionate mother   DP Madison.

To J. P. Todd

Montpelier

Orange Cy Va

EXTRACT FROM THE NATIONAL INTELLIGENCER

"The Washington Correspondent of North America, in noticing the late signal mark of respect shewn to Mrs: Madison by the House of Representatives, in offering her the privilege of a seat within its Hall whenever she may chuse to attend the sittings of that body, expresses precisely our own view of that act when he describes it as "a homage unasked, un for unprompted by any unworthy party or personal aim, directed towards no one almost forgotten, except for those gentle and elegant qualities, that bless a husband in private life and even adorn an elevated station, but bring with them no power, no influence, nothing that could ever have made adulation profitable."

Mrs: Madison revisited Montpellier several times after she became a resident of Washington—as age crept upon her, she found the journey too fatiguing, so this beautiful place was sold, and the colored population with it, to below their value, to prevent separation from their homes. The purchaser (Mr: Moncure of Richmond, Va.) courteously reserved apartments for her in case she should incline to return— She did "incline to return" and would have done so had her life been spared— Most of the precious souvenirs from Montpellier were removed to Toddsbirth, the residence of her eccentric son—we might say residences for the principal building had been burnt—and he had caused to be erected numerous smaller ones—to a large round, towerlike building, called the ball room, were trunks cases of papers, books busts and every thing else of value had generally removed— and so remained under charge of a faithful Cerberus who would sooner have parted with his right hand than the key entrusted to him. When the executor we had almost said executioner found it necessary to have a sale— the negroes stood by in astonishment and indignation, but [MC: &] dared not speak—but when the likeness of Mr: Madison was put up, the faithful one who had been charged with the building exclaimed with suddenly exclaimed, with a loud voice "Great God Almighty, you are not going to sell ole Massa" the people looked round to see from whence came the voice, but the old man had departed to hide his grief.

We looked on those building with sadness, for tho' ridiculous in the eyes of a stranger, they were built with his [MC: Mʳ Todd's] quaint ideas to add to the comfort of his mother, whom he always intended should pass her last days with him—several buildings [MC: were] intended for parlors and chambers, Mʳˢ⠶ Madison accustomed to [. .] [MC: have her private apartments] on the ground floor at Montpellier always disliked the fatigue of a staircase; to obviate this, as much as possible, to one of the cottages there are large wide stairs, the ascent very gradual, so that she might go *in at the window* after walking from the dining room—seeming to forget, in his recollections of her love of sunshine, that even in this sweet spot, wintry winds would come and she could not brave the tempest—this and many other such preparations for her comfort, she never saw—but she was grateful and felt that he loved her to the last— When spoken to, about his follies and extravagancies she would say "My poor boy, forgive his excentricities, his heart is right" she thought Mʳ⠶ Madison's favorite quotation, was well applied to her son:

"Errors like straws upon the surface float
Those who would seek for pearls, must dive below."

About this time she had a Providential escape from fire, an attempt was made to burn her residence by placing matches between the shutters and sash of her hall window, close to the staircase—towards morning, as the flames began to ascend, it was discovered by an early rising neighbor, who instantly awoke her son and, sent him to alarm the family, her servant man, Ralph, who slept in the basement was aroused. He ran up to the door of his mistress, which was as usual locked from within. After some difficulty he succeeded in getting admittance his efforts to obtain admission—the room was filled with smoke "Mistress" he exclaimed "I have come to save you, the house is on fire"! she Awakened from a sound sleep, as soon as she became conscious of the danger, she said "the papers, the papers first" nor would she consent to move until the frightened servant promised to save them also; then he seized her in his arms, rushed down the burning staircase, with his precious burthen, out of the side door, which led into the garden and placed her safely on the grass plot— He then returned to her chamber and threw from the window a black velvet dress for her covering, and afterwards rescued the trunks containing the papers (those recently purchased by Congress) from what appeared destruction. The fire, after the tocsin of danger was sounded, was soon extinguished by her kind neighbors—and the event caused her to laugh heartily, whenever she remembered the unceremonious way in which she was translated from a warm bed to the cold grass, with her bare feet—and her best velvet thrown for her to put on at three in the morning!—likewise it was a gratification to be so well assured of the fidelity of her trusted servant. The perpetrator of this evil deed was never known, nor would M^rs: Madison allow any efforts to be made towards the discovery.

M^rs: Madison always attended St. John's (the episcopal church) it was built during her husband's administration and her personal friend, Reverend W. Hawley was still the rector on her return to Washington. In July of 1845 she was confirmed as member—in writing to her nephew R. D. Cutts she says, "and now, my dear Richard I must tell you on what our thoughts have dwelt a great deal—it was to become worthy of membership in the church which I have attended for the last forty years, and which Anna has attended all her life. Yesterday this wish was consumated as far as confirmation extended— Bishop Whittengham performed this ceremony as far as confirmation extended as well as that of Installing M^r: Pyne, our Rector— we had an excellent sermon from the Bishop of New Jersey—a fine preacher and beautiful champion for Charity 'which suspects not, thinks no evil &c'".

Soon afterwards she received the right of baptism, in S^t: John's church from the Reverend S. Pyne.

In 1846 M^rs: Madison offered to Congress the additional letters and private correspondence of M^r: Madison, at the same time thoes of M^r: Hamilton and M^r: Jefferson were presented— Congress libe liberally purchased them all for 25,000 each—but their dictation in M^rs: Madison's case was extraordinary— She did not come before that body as a supplicant—she felt that the writings of her illustrious husband, were worthy of their price— Her circumstances were reduced, she was in debt—Congress paid 5000$ to go towards liquating them it and 20,000 they settled upon her so that she could only receive the interest—subject to her will, [MC: and] if she should make none, to revert back to Government. Altho' she knew the motives of this act to be good and as her friends thought for her interest, yet she could not feel otherwise than astonished—but rebellion was useless so she bore it, as she had borne every change in life, for good or evil, with her hands meekly crossed, and without allowing a murmur of discontent to pass her lips—she felt that she was powerless— and the Necessity alone caused her to accept on the terms dictated To this lady of whom it might be said, and truly, that the "Inca's blood flowed in her veins," [MC: it was a grievous trial.] Did not her friends know that a mother, such a mother, would share even the crumbs with her only child!—but it was so arranged to preserve it for her use, from "the prodigal son". How long did they think she would live?—eighty years had already passed over her head—why not have made her comfortable for the few years in prospect than to save it for Congress or, they knew not whom?

The eighty third and last year of her life, her memory was buisy with the past, she caused old letters to be reread to her, and they brought in their [. . .] associations unknown to those around her— She seemed dreamy and her characteristic benevolence and good feelings were prominent. She was very fond of having the bible read to her, and when asked what part she preferred, would always say S "the gospel of S^t. John," and it was while this was being that read to her, that her last sleep came upon her. It This sleep lasted near eighteen hours, before the family were aware it was too long. Doctor J. Thomas, her attending physician was sent for, he pronounced it slow appoplexy. D^r. Hall and other skillful practitioners were immediately summoned, and coincided with D^r. Thomas— Remedies were given but without avail, all saw that the hand of death had been gently laid upon her—she lingered two days, seemingly without suffering, only waking, when arroused, to momentary consciousness, she would then smile, her loving smile, put out her arms to embrace those whom she loved and who were near her, and gently relapse into that rest which was peace—

A few days before her death, she said to a neice, who had gone to her, as she usually did in any difficulty, and on this occasion had lost something she prized "My dear, dear do not trouble yourself about it, there is nothing in this world worth caring for" her neice a bitt struck by her tone, said, "Aunt, you who have lived so long—do you think so?" "Yes!"—she again said, with emphasis, "believe me, I who have lived in it so long, repeat to you, that there is nothing in it worth caring for." She looked intently while she spoke, then turned and walked to the window. For the last year of her life she suffered from extreme debility, her mind was not in the least impaired [MC: but] she was confused and annoyed by the conflicting advice of those who considered themselves her friends. she could not do as she wished "Oh, for my councillor" she would say, as if thinking aloud.

Her death occurred, with little suffering the eight of July 1849—M^r. Todd M^r. Todd had been with her some time previous to the last sad event.

When he approached the couch, where she reposed, and she heard the sound of his voice—the magic of maternal love caused her to shew signs of consciousness, sometimes by heavy breathing and sometimes she gave utterance to these words "my poor boy". She felt that she was his best friend, that when she left there was none to fill the void of left by so good, so kind, so enduring a mother!

M^rs: Madison's mortal remains were placed in a Sarcophagus, sent from New York, for that purpose It was exposed to view for several days. It was visited by many of her friends, who gazed sadly and tearfully at that placid countenance, they had loved so well and so long!—

The funeral proceeded from S^t: John's church, of which she was a member and from the hands of whose rector she had received her first and last communion. Her body, at the desire of M^r: Todd, was placed in a vault in the Congressional Cemetery, previous to being removed to the resting place of M^r: Madison, at Montpelier.

M^rs: Madison's handwriting was the Italian, but late in life it became laborious and painful for her to write; so much so that after M^r: Madison's death, when his, as well as her own correspondents overwhelmed her, she taught her neice Miss Payne to imitate it. After much practice, she was so successful that none but those perfectly familiar with the penmanship of both, knew the difference. This was of great assistance. The letter M^rs: Madison would begin: as soon as her as her eyes ached, the pen would be transferred to Miss Payne, who continued to write under her dictation: then she would herself add the last words and the signature: This dependance we think, was the cause of her delay in making a testament, entirely satisfactory to herself— As in life, so in death, she was considered public property. A will was made for her, by those who believed, they were fulfilling her wishes, and her poor senses were recalled to sign it.

This instrument caused great surprise as well as dissatisfaction to M^r: Todd—as a few months previous she had made one constituting him her sole heir. He did not consider the last legal, nor did the eminent counsel whom he consulted It divided the $20,000 in trust, between himself and Miss Payne. The friends of the latter were extremely anxious that its provisions should be carried into effect, and so urgent were they on this point that, after a delay of many months, M^r: Todd consented to allow the whole matter to be referred to arbitrators an arbitrator— This gentleman decided that the instrument in favor of Miss Payne should be accepted a decision from which M^r: Todd did not appeal. He declined undertaking the administration, from a knowledge of his individual creditors, and a firm resolve, repeatedly expressed, that nothing was his or should be expended until his mother's debts were paid. He named one of the creditors in his stead, as this person followed the respectable and responsible calling of an auctioneer, no difficulty or delay was apprehended in the settlement of the estate, so the friends of M^rs: Madison and her creditors concurred in the wishes of the son

The bond of union between M^r: Todd and the administrator was a mutual fine taste for paintings, and we may add, an acomodating spirit on the part of the latter with respect to loans, as well as a desire for souvenirs and autographs, many of which belonging to the estate were not only exceedingly interesting, but valuable. Upon these souvenirs and autographic letters, advances were made, as the necessities of M^r: Todd increased—never to be redeemed. The private letters and and papers of M^r: and M^rs: Madison remain in the hands of the Administrator, with the exception of some of minor importance, which he has chosen to return to their respective writers.

We have been thus explicit as we are frequently asked, with expressions of astonishment, how M^r: McGuire was so fortunate as to obtain these invaluable papers, [MC: from] among them, we are told, he has culled letters from General Washington to M^r: Madison, sufficient for a large bound volume, yet so we hear, from strangers, though we have never had the gratification of seeing them and others, perhaps, more valuable to ourselves.

Soon after the arbitration M^r: Todd was very much injured by a fall, from which he recovered slowly, as soon as he was able to travel he went to Boston, for additional medical advice, he was taken with the typhoid fever— which detained him sometime. On his return to Washington, he was ill, partly owing to exposure in returning at an inclement season. He took rooms in the house of a respectable Virginia gentleman, M^r: Shelton, which were furnished with Montpelier furniture, his mother's servants were with him, and faithful to the last. As due to the memory of M^rs: Madison we saw M^r: Todd frequently during this, his fatal [MC: final] illness. He was composed and prepared, as well as we could judge, from his own words, to appear before the high tribunal, to which, he was well aware that he [MC: had] been summoned. He lingered long and had time for meditation. We urged his seeing a clergyman, to which, to give us satisfaction he consented, Although he said, "I have always believed in the Quaker doctrine, I believe the work of reconciliation is between the Creator and Created

"Aunt" Dolley Madison, sketch by Mary Cutts. (The White
House Historical Association [White House Collection])

alone."— "I forgive my enemies, if I have any. I have never wilfully injured
anyone—but myself—I have been my own worst enemy" these words were
said slowly and emphatically.

Availing ourselves of his consent to see a member of the Gospel, we
named several—whom he declined seeing, when we mentioned the Reverend M^r: French—he said decidedly—"Let him come, I believe him to be a
good and sincere man." We went for him immediately and have the gratification of knowing that his last moments were soothed by prayer and holy
thoughts.

The slaves were fortunately freed, owing to an inadvertence, or design,
on the part of M^{rs}: Madison, to have their names registered at the City Hall,
as the laws of the district required.

With the death of her only child, ends our "life of M^{rs}: Madison." We lay
down the pen *dissatisfied!*—feeling how inadequately we have performed
the duty assigned to us—totally unaccustomed to composition of any
kind, we have sadly and mournfully undertaken this poor tribute to her
memory—for her sake we have untied the [MC: faded] ribbons, from let-

ters, which had been bound by those hands, long crumbled into dust! Our friends have cheered [MC: us] by their promised indulgence in consideration of their own abiding love for Mʳˢ: Mrs: Madison—and our [MC: own, perhaps,] overwhelming attachment, will be pardoned in remembrance of the unforgotten past! dead!

End of Cutts Memoir II

The Last Letters

Transcribed by CATHERINE ALLGOR
and JAMES T. CONNOLLY

What follows are transcripts of two letters in which Mary Cutts discusses the publication of her manuscript.[60] In the first, dated 6 June 1856, Mary Crowninshield Silsbee Sparks, wife of Jared Sparks, the author, historian, editor, and president of Harvard University, continues a dialogue about what she thinks Mary needs to do with the piece. The letter suggests that this was not the first time Mary Sparks made these suggestions; in the second letter, we discover why Mary Cutts might not have responded to them.

Cambridge, June, 6, 1856.

My dear Mary,

I have been looking for your letter among unanswered ones, but I think it has been already discussed. You will not be unforgiving if I write without cause.

I feel that I may not have said of your MSS. what I should. You were to Lend it to me, and I was to have it edited. The expense of a hundred dollars would be well worth your while, and it would appear, in every respect, as it should. You should, my dear Mary, at once sign a paper promising this, and you can let me have it, then despatch the MSS. as soon as you can.

Thus relieved from all care, you will find time to attend to yourself.

Some one tells me you are not so well, and I hear you think of coming to Boston. Can't I [. . .] something about you, dear Mary?

It would be very gratifying to peep in at your rooms, and more so to chat over the thousand associations of which few share so many.

60. Mary Sparks to Mary Cutts, 6 June 1856, Cutts-Madison Papers, Massachusetts Historical Society; Mary Cutts to Henry D. Gilpin, [10 June 1856], Cutts-Madison Papers, Massachusetts Historical Society.

Such is the [. . .] and good old intimacy in our Families, such the old con-
nexions of friendly Kindness, and political affinities, that I feel the chain
which binds me to your peculiarly feminine nature has been strengthened
and enriched by those rare accumulations of past and present, of inherited regard, of personal kindness, and affectionate memories, as difficult
to describe as it is impossible to sever.

In my own need you were a kind friend to my children, and they have
not forgotten the cottage or its hospitality.

I told you, my dear Mary, that I had nothing to Say, and yet I have
encroached on your time. I shall hope to hear from you.

Tell me who has the large house, and whose is the report that Mrs.
Greensboro ceases to be married?

Kind regards to your brothers,
Always affectionately
Mary C. Sparks

*What follows is a draft of what may be the last extant letter from Mary
Cutts about her manuscript. She seems to have been prompted to action
by Mary Crowninshield Silsbee Sparks's letter of inquiry. Here, Mary has
contacted Henry D. Gilpin, who, among many political, historical, and
artistic accomplishments, had been editor of James Madison's papers.
"Mrs. Gilpin" is Eliza Johnson Gilpin. It is obvious that, in addition to
the Sparkses, Mary had been in conversation with the Gilpins about the
publication of her manuscript. This letter reveals that it was at the urging
of both Jared and Mary Sparks that Mary Cutts add what they thought of
as "real history" to her tale, thus explaining the possible second draft of
the memoir. Mary seems not to have resented their editorial suggestions,
regarding them as the way to publication. Here we also see what Shulman
suggests in her essay; that Mary did not want to deal with the issue of Dolley and the abolitionists.*

*That Mary, struggling with the effects of the tuberculosis that would kill
her, took the time and energy to draft, rather than just write, this letter
suggests its importance. She wrote this letter in or on 10 June 1856, only
a few days after the letter above; we do not know if the Gilpins ever saw
a final draft. Her urgency about her manuscript is all the more poignant
for our knowing that she would die only a few weeks later on 14 July 1856,
and that she would never see her "little undertaking" to fruition. All of us
involved in the compiling of this volume hope that we have come in some*

way to honor Mary Estelle Elizabeth Cutts's efforts to make history. To that
end, it may be noted, we tried to follow her suggestions for the illustrations.

Winter and spring have passed, still I we have not seen Mr Tayloe, I have
been confined—tho' through the long winter we have often wished [. . .]
especially as it should have given us so much pleasure to converse about
historical [MC: [. . . .] was near to give a peice of information—useful to one
who has have groped] his advice—as a sch learned man & especially as he
promised his aid—in my little undertaking.

My dear Mr Gilpin,

My not having answered your letter ere this was not owing to want of
gratification and gratitude at your kind offers—but a the indisposition
caused by a daily chill & fever—which choses the most useful part of my
day—I am getting and incapacitates one from any exertion much exertion
afterwards.

I gladly accept your accede to your kind proposition about my manuscript—there is no one into whose hands I would prefer to entrust[MC: ing]
it—especially as I know, dear Mrs Gilpin, is as [MC: much] interested in
itself it, as yourself, and I have long learned the value of old friends such
as yourselves—I and to be loved [MC: interested] for my "mother's sake"
touches the most tender cord in my heart! The last part

Mrs Mrs Sparks was the one who suggested two years since, the writing the memoir—when she did so, I said "if I ever do, it I will dedicate to
you["]—when I began—before it was written I wrote and [MC: first the
dedication] playfully and sent to her for which I have [MC: she wrote] a
letter of thanks.— ought I to keep this promise? Mrs Sparks has written
me several often, and given me a great many useful hints—among others to bring in as much of people of her day—and historical personages—
as I could—this I have endeavored to do with accuracy— I found without
them that the narrative would in many places flag—especially the sixteen
years—passed in Washington— Mr Sparks advised me to put in all I could
about Mr Madison to strengthen the whole—& to *strengthen* my writing
[MC: assertions] I have quoted from orations &c delivered by Mr Ingersoll
and Govr Barbour—printed only in newspapers—and forgotten— I do fear
I have put in too much about my father—and the North—but that and even
more was suggested by Mr Sparks. Mrs Sparks off suggested my writing
to Miss Quincy for ledgands, one of Lady N she sent—which I submit to

you—to see if it would do for a note— What I said about P. H.[61] I knew was common place but I thought that of Aaron Burr was ~~common p~~ new! my mother was one of the ladies who profited by his kindness— I now use the paint box he gave her—and this little Ivory pallette I now use is the only one I ever used.

I Every thing, through out the naration is true, dear M⁻ Gilpin,—and there is very little I cannot prove— While M⁻ Madison & Jef— were P[resident]

I am quite concious of not having sufficiently noticed the Misses Murray and M⁻ [O?] Tayloe has supplied me with more material about Anapolis— but only yesterday, I told him of my plan, and he seemed desirous to have me bring in some ancestors of his own, high born dames before the Revolution M⁻ Rush, I dare say, knows all about them.

I hope you will like the pictures of Aunt, especially as they possess the charm of never having been copied— Do you not think one of M⁻ M.'s ought to be added? the one by Stuart is the best that was ever taken, we think, I have an engraving of [MC: from] it— I have an electrotype of a view of Montpelier, the one engraved for "Homes of American Statesmen" or rather it is in New York, subject to my call— We have a good likeness of M⁻ M— taken in 1817—by Wood—it is like him as we recalled him. Half the time Montpelier is spelt with two l's and the other half with one, by both its proprietors—it is named for that in the South of France— I again say, dear M⁻ Gilpin, that the summers of my early life [MC: from one to eighteen] were spent there, at M⁻ M's death I was sent for, or rather one of us, my sister was of more importance than at home, so I went, without delay and remained nearly a year—and being the most experienced and oldest of her neices there—was most strictly in her confidence I say this to assure you of the truth of my statement— Some persons in P.[62] seem to blame Aunt when they asserted M⁻ M— was an abolitionist—but I have nothing to do with that, only so far as to do *her* justice—

I had hoped to have sent my letter Saturday, but was not able to finish— tell M⁻ˢ G—I do not consider myself at all worse—if I can get rid of the chills & fever. Yesterday, as soon as one chill and fever had passed another came. This morning another [MC: came], and the fever still on me!

Ask M⁻ˢ G— please to write me, she does not know how much I love her letters. M⁻ Sparks, though he has given me so many hints has never

---

61. Probably refers to the section on Patrick Henry.
62. Probably Philadelphia, which was a center for abolitionist thought.

said kindly, as you have done, that he would take charge of it himself—
M^rs: S— proposed that I should give it up entirely to a M^rs: Fulsom[63]—as
editress—but—as she had no personal acquaintance with Aunt or any of
us—my *spirit rebelled*—at such an *entrustment* for she could not feel with
us Southerners— Tho' I only took no notice of it—and have not seen M^rs:
Sparks—I wrote her *twice* of my intention to submit it to yourself.

If I have left any thing unsaid that I should say, I will write again— Take
your own time about it so I shall be best pleased, and certainly *releived* to
have it with one in whom we have so much confidence.—

truly your obliged friend M. E. E. C.

63. This could be Susannah Sarah McKean Folsom, writer of fiction and poetry,
daughter of Joseph McKean, Boylston Professor of Rhetoric, Oratory and Elocution at
Harvard, and wife of Charles Folsom, prominent author and editor.

Contributors

CATHERINE ALLGOR is a Professor of History at the University of California, Riverside, and a University of California Presidential Chair. Her book *Parlor Politics: In Which the Ladies of Washington Help Build a City and a Government* (2000) won the James H. Broussard First Book Prize. Allgor's latest book, *A Perfect Union: Dolley Madison and the Creation of the American Nation* (2006), was a finalist for the George Washington Book Prize.

JAMES T. CONNOLLY is a transcriber for the Adams Papers at the Massachusetts Historical Society, as well as an archives and preservation consultant. Outside the archives, James is a poet and a musician who has played in many Boston-area rock bands.

LEE LANGSTON-HARRISON is the Executive Director of the Museum of Culpeper History. She previously served as the Senior Curator at James Madison's Montpelier for more than eight years, where her work focused on Dolley Madison. She was also the Curator/Assistant Director of the James Monroe Museum in Fredericksburg for twelve years. Langston-Harrison has been in the museum field for more than thirty-five years.

COKIE ROBERTS is a political commentator for ABC News and for NPR. She is the best-selling author of *We Are Our Mothers' Daughters* (revised and expanded, 2009), *Ladies of Liberty: The Women Who Shaped Our Nation* (2008), and *Founding Mothers: The Women Who Raised Our Nation* (2004). Roberts has also written two books with her husband, Steve, *From This Day Forward* (2000) and *Our Haggadah: Uniting Traditions for Interfaith Families* (2011). The Robertses are the parents of two and grandparents of six.

HOLLY COWAN SHULMAN is a Research Professor in the Department of History at the University of Virginia, Editor of the Dolley Madison Digital Edition (2004–), and Founding Director of Documents Compass at the Virginia Foundation for the Humanities. She has written or edited several books, including *The Voice of America: Propaganda and Democracy, 1941–1945* (1990); with Maureen Beasley, *The Eleanor Roosevelt Encyclopedia* (2000); and with David Mattern, *The Selected Correspondence of Dolley Payne Madison* (2003). Shulman has also published five volumes of The Dolley Madison Digital Edition, as well as various scholarly articles. As founding director of Documents Compass, she is the principal investigator on a major grant from the Andrew W. Mellon Foundation for a prosopography of the American Founding Era, and the principal investigator on a tools grant from the National Historical Publications and Records Commission (NHPRC) to create an electronic editing tool for scholarly editions. She lives with her husband in Charlottesville, Virginia, and has three children and five grandchildren.

ELIZABETH DOWLING TAYLOR's twenty-two-year career in historical interpretation has included positions as Director of Interpretation at Thomas Jefferson's Monticello and Director of Education at James Madison's Montpelier. Most recently a Fellow at the Virginia Foundation for the Humanities, Taylor is now an independent scholar and lecturer. Taylor is the author of *A Slave in the White House: Paul Jennings and the Madisons* (2012). She lives in Barboursville, Virginia.

A Note on Indexing

At the very least, indexing can be a very basic final step in a book's production, a list of proper names and places, with a few key concepts identified. At its highest form, indexing can be an art, reflecting not only a volume's content but also its argument and form. As always, Mary Cutts has pushed us, her transcribers and editors, to examine the task before us, to innovate and invent.

As with the main text, our goal has been to strike the right balance between faithfulness and usefulness; that is, to aid the curious reader while remaining committed to the fidelity of the text and the author's intention. To that end, we have retained Mary's mistakes—Virginia Randolph may not have married "Mr. Archibald Cary," as Mary asserts on page 148, but we dutifully index both names accordingly. (Virginia Randolph married Wilson Jefferson Cary and had a son, Archibald, named after an illustrious ancestor.) Mary is also a bit confused about "Ambrose Madison." While she does correctly identify one Ambrose as the grandfather of James Madison, she also simultaneously posits another Ambrose as James's elder brother, who dies as a young man (which is not correct), and as a younger brother who lives long enough to sire a favorite niece of James's (which is correct). We chose to elide both of these "brothers" under the singular heading of "brother."

When Mary misspells or misidentifies someone, we include her misnaming, even as we corrected it, so as to guide the reader who wants to read about, for example, James Madison's mother, as in *Madison, Nelly Conway ("Ellenor")* or Dolley's grandfather, *Payne, Josias ("John")*. Again, for readability, we have regularized some spelling (as in "Confucius"); we also gave familiar historical names to events, so that the "Southampton Rebellion" on page 182 is indexed as such and also as the "Nat Turner Rebellion."

As asserted in the introduction to this volume, we believe that what is left out or deleted from the text can be as important and perhaps more revelatory than what is included. For instance, the famous description of James as "the great little Madison" is in a deleted section. Hence, we also indexed deleted material. The page numbers of such text are in the strike-through tint used in the Memoirs themselves. On a page where Mary or Lucia struck out material only to rewrite it later on the page, we indexed the "final"—that is, rewritten—version.

Finally, one of the "rules" of editing is to not include an entry for a person or place that is mentioned just once in the text. But as Mary's manuscript challenged the accepted genres of history for her time, so the piece defies the conventional wisdom of editors. Mary wrote relationally, weaving her story, introducing people, and asserting her historical ideas within a context of families and places. She saw the world as a network of relations and real estate. Not only does she unabashedly include a paean to "old houses" on page 145, but all through the text, very few people stand alone as individuals. Most of her personages are "placed" by their connection with others. Mary's manuscript is unique, so we may never have enough writings like it to make a generalization, but we suspect that Mary shared this mindset with other women of her day and that women's writing may reflect this characteristic. Leaning toward the "indexing as an art" point of view, then, we have decided to eschew the rules and recorded each person mentioned. We beg the readers' patience, as they move through the webs of "Miss Tarleton"'s and "Dr. Thomas"'s, trusting Mary that they are important.

Index

Recent Books in the JEFFERSONIAN AMERICA SERIES

CPSIA information can be obtained
at www.ICGtesting.com
Printed in the USA
LVHW031928120319
610380LV00002B/206/P